C0-EFL-129

Because the Lord is Your Shepherd

1

Because the Lord is Your Shepherd

We must teach those in the next generation

Ms. Lou V. Walker

Outskirts Press, Inc.
Denver, Colorado

The opinions expressed in this manuscript are solely the opinions of the author and do not represent the opinions or thoughts of the publisher. The author has represented and warranted full ownership and/or legal right to publish all the materials in this book.

Because the Lord is Your Shepherd
We must teach those in the next generation
All Rights Reserved.
Copyright © 2010 Ms. Lou V. Walker
v2.0

Cover Photo © 2010 JupiterImages Corporation. All rights reserved - used with permission.

Scriptures were taken from the Holy Bible KJV--King James Version, Royal Publication Inc. Copyright 1964, 1965, 1968.

This book may not be reproduced, transmitted, or stored in whole or in part by any means, including graphic, electronic, or mechanical without the express written consent of the publisher except in the case of brief quotations embodied in critical articles and reviews.

Outskirts Press, Inc.
http://www.outskirtspress.com

ISBN: 978-1-4327-4585-1

Outskirts Press and the "OP" logo are trademarks belonging to Outskirts Press, Inc.

PRINTED IN THE UNITED STATES OF AMERICA

Dedication

Your tears really are just temporary (Psalm 30:5); you do not have to cry anymore. He is going to wipe all of your tears away.

This book is dedicated to those who really believe the Lord is their Shepherd in this generation because of their personal experiences with Him in the name of Jesus. He has heard your cry out to Him for help in the name of Jesus.

He heard you late in the midnight hour; now He wants to supply your healing power.

He is willing to turn your negative situations around in the name of Jesus.

This book will be greatly appreciated by anyone who is tired and brokenhearted in this generation.

Always remember your tears really are just temporary.

May the Spiritual Living God continue to bless you each and every day, in the name of Jesus.

Table of Contents

1. Because the Lord Is My Shepherd 1
2. Marriage Covenant 11
3. Women According to Scripture 27
4. Relationships with Jesus as the Mediator 33
5. She Really Should Be Feared 45
6. Why Would Any Male Access an Evil Spirit? 57
7. Seven Women to One Man 63
8. He Closes and Opens Wombs 71
9. Only the Spiritual Living God Knows the Plans He Has for You .. 89
10. They Meant It for Evil, but the Spiritual Living God Used It for His Glory 99
11. So, You Think You Do Not Need Jesus 101
12. How Should I Receive Death? 113
13. Which Do You Have, Faith or Fear? 119
14. PRIDE, Pride, Pride, Pride 127
15. Are You Caught in Sin and You "Can't" Get Loose? 137
16. The Spiritual Living God Uses Ordinary People 145
17. A New Heart and New Spirit 165
18. False Teaching and Consequences 169
19. We Need a Relationship, Not Religion 171
20. Financial Freedom Comes from the Spiritual Living God 181
21. The Presence of the Lord Is Here 189
22. Disobedience Has Consequences 193
23. You Must Believe Me to Trust Me 203

24. Until You Can Fear, Honor, and Respect the Holy,
    Spiritual Living God, Stop the Questions 221
25. How Do We Know God Hears Us When We Pray? 237
26. You Inquire of the Spiritual Living God's Will,
    but You Do Not Like His Answer 247
27. When Your Wisdom Allows You to Look Foolish 251
28. Why Should I Be Submerged for Baptism? 255
29. Sin Can Be White as Snow 263
30. SABBATH 267
31. The Spiritual Living God Is Still in the Blessing Business 273
32. Do We Really Need to Battle with Other Countries? 285
33. America Was Established for the Spiritual Living God 297

Because the Lord Is My Shepherd

He Only Loves You (HOLY) the way you should be loved by a holy, righteous, spiritual, and living God. Who loves His children (Isaiah 1:18-20) and really wants you to understand what you are going through, inviting you to trust Him? Though your reflection from sin is scarlet, He is willing to wash your sin whiter than snow. As you read Genesis 1:27 and 5:2, and Matthew 19:4-5, the Spiritual Living God speaks of how He made a man (male) and woman (female) in His image. Then, He allowed the male to provide a name for everything that exists here on Earth.

After the man (male) named all things, Adam found something was still missing. He still was not satisfied with all the Spiritual Living God had provided (Genesis 2:15-20). The Spiritual Living God decided He would create a helper for him, not a leader for man (male). He allowed the male (Adam) to experience a deep sleep and removed a part of his rib, creating a woman (female, Eve) (Genesis 2:21-25).

When Adam woke up, he observed a woman (female) and said, "She is bone of my bone and flesh of my flesh." The Spiritual Living God allowed man to reside over all things He created here on Earth.

He created males and females in His image, which means He was not confused about the genders in the generations before we were born. There were cities in Abraham's generation, Sodom and Gomorrah, that decided they would participate in homosexual lifestyles (Genesis 18:20; 19:4-7). The Spiritual Living God sent angels to destroy the cities, but Abraham tried to intercede on their behalf. He started with fifty people, and before he stopped speaking, he was down to ten people, asking the Spiritual Living God if ten people are found, would He save the cities? He actually agreed ten people were enough to save everyone in those cities (Genesis 18:22-33). The Spiritual Living God was willing to spare everyone's life, if ten people could be found who really sought the Spiritual Living God with a sincere heart. The angels only found four out of all the people that lived in those cities. The four were told to leave the cities and to not look back; otherwise, they would experience death. The cry of anguish was too much for Lot's wife; she looked back and turned into a pillar of salt (Genesis 19:24-29). Lord, have mercy; surely we have at least fifty in the United States of America who believe in the Heavenly Father, Son, and the Holy Spirit. We will tell future generations about the destruction of Sodom and Gomorrah (2 Peter 2:6), praying we do not experience your hand of heaviness.

Anytime we take the time and observe things taking place in this generation, we will see destruction (fires and floods), but lives are being spared. Do you think the Spiritual Living God is trying to warn this generation? Surely, we can learn from past generations' mistakes in this generation (Ezekiel 20:45-49).

The Holy Bible provides detailed instructions for humans to learn of the plans and purposes the Spiritual Living God has designed for their lives here on Earth.

This is why everyone that has breath (Genesis 2:7) has a

living soul from the Spiritual Living God and His Spirit (Jeremiah 31:31-35; Joel 2:28-32; 1 John 4:12-14). We need the Holy Bible to locate the plans and purpose for the Spiritual Living God's children (Romans 8; Galatians 3:24-29); it contains the blueprint for our lives here on Earth. The problems with future generations are we have become gods with the little knowledge the Spiritual Living God allows us to possess. We depend upon ourselves, thinking we can handle all things and taking credit for any success, until we are at death's door. Then, we want to acknowledge (John 4:24; 3:16) this is real and the Gospel (Psalm 22; Isaiah 53; Romans 1:16-20; Ephesians 1:13; 1 Thessalonians 1:5-6; Hebrews 1) is the Truth according to the Spiritual Living God's inspired words (Romans 1:16). Sometimes it is a little late to continue among the living, but you might be able to plant a seed for heirs or the next generation (Joel 1-3).

Observe the life of Satan (2 Peter 2:4), and the mistakes he made while residing in heaven; this was a very expensive lesson for future generations. He wanted to replace the Spiritual Living God and found himself removed from heaven.

When Satan fell from heaven, he had angels to follow him. They observed the women here on Earth one day and decided they would mate with them, creating giants here on Earth (Genesis 6:1-8).

The Spiritual Living God became displeased with the actions of all the people. This caused Him to regret creating males and females here on Earth (2 Peter 2:5). The Spiritual Living God called one man (Noah) into obedience with his family to build and enter the ARK. Noah was instructed by the Spiritual Living God to build the ARK because it was going to rain (Genesis 6:9-22). He was told to take two of every unclean animal, male and female, from each species (Genesis 7:1-3). He also told Noah to take more than two of the clean animals from the male and female genders. "In order to keep the seed alive upon the face of the Earth," which generations dropped the ball and confused the twenty-first-century generation?

The point in the above statement is the demand of the male and female genders being recognized by the Spiritual Living God's need for them to replenish the Earth after the flood (Genesis 6-7). Be sure and focus on the details in the Scripture, how many times the words "male" and "female" are found. He made sure the animals mated with the opposite gender in order to replenish the Earth for His purpose.

The Spiritual Living God placed humans created in His image above animals here on Earth (Genesis 1:28). Exactly how did we become confused regarding the Spiritual Living God's plans and purpose for the human, male and female genders? We are provided with intelligence from the Spiritual Living God (Psalm 19:7-11; Luke 24:44-47; John 1:4-5). When was the last time you observed animals of the same gender pursuing each other? They do not carry on in these manners, but humans created in the Spiritual Living God's image do and make excuses with our limited intelligence as to why we act this way (Romans 1:21-32). Hopefully, you will not try and question the Spiritual Living God's creation, but accept the homosexual lifestyle as a choice with consequences. Pray the Spiritual Living God will have mercy on you in the name of Jesus, for whatever reasons you made the choice. He really does have healing hands with the power to change anything going on in your life anytime we are willing to give the sins up in the name of Jesus (Psalm 19:12-14; 1 John 1-2). Remember, we will not give up anything we enjoy; we will make an excuse and blame someone else for our mistakes in life.

We are currently in a century where males are marrying males and females are marrying females. This is not the Spiritual Living God's plans for those created in His image. We need to reference the Holy Bible and follow His guidelines for relationships. If we are confused in this generation, just think of the consequences the future generations will experience for thinking those outside the will of the Spiritual Living God were making the right decisions. The other spirits that exist in this world (1 John 4:1-6) will not have to work very hard to deceive future generations. Remember the Holy Spirit is provided by the Spiritual Living God, in the name of Jesus; He will never compete for your time. Anytime we find time to read and pray for spiritual guidance while reading the inspired words of the Spiritual Living God, the Holy Bible will always provide the inspired words we need to have peace in the midst of the storms of life. There you will receive the promises made by the Spiritual Living God (1 John 1-5), for His children and their heirs in future generations. Anytime we sincerely love Him as our Heavenly Father in the name of Jesus, we will make an honest effort to STOP saying and doing things outside the will of the Spiritual Living God, refusing to quote this is LOVE when it is called SINS (Psalms 14, 53; Proverbs 24; Romans 1:21-32; 9; 1 Corinthians 1:18-31). Ignorance is bliss; now you have insight regarding your lack of spiritual knowledge.

Here we are many centuries later and still refusing to use the original blueprint for our lives here on Earth. This is what the Spiritual Living God provided for His design of humans, male and female genders. When the Spiritual Living God designed the male and female genders in His image, He provided instructions for them to multiply and replenish the Earth (Genesis 1:26-28).

Guess what? He never stated male and male or female and female should become one flesh (Genesis 2:24-25) to replenish His Earth. He asked opposite genders to take this responsibility. We have become so intelligent in this current century, until we have decided "that was then; this is now." Do we really think the answers to spiritual questions can be found in a textbook written by man without the guidance of the Holy Spirit?

Someone needs to pinch you and remind you the Spiritual Living God does not change to accommodate each generation or century (Isaiah 40:6-8; Hebrews 13:8; 1 Peter 1:24-25). *Someone once said, "Men of higher intelligence decided to confront the Spiritual Living God about designing and creating something here on Earth. It was said, He agreed to the challenge; man began to pick up things needed for the venture. Then, the Spiritual Living God observed man needed dirt, and He politely stopped man and said, 'You must use your own dirt.'"* OOPS!

When you were younger, people did not die at the rate we are observing death take place at in this day and time. According to man, we are more advanced in technology and medicine. Nevertheless, we are more sinful and disobedient than previous generations (James 4-5). We have so many little gods, including ourselves with a prideful heart, thinking more highly of ourselves than we ought to (Luke 7:7-14; Romans 12:3-8). Man will never have the power to stop the Spiritual Living God's consequences provided for humans anytime we choose to be disobedient. Jesus called them an adulterous generation during His time here on Earth (Matthew 13:38-41). Do you think we have multiplied (Proverbs 1:20-33; Proverbs 30; Isaiah 66:4; Jeremiah 7:13-20; 8:17-22; Zechariah 7:8-14; John 9:31) the sins that were taking place in those generations? Therefore, future generations will leave here at a much faster pace than previous generations. Someone forgot to teach the next generation, the Spiritual Living God only provided blessings (Proverbs 8:32-36; Hebrews 6:13-20; 12:12-17) when the people decided to obey His instructions. Whenever we choose a life of obedience (Luke 14:25-35), according to His inspired words found in the Holy Bible, and follow the standards set by His only begotten Son (John 1; John 3:16-21; John 14-16; Acts 2). Jesus Christ is our only spiritual connection with spiritual guidance provided by the Holy Spirit (1 Corinthians 2; Ephesians 1:3-5, 13-14; 1 Peter 1:13-25), then, we can be blessed in this generation.

We really need to stop and observe our lives in general; they can become very difficult to live without the Spiritual Living God (Luke 6:46-49). It is impossible for a man (male) or woman (female) to accomplish anything that will last; men and women need Jesus as their mediator to intercede on their behalf (Hebrews 1). We are reminded in Job (4:17-21), we will never be more than the Spiritual Living God, our Maker. Choosing to live life without Him provides physical or spiritual death without experiencing eternal life (Proverbs 9; 1 John 5). Wisdom, knowledge, and understanding are available to those who have access to the guidance of the Holy Spirit (John 14-16; 1 Corinthians 2). Then, we can

BECAUSE THE LORD IS YOUR SHEPHERD

live according to the Spiritual Living God's plans and purposes for our lives here on Earth. Tell me again why we do not need the blueprint of our lives, the Holy Bible? I get it, my Spiritual Living God, who allows you to have a spiritual relationship with Him through His only begotten Son (John 3:16), Jesus Christ, with guidance provided by the Holy Spirit (John 14-16; Acts 2), because He is a Spirit (John 4:23-24). He provides so much patience (Hebrews 5:11-14), until you have time to make up your mind about His Deity (Hebrews 6). He is totally different from the god you know and serve, right, got it! When you decide you would like to get to know the Spiritual Living God, just travel to many areas of the Bible (John 1:1-18; 3; 4:23-24; 6:44-65; 10; 14-16; Acts 2; 1 Corinthians 2; Romans 1:16-20; 8; 9:5-26; 10:9-21; 1 Peter 1:13-25), hang out in 1 John (1-5). Welcome aboard; we are glad to have you as part of the spiritual family of the Spiritual Living God, who resides in heaven with His Son seated on the right as our Mediator, interceding on our behalf to the Spiritual Living God (Romans 8; Galatians 3:24-29; 4:6-7; Ephesians 1:5; Hebrews 1; James 2:5), known to His children as their Heavenly Father. Remember, it helps to stay focused (Proverbs 3:5-6; Matthew 6:25-33; Galatians 5:16-26; Ephesians 6:10-20; Colossians 1:3-22; Hebrews 8-12; 2 Peter 1:12-21), realizing it is possible to do all things (Philippians 4:6-9, 13, 19) with guidance from the Holy Spirit; we are truly being blessed (Ephesians 1:3-5).

Anytime you have any knowledge about building or designing anything here on Earth, you will find it is necessary to provide the details in print for others to visually observe. Otherwise, it will be hard for others to follow your thoughts about the future plans. This design is called a blueprint;

everything you present is based on your knowledge or information provided by the person interested in the design.

Once everything has been agreed upon about the design, it is used to create exactly what was requested or needed. Any deviations away from the original design cause future problems.

Does this sound familiar? The Spiritual Living God created us with a blueprint. He was pleased with His creation until we decided to deviate away from His plans and purpose for our lives found in the Holy Bible. Now, we have all kinds of problems, suffering many consequences for being disobedient here on Earth. Heaven help those without spiritual knowledge because they will blame the Spiritual Living God for their lack of knowledge, out of ignorance (Psalm 14; 53; Proverbs 1:20-33; Romans 1:21-32; 1 Corinthians 1:18-31). Nevertheless, there were generations before we were born, in Hosea's generation, with the same problems that exist today, in the twenty-first century. The Spiritual Living God provided inspired words for them and future generations (chapter 4). He reminded them sins would have consequences and the people would perish for lack of knowledge regarding His Deity.

Marriage Covenant

The Spiritual Living God established in the beginning His standards for a marriage covenant, found in Genesis (2:18, 21-25; Matthew 19:4-6). Anytime we make a covenant with the Spiritual Living God, He is the only One with the power to release you from this covenant--which is a binding agreement, which became spiritual when the Spiritual Living God became involved. We must remember, He is a Spirit and only deals with Spirit and the Truth (John 4:23-24). This is why those who chose to be married with His blessing are still married, until He releases us from the marriage covenant (1 Corinthians 7:39; Ephesians 5:22-33; Hebrews 13:4). Remember, there is physical and spiritual death human beings can experience (Matthew 19:8-9; 5:32; Romans 7:2-3).

The Spiritual Living God has plans for those who desire a mate. They should reference Ephesians (5:18-33); there you find the explanation of a man (male) and his wife (female). Choosing to ignore His plans and purpose for the marriage (1 Corinthians 7:1-10) covenant allows us to look forward to being burdened with problems.

We are hindering our spiritual personal relationship with the Spiritual Living God, who acknowledges those who believe the Gospel (Psalm 22; Isaiah 53; Romans 1:16-20; Ephesians 1:13; 1 Thessalonians 1:5-6; 4:3; 5:19; Hebrews 1; 1

BECAUSE THE LORD IS YOUR SHEPHERD

Peter 1:13-25) as His children (Romans 8; Galatians 3:24-29; Ephesians 4:14-32).

A spiritual relationship with Him as the Heavenly Father and His Son, Jesus Christ, provides a Helper, the guidance of the Holy Spirit (John 14-16; Acts 2; Hebrews 1). Sometimes we use the cliché "The way to a man's heart is through his stomach." Just think, if a woman can deceive you with her cooking skills, how do you petition the Spiritual Living God for help when things fall apart in the marriage? No way! You cannot use Adam's line, "That woman you gave me." Knowing you made the call without the guidance of the Holy Spirit, choosing to lie will not work; just come clean and say, "Lord have mercy on me. I failed at reading and heeding Your instructions found in the Holy Bible with the guidance of the Holy Spirit." Hopefully, men being led by the Holy Spirit will not fall for this temptation (Proverbs 9; Ecclesiastes 7:26) and will follow the inspired words found in the Holy Bible (1 Corinthians 11:3; Ephesians 5:22-33). In the end, you will find grandma, mom, aunt, or a sister's meal would have been less expensive, without the heartache and pain associated with relationships outside the will of the Spiritual Living God.

Whenever we choose mates for marriage outside the will of the Spiritual Living God, we find ourselves in a divorce court, breaking the marriage covenant we made with the Spiritual Living God's blessings. We asked Him to accept our marriage covenant according to His words found in the Holy Bible (Matthew 19:3-12). Then, we go to man within the judicial system for permission to dissolve the marriage covenant with the Spiritual Living God (1 Corinthians 6). Anytime we make a covenant with the Spiritual Living God,

MARRIAGE COVENANT

who is a Spirit, about anything, we need to seek Him to break the covenant (Numbers 30). If He refuses to release us from the marriage covenant, and we choose to follow the world's standards for being released (1 Corinthians 7), we will be like the woman at the well having a conversation with Jesus (John 4:7-42).

Keeping covenants made with the Spiritual Living God allows us to have the guidance of the Holy Spirit, and our prayer life will not be hindered, just like David's in Psalm 25. This is why it is necessary for "women to become whole again after breaking a marriage covenant with the Spiritual Living God." According to Deuteronomy 21:14b and 22:28-29, the male has taken a part of her. This will be restored in a marriage covenant, because he completes her (1 Peter 3:7). If we choose to ignore the Spiritual Living God's inspired words regarding a marriage covenant without being spiritually released, get ready to become like a road lizard, doing the same thing, the same way, and expecting different results, or a dog chasing his tail; it makes you dizzy observing the dog going around and around until he becomes tired without becoming successful.

Remember, the woman at the well (John 4:7-23) had married husband number five and was working on number six. Hopefully, the message found in my first book, **How to Become Whole Without the Better Half**, provides insight about restoration after experiencing a broken marriage covenant.

A successful marriage requires a triangle just like the Heavenly Father, Son, and the Holy Spirit (1 John 5:6-12). The marriage covenant requires man (male), Jesus Christ (Mediator), and a wife (female) in order for us to experience a successful marriage without a divorce and have peace. When we begin to experience a rumble, get ready to go to the Spiritual Living God, praying in the name of Jesus (Philippians 4:6-9). If there is any sin, past or present, you committed, ask for forgiveness in Jesus' name. Always remember, the flesh is greedy and very demanding. If you feed it at any time, it will become aggressive and controlling (2 Corinthians 7:1; Galatians 5:16-6:10; Ephesians 6:10-20). It requires more attention and commitments without your approval.

In other words, you find yourself participating in things you thought you gave up in life (James 1:12-18; 2 Peter 2:9).

You know, you prayed and asked for forgiveness in the name of Jesus, praying the Spiritual Living God would have mercy on you, in the name of Jesus.

Do you think we can be identified as the adulterous generation (Proverbs 30) of the twenty-first century (Matthew 12:39)? Women have become very aggressive and decided they should lead and men shall follow their leadership (Genesis 2:21-25; 3:16; 1 Corinthians 11:3, 7-12; Ephesians 5:22-33; 1 Timothy 2:3-6, 13-15). This decision will cause much heartache and pain because the standards the Spiritual Living God provides states the male shall lead and the female shall follow (Genesis 3:12-19; 2 Corinthians 6:14-18; Ephesians 5). Spiritually, there is no difference between a male and a female when the Spirit of the Lord provides wisdom, knowledge, and understanding for His children (1 Corinthians 11:8-12; Galatians 3:28-29). Nevertheless, the Spiritual Living God has an order for all things (John 14:24-31; 1 Corinthians 7:1-9; 11:3; Ephesians 5:22-33). If we do not

MARRIAGE COVENANT

want a male to lead in a relationship, we need to be like Paul and devote our life to spiritual growth (1 Corinthians 7:7-11). The Spiritual Living God reminded those in Isaiah's generation, thy Maker is thine Husband (Isaiah 54:5-7). Surely, we can trust Him in this generation to be our Husband with the guidance of the Holy Spirit, until He provides your soul mate. Whenever we think about past problems with following a man (male), it usually comes from following a man who was not following Jesus Christ (1 Corinthians 11:3; Ephesians 5:22-33).

Anytime a male does not have the guidance of the Holy Spirit, he will totally abuse his ability to lead others. This situation will always cause you to build a wall around your heart, refusing all male leadership. Geez, I wonder if you remember which male caused this original problem with you, hardened your heart (Hebrews 3:7-15) against male leadership. Always remember, there are right and wrong ways to do things here on Earth (John 16:13; Philippians 4:6-9, 13; 1 Timothy 4:1). Nevertheless, you must be a child (Romans 8; Ephesians 4:14-32) of the Spiritual Living God to experience the promises found in the Holy Bible. We need to choose a life of obedience according to the Spiritual Living God's purpose and plans for our lives. Otherwise, we will miss out on receiving our blessings according to the Spiritual Living God's plans and purpose for marriage covenants (1 Peter 3:1-12).

Remember, the man (male) must follow Jesus Christ before he can lead his wife and family (Ephesians 5:18-33). Nevertheless, we really need to stop being unequally yoked in all things (2 Corinthians 6:11-18). Paul provided the warning in his generation; surely, we can learn from

BECAUSE THE LORD IS YOUR SHEPHERD

their mistakes in our generation. Maybe these Scriptures will provide some insight regarding the stress you are experiencing in this generation. Any woman (female) who decides not to follow the Christian teachings of Jesus Christ regarding this Scripture (1 Corinthians 11:3, 7-11; Ephesians 5:22-33) should be like Paul and devote her life to spiritual growth and teaching.

She really needs to inform any male she decides to interact with spiritually; otherwise, he can look forward to (Ecclesiastes 7:26) this experience without the guidance of the Holy Spirit. He always provides spiritual insight about her ability to tear down and destroy all things, until she surrenders her life to Jesus Christ and receives the guidance of the Holy Spirit.

We have changed the Spiritual Living God's original plans for the family in this generation. The world states, "You can live together without a marriage covenant and according to a certain time frame, you are considered husband and wife." Most females allow the male to walk away from his responsibility as her husband. She knows within her heart of hearts she was never his wife in the eyes of the Spiritual Living God. Therefore, she begins to experience what was said before her birth. The male removes a part of her during sexual activity that can never be replaced by man's standards, and he is responsible for completing her in the eyes of the Spiritual Living God. This is why the cliché "Why buy the cow when the milk is free" causes severe pain. Just remember, we are going to suffer the consequences just like David and Bathsheba in his generation (2 Samuel 11).

David was blessed with many wives and a man after the Spiritual Living God's heart (Acts 13:22). The day he

MARRIAGE COVENANT

observed Bathsheba with part of her plans to become noticed by him, David's life began to crumble; his desire for another man's wife caused him many sorrows and pain (2 Samuel 12). Exactly how can we commit adultery (Luke 16:15-18; 2 Peter 2:14) in this generation without experiencing consequences? If the Spiritual Living God had to discipline David, we will not escape this reminder of His being displeased in this generation (Hebrews 12:3-11).

He suffered the loss of his firstborn child with Bathsheba, which they conceived in adultery. David's older children caused him much heartache and pain by being disobedient also. The experience was like dominoes falling after the first one fell. When David finally came to a spiritual understanding about the holiness of the Spiritual Living God, who refuses to accept sin from anyone, David repented and asked for forgiveness for his sins against the Spiritual Living God, remembering his relationship before Bathsheba's arrival.

The Spiritual Living God forgave him and restored His relationship with David; He blessed him with another son, Solomon. This son was the most intelligent man that lived here on earth before Jesus' appearance as a human (1 Kings 3:3-15; Matthew 12:42; John 1:1-15; Hebrews 1; Philippians 2:6-12).

When we accept the Spiritual Living God's only begotten Son (John 1:18-31; 3:16-21; 5:17-47; 10; Romans 10:9-21) as our Lord and Savior, Jesus Christ, who died and rose and is seated at the right hand of our Heavenly Father, the Spiritual Living God (Hebrews 1; 1 John 1-3), we are provided with the guidance of the Holy Spirit to make better decisions regarding our lives here on Earth. Otherwise, the consequences of sin are experienced with sorrow and pain, affecting those related to you personally and those who follow your leadership. Nevertheless, we are forgiven just like David because of our relationship with the only begotten Son (John 3:16-21; Romans 8; Ephesians 4:14-32; Hebrews 8). Therefore, our relationship is restored in the name of His Son, Jesus Christ, when we repent, asking for forgiveness for sinning against the Spiritual Living God (Luke 13:3; Acts 2:38-40; 17:30; 26:20; 1 John 1-2).

The current and future generations are being placed at a disadvantage when we forget all sins have consequences. Jesus came into this world so we could experience an abundant life (John 10:10; 1 Timothy 2:2-8). Anytime we have a spiritual personal relationship with the Holy, Righteous, and Spiritual Living God (Hebrews 10; 1 John 1-2). Jesus' blood was shed on Calvary's cross; it is used for cleansing us from all unrighteousness (1 Peter 1:13-25). Whenever we choose to ask for forgiveness for our sins, in the name of Jesus (1 John 1:7-10), we are forgiven. Just like David had to recognize the holiness of the Spiritual Living God and receive restoration, we need to learn we must honor, respect, and acknowledge the holiness of the Spiritual Living God (John 10) in this generation also.

The Spiritual Living God is too holy, righteous, and spiritual to have a relationship with those who refuse to acknowledge His Son. Anytime we decide to surrender our lives to the guidance of the Holy Spirit, life becomes so much easier to live. The Helper, who provides wisdom, knowledge, and understanding about all things, especially spiritual things (1 Corinthians 2). Jesus provides this access (John 14-16; Acts 2) for the children (Romans 8; Galatians 3:24-29; Ephesians 4:14-32) of the Spiritual Living God. We need to make better

MARRIAGE COVENANT

decisions about all things (John 16:13; Philippians 4:6-9, 13) that are pleasing to the Spiritual Living God, who claims us as heirs (Romans 8:17; Galatians 3:26-29; Ephesians 3:4-9; Titus 3:3-8), because He is our Heavenly Father. It is impossible for humans living in the flesh to communicate with the Spiritual Living God (John 4:23-24); we have been reminded to test the spirits by the Spirit (1 John 4:1-6; Acts 19:11-19). Otherwise, they are powerful enough to deceive you without the guidance of the Holy Spirit.

Just like the Spiritual Living God spoke to Adam about the trees in the Garden of Eden, "Do not eat from this tree but enjoy the others," the snake knew whom to communicate with in order to deceive; he knew Adam would not give the conversation any time or thought. Nevertheless, Eve as his wife was able to accomplish the deed because of their connection of being one flesh, as his wife (Genesis 2:24; Ephesians 5:31). This is a very powerful connection, when a relationship causes you to forget what the Spiritual Living God spoke to you personally (Genesis 3:12-13). This is the first warning to man about the power and influence of any female. Adam had directions straight from the Spiritual Living God. He did not need a mediator or anyone delivering the message from the Spiritual Living God.

Just think, if Adam could be deceived after communicating directly with the Spiritual Living God, in the beginning of creation, men in future generations do not have a prayer without Jesus Christ providing a Helper, the guidance of the Holy Spirit. The male will be destroyed by any female who decides to use her power (Ecclesiastes 7:26). Eve was the tip of the iceberg; women in the twenty-first century without the guidance of the Holy Spirit are the iceberg. The power and force are so great,

BECAUSE THE LORD IS YOUR SHEPHERD

you can feel the coldness; before she touches her next victim (Proverbs 5-7), consider yourself warned.

Remember in the commercial in the 1980s, "She can bring home the bacon and fry it up in the pan and never forget, who is the man." Guess what? The bacon is burning in the twenty-first century. Women have too many irons in the fire; they forgot you are the men. Look around; in this generation, some men are staying home and raising the children because the woman's salary is greater than his salary in some cultures. Whenever we live according to the Spiritual Living God's plans and purposes for our lives, the Spiritual Living God can multiply anything and everything to meet the needs of those who truly belong to Him as His children (Romans 8; Galatians 3:24-29; Ephesians 4:14-32). Otherwise, we are in control of things and will always work hard and not smart.

Statistics state things change drastically since women began to leave the home without training up their children (additional thirty sexually transmitted diseases, many without a cure, drug usage experienced by those under the age of sixteen, perversion (child) sexual interest for both genders, children have total disregard for any adult with authority, disobedience is off the history-making chart, they are building prisons faster than schools for a formal education). We were warned in Proverbs 30 and 2 Peter 2:14 about the consequences of an adulterous generation.

As females, if we do not have any desire to follow the inspired words of the Spiritual Living God in each generation regarding motherhood, we should stop conceiving children, when we know in our heart of hearts, we have no desire to train up a child according to the inspired words found in

MARRIAGE COVENANT

the Holy Bible. Agur's prophecy was spoken with inspired words in his generation; they are currently taking place in this generation of the twenty-first century (Proverbs 30). Your children have no respect for you as a parent, which is probably a generational curse (Proverbs 30:11-17; Matthew 15:3-6), and we keep bringing more children into this world out of disobedience. Does anyone know what happened in America from the 1960s until this present day and time? Probably past generational sins coming back (Exodus 20:5-6), with the current generation choosing to experience a life of disobedience.

What ever happened to the leadership provided according to the Scriptures (1 Corinthians 11:3; Ephesians 5:18-33) in the mid-twentieth century? Yes, it was wrong for males to disrespect females because of their gender. Geez, any male without the guidance of the Holy Spirit who decides to interact or have a personal relationship with a female (Ecclesiastes 7:26) can look forward to experiencing some heartache and pain in this generation. Anytime a female chooses to accept the Spiritual Living God as her Heavenly Father, the Son, and the guidance of the Holy Spirit, she has the male gender beat with spiritual guidance (Ephesians 5:1-21). The Scripture states the Holy Spirit provides insight for both genders on the same level spiritually (1 Corinthians 11:8-12; 2 Corinthians 6:14-18). Nevertheless, those who have spiritual guidance must follow the guidelines for male and female relationships. Otherwise, there is no spiritual guidance for males or females who do not need a spiritual personal relationship with Jesus Christ--which means you are just like a deer caught in the headlights of a vehicle competing with evil spirits leading any males or females

BECAUSE THE LORD IS YOUR SHEPHERD

(Ecclesiastes 7:26). You can only ask the Lord to have mercy, if the female decides not to follow Jesus Christ with the guidance of the Holy Spirit. Nevertheless, you have never experienced the EV in evil with Satan leading a woman or a male. We must tell the truth in order to shame the devil. This will never be a nice learning experience, so get ready for turbulent times (Proverbs 5-7).

Otherwise, try surrendering your life to Jesus Christ, asking for forgiveness for all sins. The Holy Spirit brings to your remembrance and allows your Heavenly Father, who resides in heaven, who acknowledges you as His child (Romans 8; Ephesians 4:14-32) to provide the spiritual guidance needed to meet our needs in this generation. Just like past generations, who did not have the little gods (the different technology and materials things) available in their generation (Ecclesiastes 7:29), we need to remember, their success came from being obedient to the Spiritual Living God's commandments (Matthew 22:36-40; John 3; Romans 13:8-10). They believed (1 John 1-4; Romans 10:9-13), and accepted these Scriptures, reminding the next generation, we can also look forward to experiencing eternal life (1 John 5). Whenever we choose a life of obedience, we can look forward to being blessed (Proverbs 3:5-6; Matthew 5:1-12, 17-20; 6:25-33; John 10; James 1:12-18; 2 Peter 2:9) while living here on Earth until Jesus returns for the Spiritual Living God's children.

The past generations did not have to struggle like we do today in order to stay focused on the Spiritual Living God and grow spiritually.

Lord, have mercy on the generations after the twenty-first century, if we have problems believing in the Heavenly

MARRIAGE COVENANT

Father, Son, and the guidance of the Holy Spirit in this generation. The current technology is supposed to make life easier, but it is also interfering with our spiritual growth (Ephesians 3:14-21). We are actually relying on man-made devices in this generation. This allows us to replace the spiritual personal relationship with Jesus, which is needed to experience the guidance of the Holy Spirit, therefore, forgetting the Spiritual Living God, through His darling Son, Jesus Christ, with the guidance of the Holy Spirit (1 John 1-5), who is the only reliable Source of strength (John 16:13; Philippians 4:13), which is always available and will not change with each generation.

The past generations, who were grounded in their faith, always floated and did not sink during the storms of life. They could testify about the Spiritual Living God's mercy and grace, encouraging others to hold on to their faith because the storms were only passing over (Hebrews 11). Jesus Christ provided the anchor with the guidance of the Holy Spirit for the children (Romans 8; Galatians 3:24-29; Ephesians 4:14-32) of the Spiritual Living God. Those who had a personal relationship with the Spiritual Living God were actually able to experience the guidance of the Holy Spirit personally. Therefore, they became grounded in their faith and belief (Proverbs 3:5-6; Matthew 6:25-33; 13:18-23; 1 Peter 13-25; 2 Peter 1:12-21). They did not follow the wind and become confused about the difference in having a spiritual personal relationship with the Spiritual Living God and those who had **religion** in past generations. Do the research. We have more man-made **religions** in this century than in past centuries. Anybody can get people who are confused and disillusioned spiritually in this day and time

BECAUSE THE LORD IS YOUR SHEPHERD

to follow him. If they have experienced heartache and pain at the hands of someone, they trust putting all their faith in this human. Who said they were guided by the Holy Spirit, only to be misled and confused by the decisions their leaders are making?

They really need to experience the Spiritual Living God (1 Corinthians 2) for themselves with the guidance of the Holy Spirit, which can only be accessed through Jesus Christ. Then, they would have spiritual discernment and never experience this deception about spiritual things (1 Corinthians 2-3). If, the inspired words of the Spiritual Living God have been planted in our hearts, it will be impossible to intentionally sin against the Spiritual Living God (James 1:12-18; 1 Peter 2:9-10; 2 Peter 2:9).

Nevertheless, if we are on the fence (Revelation 3:15-17) and refuse to make a choice about the Spiritual Living God having a spiritual relationship with those created in His image (Genesis 1:26-28), the message has been provided. We need to be mindful to always sincerely bring all things that easily beset us to the altar and lay them at the feet of Jesus. Surely, we do not need spiritual reminders daily; you realized you must give up all things outside the will of the Spiritual Living God (Proverbs 3:5-6; Matthew 6:25-33), which cause us to choose to be disobedient. We need to walk in the Spirit and put on the whole armor of the Spiritual Living God, so we can be restored daily with spiritual strength (John 16:13; Galatians 5:16-26; Ephesians 5:1-21; 6:10-20; Philippians 4:4-19).

According to the promises made before and after the arrival of Jesus Christ as His only begotten Son, for the children (Romans 8; Galatians 3:24-29; Ephesians 4:14-32) of the Spiritual Living God, the Spirit (Jeremiah 31:31-35; Joel 2:28-32; 1 Corinthians 2; Hebrews 8:6-13; 1 John 4:12-14) that is within you will be enlightened with guidance provided by the Holy Spirit (John 14-16; Acts 2) about spiritual things. Remember (John 14:26) Jesus' promise to reveal things to us in times of need by the Holy Spirit; there is no need to stress yourself if you believe in the promise.

The question is, "Do you have a spiritual personal relationship with the Spiritual Living God or **religion**?" It really does make a difference. We must have a spiritual personal relationship with the Heavenly Father, Son, and the guidance of the Holy Spirit to be enlightened regarding spiritual things in this generation (John 14-16; Acts 2; 1 Corinthians 2; Hebrews 1).

Otherwise, we will experience the different spirits (1 John 4:1-6) available for humans to experience oblivion for a while, and then return to reality. There are many man-made medicinals, legal and illegal drugs, that only the Spiritual Living God can release humans from. Remember, drugs are a spirit and the Spirit of the Spiritual Living God is the only One who can defeat this spirit. We need to remember the Spiritual Living God is still in control in this generation (Psalms 46-50). Otherwise, we could fix the problems that exist without man-made medicinals, alcohol, and non-pharmaceutical drugs we use to escape this world's problems, forgetting whenever we return to reality the problems did not clear themselves up. If anything, we probably compounded the problems with additional problems. Anytime we indulge in things that are harmful to our bodies, outside the will of the Spiritual Living God, we hinder our spiritual relationships (1 Corinthians 3:16-23), therefore, quenching the Holy Spirit,

BECAUSE THE LORD IS YOUR SHEPHERD

when we have been asked not to participate in these things (Ephesians 4:29-32; 1 Thessalonians 5:19) that interrupt spiritual communication with the Spiritual Living God, in the name of Jesus. The spiritual relationship (Romans 8; Ephesians 4:14-32) we have with the Heavenly Father (John 4:23-24), Son (John 14-16), and the guidance of the Holy Spirit, who leads, and we follow the Spiritual Living God's instructions found in the Holy Bible, are promises made for those who can be identified as His children (Galatians 3:24-29; 4:1-7; 1 Thessalonians 4:1-12).

If you do not receive your spiritual breakthrough (1 John 1-4) as a child of the Spiritual Living God, there must be something hindering your spiritual relationship (Psalm 19; Matthew 10:34-42; Luke 12:49-53); we must put all things into perspective to become His children and be claimed as His heirs. We cannot love anyone or anything more than the Spiritual Living God. We need to continue to repent and ask for forgiveness (Psalm 51), go back and pray without ceasing in the name of Jesus (1 Thessalonians 5:17-23), speaking about the promises He made for those who love Him and are willing to keep His commandments (Exodus 20:5-6; Matthew 22:37-40). Only through Jesus Christ with the guidance of the Holy Spirit are humans allowed to find their soul mate, which removes the need to fornicate and commit adultery in this generation (Romans 12:2; 1 Corinthians 5:9-13; 7:1-9; Galatians 5:16-26; Ephesians 1:3-23; 5:22-33; 6:10-20; 1 Thessalonians 4:3; 2 Peter 2:14).

Women According to Scripture

Women can be enlightened by the guidance of the Holy Spirit, but it is obvious, we can be a force to be reckoned with, without the guidance of the Holy Spirit (Proverbs 5-7). Solomon should know; he had 700 wives and 300 concubines (women on the side). They changed his heart, which was originally right with the Spiritual Living God (1 Kings 8:60-61; 9:4-9); "then old age set in and his heart was changed" (1 Kings 11:1-8).

The Spiritual Living God does not speak a lot about women receiving His instructions regarding leadership in the Holy Bible. There are a few women found with a sincere heart, but they mostly performed or informed the male the Spiritual Living God needed them.

This information helps the reader understand His plan and purpose for the male gender holds great responsibility. The twenty-first century is presenting and accepting women are men's equal in all things. Only by the guidance of the Holy Spirit, the Spiritual Living God presents spiritual knowledge to those who are His children (Galatians 3:24-29). Nevertheless, He presented an order for instructions regarding leadership according to His plans and purposes before we were born. Jesus will follow the Spiritual Living God, man will follow Jesus, and women will follow men (1 Corinthians 11:3; Ephesians 5:22-33). We can change anything we desire, but according

BECAUSE THE LORD IS YOUR SHEPHERD

to His plans and purpose. This is acceptable to Him as our Heavenly Father, for His children. We need to follow His leadership and not the world's. The world cannot help you in times of need, when you need to hear from heaven, regardless of the situation. The worldly decisions can get you in trouble; Jesus is the only One who can intercede on our behalf to the Holy, Righteous, and Spiritual Living God, to have mercy in His name. Before Jesus Christ's arrival as the only begotten Son, the Spiritual Living God provided instructions to males and females about making a vow (promise) to Him (Numbers 30). We should never make a promise to the Spiritual Living God, unless we have every intention of keeping the vow (Ecclesiastes 5:1-7).

He also stated certain things were to take place according to His inspired words found in the Holy Bible. He did not give us permission to change things according to each generation's desires to take place at that time (Hebrews 13:8). This is like the Scripture states the Bishop must be the husband of one wife (1 Timothy 3:1-7; 1 Peter 5:1-4). Oh! I get it, "That was then; this is now." Right. We will soon find out if our logic is the truth according to the Holy Bible. Surely, there are enough things going on in the world today to keep us busy enough not to challenge the inspired spoken words before our birth. Just think of the future generations making changes to accommodate their generation (ooh, that is scary!). This can be very shocking to the mind-set for those who believe, if it was good enough for past generations, it should be sufficient for the next generation also (Joel 1:1-4). Just remember, the Holy Bible is the inspired words of the Holy, Righteous, and Spiritual Living God. He could have used the husband of one wife or the wife of one husband if this is what He wanted future generations to follow regarding a bishop (something to think about). Only by the guidance of the Holy Spirit are we allowed to have wisdom, knowledge, and understanding regarding spiritual things (1 Corinthians 2).

The Spiritual Living God knows the heart and mind of each person He created in His image (Proverbs 23:7a, 12). Females tend to be more emotionally driven, therefore confusing the truth more easily. The male usually does not have this disadvantage regarding emotions, so there can be less confusion; remember the Scripture states the woman (Eve) was deceived, not the male (Adam) (1 Timothy 2:13-15). (STOP, I feel your anger; SMILE, IT IS THE TRUTH!) Therefore, they can waver in their faith, but with guidance from the Holy Spirit, they could probably take a stand for righteousness according to the inspired words of the Spiritual Living God. I personally think a male could handle the Scripture in Matthew 10:36 easier than a female, after carrying a child for nine months next to your heart and being told to go and perform an Abraham and Isaac sacrifice (Genesis 22:1-19). Remember, when the Spiritual Living God spoke to Abraham in detail about the promised son, Isaac was to be conceived by Abraham's wife, Sarah. After waiting according to Sarah's time clock and not being able to conceive, she decided to give the Spiritual Living God a helping hand with His plans regarding the promised son, Isaac (Genesis 13:15-16). She provided her servant (Hagar) for Abraham to mate with, so they could have the promised son--which she thought worked until the female personalities showed up. The servant decided to despise her, and Sarah became upset (Genesis 16:1-6).

What did I say about women and the ability to become

BECAUSE THE LORD IS YOUR SHEPHERD

deceitful? Do you think? This is why Abraham never told Sarah where he was going with Isaac (think about it). Sarah's response would probably be, "Leave the boy and go have a little talk with the Spiritual Living God about an alternative now, or I will go and help out God again!" This would probably be the straw that breaks the camel's back. There is a difference in the male and female leadership of the church, according to Scriptures in Titus (1:5-16).

Yes, spiritually, the Holy Spirit provides the same wisdom, knowledge, and understanding about spiritual things (1 Corinthians 11:7-12; Galatians 3:26-29), by the guidance of the Holy Spirit, to both genders, but the male shall lead, according to this Scripture (1 Corinthians 11:3; Ephesians 5:22-33). Geez, nothing would ever be accomplished if everybody was a chief and there were no Indians. Jesus came so we might learn how to become servants and stop looking for others to serve us (Luke 22:24-30; John 10; 13:1-20). Remember, charity covers a multitude of sins (1 Peter 4:8-10). "You cannot beat the Lord GOD's giving no matter how hard you try; the more you give, the more He gives to you. Just keep on giving. It is really true; He gave His Son--what more could He give?" Which one of us without the guidance of the Holy Spirit could perform this activity (John 13:1-20)? Only the Spirit of the Spiritual Living God allows us to get past our personal roadblocks and choose to be like Jesus Christ. Then, we can receive the spiritual guidance needed to follow in Jesus Christ's footsteps, so others might see Him through you.

The Spiritual Living God stated, He would use rocks (Luke 19:38-40) if a man was too busy to worship Him. All thanks be to the Spiritual Living God, He still has some men that are available to answer the call into obedience with the guidance of the Holy Spirit in this generation (2 Chronicles 7:14) to lead His church. Do you think this is why women are preaching and leading churches in the twenty-first century? Keep listening; there is a difference in the preaching and exactly how the message is being delivered. We must be able to receive spiritual insight before the difference is recognized.

We must always remember, the Spiritual Living God has an order for all things to keep down confusion among His children. Division among believers can create strife among those who believe the report of the Gospel (Psalm 22; Isaiah 53; John 12:38-50; Matthew 6:25-33; Romans 1:16-20; Ephesians 1:13; 1 Thessalonians 1:5-6; Hebrews 1; 1 Peter 1:13-25) when we take our eyes off the teachings of Jesus Christ. We need to reference Philippians 4:3-9,--the women assisted Paul; they did not lead Paul. Just think about these things. Fathers have the responsibility to teach the males, their heirs, about having a spiritual relationship with the Spiritual Living God (Proverbs 3-5) anytime they desire to become spiritual leaders in each generation. Otherwise, they are set up for destruction regardless of their worldly wisdom (Proverbs 9; Ecclesiastes 7:26).

There is a female that exists without the guidance of the Holy Spirit that can actually break his spirit (Proverbs 6:20-29; 7; 22:14; 25:24). They should teach their sons to pray for the woman that uses her tears at a distance; otherwise, she just might have him experiencing some tears without the guidance of the Holy Spirit. Most women that are honest will tell you, women have the male gender beat when it comes to deception. Only by the guidance of the Holy Spirit

BECAUSE THE LORD IS YOUR SHEPHERD

with the fear of the Spiritual Living God will women choose not to venture in the area of deceit. There is a female waiting to make a believer out of you. Just hold on; she will rock your world and ask you what happened (Ecclesiastes 7:26). Fathers here on Earth need to stop spoiling their little girls, who can turn out to be women found in Proverbs 5-7. They are being set up to experience the hand of heaviness provided by the Spiritual Living God. This hand is for their hardened hearts (Hebrews 3:7-11), which encourages them to use deceit and drama to their advantage.

Relationships with Jesus as the Mediator

According to 1 Peter 2:4-8, insight is provided regarding access to the Heavenly Father, the Spiritual Living God, through His Son, Jesus Christ (John 1:1-18; 3:16-21; 4:23-24; 14-16; Acts 2; Hebrews 1), a definition for those whom the Spiritual Living God considers His children (Romans 8; 1 Corinthians 2; Galatians 3:24-29; Ephesians 1:13-23; 4:14-32; 1 Peter 2:9-10). The Spiritual Living God has expectations for those who sincerely belong to Him (Isaiah 56:3-8; 2 Corinthians 3-4; Galatians 5:16-26; Hebrews 10-12; Titus 3; 1 Peter 2:11-17; 1 John 1-5). He also speaks of the foolishness of men (Psalms 14 and 53; Romans 1:21-32; 1 Corinthians 1:18-31; 2 Corinthians 2:11; Galatians 3:1-5) who choose not to follow Him. He reminds those who can be identified as His children, the Light will silence their ignorance (Isaiah 49:1-6; John 8:12-30).

If the male follows the steps of Jesus Christ (1 Corinthians 11:3; Ephesians 5:22-33), presenting himself before others with a Christlike Spirit, What would Jesus do in this situation? There is no reason for others not to observe your life and follow your leadership here on Earth.

The Spiritual Living God's children must always follow the Scripture providing instructions for spiritual relationships in marriages (1 Corinthians 6:15-7:40; 11:3; Ephesians 5:22-33; 1 Peter 3:1-12). There is never any confusion about

BECAUSE THE LORD IS YOUR SHEPHERD

the husband's and wife's position in this relationship (2 Corinthians 6:14-18). If they are equally yoked, when he says jump, the wife asks, "How high, lord husband?" because you trust him to lead you according to Christian principles. There is no need for you to concern yourself when he is accountable to the Spiritual Living God, in the name of Jesus. According to the promises of the Spiritual Living God, He is our Heavenly Father, and He provides for His children (Romans 8; Galatians 3:24-29; Ephesians 4:14-32). Just go to the Spiritual Living God in prayer and watch the changes take place before your eyes. Remember, the husband must follow Jesus in order for the wife to follow her husband (1 Corinthians 11:3; Ephesians 5:22-33). Whenever we choose husbands outside the will of the Spiritual Living God and try to follow spiritual instruction found in the Holy Bible, which is inspired words by the Spiritual Living God, we become totally confused for being unequally yoked in all things (2 Corinthians 6:11-18). The male is not capable of making the right decisions without the guidance of the Holy Spirit so he can lead you according to the promises the Spiritual Living God made to His children (Romans 8; Galatians 3:24-29).

Whenever we allow the Holy Spirit to guide us, every single decision will line up with the Spiritual Living God's plans and purposes for our lives here on Earth. He will bless you for being obedient according to His inspired words found in the Holy Bible.

This is why being unequally yoked in marriage causes so much pain and heartache (2 Corinthians 6:14). Any woman misused and abused will one day rise up and become tired of being a doormat (Proverbs 5-7; Ecclesiastes 7:26), reminding you of her wrath.

RELATIONSHIPS WITH JESUS AS THE MEDIATOR

Anyone who thinks times have changed, "That was then; this is now," believe me, the women in this generation make the women in past generations appear very meek. The Scriptures have already been provided about the power women have to be deceitful without spiritual guidance (Ecclesiastes 7:26).

Being equally yoked is of the highest importance to a marriage covenant (2 Corinthians 6:11-18; Ephesians 5:22-33). If you do not have the guidance of the Holy Spirit, another woman can trap your husband like a deer caught in headlights. The evil ways she possesses will totally confuse and disillusion him as the male gender, but look out if he allows an evil spirit to possess him.

The male begins to disrespect you as his wife, the woman who respects his authority as her husband. According to Scripture (Genesis 2:24-25; Matthew 19:5-6; Mark 10:6-12; Ephesians 5:22-33), the two become one in marriage. Their flesh is tied (bonded) to each other (1 Corinthians 6:15-20; 7). Remember Paul, not the Lord, said, "It is possible to save the other spouse who does not believe they should stay together" (7:12-14). This is one of the consequences for choosing a spouse for marriage without consulting the inspired words of the Holy Bible (2 Corinthians 6:11-18). Just remember Paul's conversation with the Lord during his distress (2 Corinthians 12:1-10).

Problems begin to present themselves when the husband or wife commits adultery (sins) against the Spiritual Living God (Matthew 19:7-10; 1 Corinthians 6:13b-20; 2 Peter 2:14). Anytime the wife or husband accepts the sin of adultery without rebuking the other spouse in a Christlike manner, somebody is going to seriously suffer the consequences

BECAUSE THE LORD IS YOUR SHEPHERD

for ignoring the other spouse's activity of adultery. Lest we forget, the two become one in the eyes of the Spiritual Living God (Genesis 2:24). If the wife is not strong enough to communicate with her husband, she should seek help from the elders of the church (1 Peter 5:1-11). This is why the leaders must follow the teachings of Jesus found in 1 Timothy 3:1-13 and Titus 1:5-9. Otherwise, your counseling can be ignored in this rebellious, adulterous generation of the twenty-first century.

We must be able to follow the inspired words found in the Holy Bible. We should never underestimate the ability of others who observe our lives and hold us accountable in each generation, in order to lead them according to the inspired words found in the Holy Bible. Otherwise, it will be impossible for others to accept your counsel, when you have not allowed the Holy Spirit to lead you (2 Peter 2:9). Choosing not to be the husband of one wife sets the leader up for destruction and discourse among those seeking spiritual counseling. Nevertheless, if the husband refuses spiritual counseling according to the Spiritual Living God's standards, choosing to ignore his marriage covenant with the Spiritual Living God, get ready to experience some turbulent times, but know your anchor will hold in the name of Jesus if you are the Spiritual Living God's child (Matthew 8:23-27; Romans 8; Ephesians 4:14-32). The spouse will become a thorn in your flesh, but remember Paul's conversation with the Lord, "My grace is sufficient" (2 Corinthians 12:1-10).

As a wife, you are probably only experiencing Zipporah's quick thinking. Observe when the Spiritual Living God was about to discipline Moses for not circumcising his son (Exodus 4:24-26). The Spiritual Living God created a helpmate for

RELATIONSHIPS WITH JESUS AS THE MEDIATOR

Adam, someone to complete the part he was missing in life.

Adam's other half (wife) decided to inform Adam of something God spoke to Adam about before her existence (Genesis 2:15-20). This is really a conversation they should not be communicating about, if she is going to question him. This is an opportunity for this generation to observe the benefits of being unequally yoked in this generation. As children of the Spiritual Living God, the Holy Spirit will always provide wisdom, knowledge, and understanding to both children without any confusion. Whenever the Spiritual Living God speaks to you as a husband (1 Corinthians 11:3; Ephesians 5:22-33), you should be still and wait for the directive from the Holy Spirit. The directive to the husband should be followed according to the Spiritual Living God's plans. Anytime we allow others to influence things provided by divine guidance of the Holy Spirit (1 John 4:1-6), problems can present themselves and cause much heartache and pain. Remember, the Spiritual Living God had a conversation with Abraham about conceiving the promised son by his wife, Sarah. He told him the child would be a nation (Genesis 22:17-18). Abraham was to observe the stars in the sky for his visual of things to come. Sarah decided to help the Spiritual Living God because she was not getting any younger; she provided someone to take her place (Hagar) (Genesis 16).

Sarah decided the Spiritual Living God needed some help to speed along the process, so she provided her servant (Hagar) for her husband. The results of Sarah helping the Spiritual Living God are still being experienced today, in the twenty-first century (Genesis 22). A long story short, we

BECAUSE THE LORD IS YOUR SHEPHERD

have two nations instead of the original promised nation established by the only promised son. Hagar's son Ishmael was never the promised son (Genesis 21). Those interfering females, Sarah and Hagar, caused this situation to take place. What did I say about women and the ability to deceive? "What a tangled web we weave, when first we practice to deceive." Yes, Abraham forgot as a male, his gender has been provided with two heads, but only one contains the brain, which allows you to make intelligent decisions without future consequences.

We are still experiencing this confusion in the twenty-first century, because the nation with Ishmael's descendants still think they are the chosen nation (ignorance is bliss). Just think, if they had the intelligence to receive the guidance of the Holy Spirit (Romans 8; 1 Corinthians 2; Hebrews 1), they could read the inspired words found in the Holy Bible. The inspired words of the Spiritual Living God (2 Timothy 3:16) provide wisdom, knowledge, and understanding about all things here on Earth. As children (Romans 8; Galatians 3:24-29; Ephesians 4:14-32) of the Spiritual Living God, we are allowed to have a full understanding about the Spiritual Living God's original plans and Sarah's plans to help the Spiritual Living God. When the Spiritual Living God places a male in a position as a leader, he should always go back to original sources for answers, not a female with a hidden agenda (1 Corinthians 11:3; Ephesians 5:22-33; Titus 1:5-16). Just think, if we had one wish to change anything before Jesus Christ's appearance as the Spiritual Living God's only begotten Son, the majority of Americans with a spiritual personal relationship with the Spiritual Living God would probably wish to remove the Hagar and Ishmael

RELATIONSHIPS WITH JESUS AS THE MEDIATOR

connection to Abraham, without a doubt. Geez, we could probably have a better world with less confusion about the promised son to be conceived by Sarah and Abraham (Genesis 17:15-19; 18:9-15; 21:1-8).

Do you think the Spiritual Living God had a good reason for insisting fathers instruct their sons, leading them with the guidance of the Holy Spirit (Proverbs 4)? Otherwise, they could look forward to experiencing deception (Proverbs 5-7; Ecclesiastes 7:26). It is really amazing how we can learn the hard way or the easy way when it comes to lessons learned about life. Remember, it was Eve, not Adam, who was originally deceived (1 Timothy 2:13-15). How did we become confused in this generation about the leadership of the male gender?

(Do not answer--women taking charge and males assuming the weaker role in the relationships, right?) Males should never underestimate the power of a woman; you were warned from past generations' mistakes. Surely, the Spiritual Living God did not bless you with a son for a female to destroy your heritage, without a son, it is the end of the line for you (Ecclesiastes 7:26).

This generation is accepting a female using her father's last name and continuing the heritage of the family, but that is not scriptural. Two females already tried this before you were born and created nations of disobedience, according to the Spiritual Living God's inspired words, disrespecting His plans and purposes (Genesis 19:30-38). Surely, we can learn from their mistakes.

These two females made a decision without spiritual guidance from their leader in their generation, before Jesus Christ, who provides the Helper in our generation.

BECAUSE THE LORD IS YOUR SHEPHERD

They decided the Spiritual Living God needed their help in preserving their father's seed after the destruction of Sodom and Gomorrah by the Spiritual Living God (Genesis 19:24-29). The heritage always stops without a male offspring, which is considered a blessing from the Spiritual Living God. When the Egyptians wanted to stop the Hebrews from multiplying, they set out to destroy all male babies (Exodus 1:16-22). Anytime a culture would like to diminish another culture in this and past centuries, they always kill the males, and some cultures go as far as impregnating the female with their seed to expand their culture (Genesis 34:25; Numbers 31:17; Judges 20:13-48; 21). Jeremiah reminded those in his generation about the male child being a blessing (49:1). Jacob also speaks to his sons before his death regarding their future (Genesis 49). It is really amazing how he never said anything about his daughter; she was not mentioned during his prophecy about his children's futures.

In Moses' generations, there was a command that all males went before the Spiritual Living God three times a year (Exodus 34:23). Do you think the Spiritual Living God had His reasons for excluding females? We are currently accepting the weakness of the male gender with female characteristics as pleasing to the Spiritual Living God. (He was called a Peter Pan Man; now he is called Metro Man in the twenty-first century.) It is probably a dominant female's influence in their lives that causes their confusion in this generation (Ecclesiastes 7:26). This is why the homosexual lifestyle is acceptable in this generation. When was the last time you observed a male insisting his daughter has a right to participate in the homosexual lifestyle?

They are usually not confused in this matter, but women

have this negative influence over their sons and daughters causing this mass confusion in this generation about the homosexual lifestyle. Their devious ways for reasons unknown can be a heavy influence on both genders. We can make all the excuses we like for the choices people make. Just pray the Spiritual Living God does not become angry and reveal His hand of heaviness to our generation, trying to get our attention for this abominable (hated very much) sin. Yes, all sins cause the Holy Spirit to grieve (Ephesians 4:29-32; 5:1-21), but the Spiritual Living God made it a point to attach the word "abomination" (totally detestable) on some of the things we do. We must stop sugarcoating things in this generation, when sin affects those by blood relationships (2 Peter 2:9).

When you surrender your life to the Spiritual Living God, we must take a stand for what is right and pleasing to Him (Matthew 10:34-39; John 16:13; Romans 16:25-27; Philippians 4:6-9). He really can deliver anyone from the homosexual lifestyle, but the person must be willing and ready to give it up (Psalm 19; 51). We must remember, the Spiritual Living God's decisions will never be manipulated by man's devices and bring positive results (Proverbs 4). Yes, females are definitely needed, but they cannot take the place of males' expectations, according to the Spiritual Living God's inspired words found in the Holy Bible.

Those in the twenty-first century that say, "That was then; this is now," get ready to experience some devastating pain for trying to change the inspired words provided to benefit your generation (John 5:39-47; 8:12-30). Remember, the Spiritual Living God has already commanded, His words will stand forever (Isaiah 40:8; Acts 5:29; 1 Peter 1:22-25).

BECAUSE THE LORD IS YOUR SHEPHERD

Surely, we can learn from Lot's daughter's mistakes and the destruction of Sodom and Gomorrah in this generation. The whole Book of Proverbs was written for males in the future generations. Men must always accept the inspired words of the Spiritual Living God as the Truth (1 Corinthians 11:3; Ephesians 5:22-33); they provide spiritual insight. Whenever males follow Jesus Christ according to the plans of the Spiritual Living God, a woman without the guidance of the Holy Spirit will never challenge and intimidate his ability to lead and become successful. The Holy Spirit will always come to your defense (John 14:26) when speaking with those other spirits that exist in this world (1 John 4:1-6). There are some women who have a Spirit like the description found in Proverbs (18:20-24; 31:10-31). Always remember, it is a blessing to interact with a woman (female) who can identify the Truth and relate to it. If the Spiritual Living God created you in His image, then you are considered that gender in His eyes, as a male or a female (yes, my mind is narrow; I can only accept the inspired words of the Spiritual Living God as the Truth) (John 4:23-24; 1 Corinthians 2). Those who accept sex change operations to change their gender are recreating what they desire to live as in this world. Always remember, the Spiritual Living God does not make mistakes. ANYTHING HE DESIRES TO CHANGE DOES NOT REQUIRE ASSISTANCE FROM MAN; HE HAS ANGELS TO CARRY OUT HIS AGENDA (Exodus 23:20-25; 2 Samuel 23:15-17; Psalm 91; Ecclesiastes 5:1-7; Isaiah 37:35-38; Daniel 3:28-30; 6:21-27; Hosea 12:1-6; Matthew 1:20; 4:10-11; 18:10; 24:36; 28:2; 26:47-56; Luke 1:11-13, 26-38; Hebrews 1; 2 Peter 2:11; Jude 9); He is the Spiritual Living God all by Himself (Job 36:5-33).

RELATIONSHIPS WITH JESUS AS THE MEDIATOR

When the Spiritual Living God gave the Israelites the land of Canaan (Genesis 15:18-21; Exodus 23:20-33; Numbers 33:50-56; Deuteronomy 11:8-32), they were warned ahead of time about the strength of the Canaanites. He told them to never mingle with those outside His covenant. He also warned them not to marry the strangers because they would turn their hearts away from Him, the Spiritual Living God. They are powerful enough to have you worshiping their gods. The Spiritual Living God reminded the Israelites, they did not want to experience His anger because He would destroy them on the spot (Deuteronomy 6; 7:1-5; 8:11-20). If the people were warned in Moses' generation, and He provided His only begotten Son to help us make the right decisions in our generation, so we could receive His promises provided for those who are His children (Deuteronomy 12:25-28; Romans 8; Ephesians 4:14-32).

Who told this generation, we could be blessed in our disobedience, in this day and time? Anytime we take the time and acknowledge the Heavenly Father, who sent His only begotten Son, who provided a Helper, the Holy Spirit, we need to rejoice (Philippians 3:1-3; 4:4-9) for this blessing of being enlightened about past generations' mistakes. Now we should be able to make better decisions without suffering consequences for choosing a life of disobedience (Ephesians 5:21). Nevertheless, you need to personally experience the Light (John 1:1-34; 3:16-21; 4:23-24; 5:17-47; 10; 14-16; Acts 2; Romans 8; 1 Corinthians 2; Ephesians 1:13; Hebrews 1; 8; 1 John 1-5) in order to realize you are walking in darkness (Psalm 34; Galatians 5:16-26).

She Really Should Be Feared

We are reminded in Scripture (Genesis 2:15-25; 1 Timothy 2:13-15), Adam was created before Eve. Nevertheless, women should be feared out of the respect of her ability to tear down and destroy things when they choose to indulge in being evil (Ecclesiastes 7:26). A woman has so many MO's (modi operandi), only the Spiritual Living God knows which one she will expose during your encounter (sweet-spirited, lady, madame, aggressor, trophy wife, passive, destructive, a call girl, or virtuous and God-fearing, respecting Him as her Heavenly Father).

Therefore, the Spiritual Living God's conversation was between Adam and Himself, regarding His plans for things to come, including the instructions about the Garden of Eden (Genesis 2:15-17, 3: all). The male gender needs to stop thinking every female they meet is just like the women in their lives that had a positive influence (Ecclesiastes 7:26). Any male that has been determined in his decision about steps to take in order to accomplish anything, only to be convinced by a female her decisions to help or change the plan were better, and faced a disaster, probably can relate to the power Eve had to convince Adam, Yes, the Spiritual Living God said, but did He really say we could not eat from this one tree only?

Just like Adam, you have become confused because she agreed, and then she questioned your decision with another question. This threw you off track with the first question. This is how males become like a deer caught in the headlights of a moving vehicle. Before Eve's arrival, Adam was obedient regarding all instructions provided by the Spiritual Living God. It appears he followed his wife regarding the instruction about the trees, like a sheep going to slaughter (Proverbs 31:3). When the lights came on, and the fog cleared in his mind, he began to think again. He realized he had been tricked by the serpent through his wife.

This generation loves to analyze things, so for the sake of listening to your points, let's say Adam told his wife, Eve, what the Spiritual Living God said about the trees in the Garden of Eden (Genesis 2:15-18). Anytime knowledge has been provided from the Spiritual Living God (John 4:23-24), there should never be a doubt about the source (John 16:13; Philippians 4:8-9) of information. If the message lines up with the teachings of Jesus, just take a stand. Eve was dealing with a spirit (1 John 4:1-6) when the snake spoke to her, but she had no idea of the test. Sometimes evil spirits are more convincing than the Holy Spirit, when you feed the flesh more than the Spirit.

In order to gain spiritual knowledge, the Spirit must be fed by the Holy Spirit. A female can have overwhelming curiosity, which allows her to experience things that should not pull her interest. Let's say Adam forgot to tell his wife (Genesis 3:1-13), sorry, that rebuttal will not work. You have to love Adam's response to the Spiritual Living God: "The woman whom thou gave to be with me, she gave me of the tree, and I did eat." This is why someone must lead, and someone must follow (2 Corinthians 6:11-18); otherwise,

SHE REALLY SHOULD BE FEARED

nothing will ever be accomplished in a marriage (Genesis 3:16-19). We have been provided with an order for things to take place in a marriage (Ephesians 5:22-33), but the husband must follow Christ before he can lead his wife (1 Corinthians 11:3; 1 John 1-5). The male must have a spiritual connection, receiving his help from the guidance of the Holy Spirit; otherwise, it will be impossible to lead others (John 14-16; Acts 2; Romans 8). It is obvious, everything worked according to the Spiritual Living God's plans and purpose until the female arrived in the Garden of Eden.

Many generations later, the Spiritual Living God spoke to Abraham about His plans to bless and multiply his seed conceived by his wife, Sarah. He told Abraham he would have a son, which would be like the dust of the Earth and stars in the sky (Genesis 13:14-15; 15:1-6; 22:15-18). Abraham shared this conversation with his wife, Sarah. After what she felt was a long enough waiting period because she was not getting any younger, she decided to help the Spiritual Living God with His plans (Genesis 16:1-6). Just in case this generation forgets (Psalm 121), the Spiritual Living God never slumbers or sleeps (2 Peter 3). During Sarah's impatience, she provided another female to try and help conceive the promised son.

This action eventually would prove to be a very expensive lesson (Galatians 4:22-31). Look at the results still being felt in the twenty-first century. The people are still confused in some nations about the promised son being Isaac (Genesis 22). The son Sarah and Hagar manipulated out of Abraham was not the Spiritual Living God's promise taking place, but two women helping the Spiritual Living God out. Yes, the Spiritual Living God spoke to Abraham and not Sarah, but what male would turn down a chance to have a sexual encounter with a beautiful woman (Proverbs 9; Ecclesiastes 7:26)? The consequences were experienced for his actions back then, but the Spiritual Living God kept His promise (Genesis 18:9-15). He allowed Abraham and Sarah to eventually conceive the only son with the original promise (Genesis 15:1-6; 16:1-6; Hebrews 11). Take the time and think about the strength and power Sarah had to cause a mass confusion, still being felt today.

Let us also look at Miriam, Moses' sister. Remember, the Spiritual Living God called Moses into obedience, and he insisted his brother Aaron was a better choice for the Spiritual Living God to use (Genesis 3-4).

When Miriam decided to voice her opinion against the wife of Moses, it cost her greatly (Numbers 12). After the Spiritual Living God set the record straight about Moses, He allowed Miriam to experience leprosy and told Moses to put her out of the camp. Moses had to intercede on her behalf to the Spiritual Living God, but she still experienced consequences for disagreeing with the Spiritual Living God's choice of a wife for Moses. We really have to be careful about speaking against those the Spiritual Living God calls into obedience, according to His plans and purpose for their lives here on Earth (Psalm 105:15); take my advice, this is really true.

Samson was a child promised by the Lord; his mother constantly prayed to the Spiritual Living God to bless her with a child (Judges 13). The Spiritual Living God sent an angel with a message, she would conceive a son after being barren (Judges 13:5-7), with instructions about the future. The Spiritual Living God also told Samson's mother

SHE REALLY SHOULD BE FEARED

what not to consume while carrying this child. Samson's strength was revealed when he experienced the lion, and what it would take to maintain it by his parents. To make a long story short, the men in that generation outside the will of the Spiritual Living God actually feared him because of his strength (Judges16). So, they found a devious woman to find out the source of his strength. When he met the woman, named Delilah (devil in disguise), she played the game "fool me once, shame on you; fool me twice, shame on me; fool me three times, my interpretation for Samson, say it isn't so."

Lord, have mercy, she was able to deceive him with her drama, revealing to him her plans about the Philistines being upon him. The third time was a charm because he revealed his source of strength after experiencing her plans before he told her the truth. Do you think it was love or his lusts that caused him not to realize she was planning to deceive him? It does not matter; if you receive a message from the Spiritual Living God and are told never to reveal the secret about your strength, how can a woman overrule this message? Praise the Spiritual Living God, Samson eventually humbled himself and prayed, asking for forgiveness for his mistake. He was blessed with the return of his strength, but not his sight (Judges 16:23-29). He redeemed himself by killing more men outside the will of the Spiritual Living God, without his eyesight. The number of men killed this time outnumbered his original destruction with the jawbone of an ass (Judges 15:14-20).

What if you found yourself being spiritually tested? Sometimes it helps to see where we are spiritually; Satan will need permission to test you before a test can take place

49

BECAUSE THE LORD IS YOUR SHEPHERD

from him (Job 1:6-2:8). If you have a spouse, pray she is not like Job's wife. The words she spoke during Job's test could break a man if he is not grounded in his faith and the Truth (Job 2:9-10; Hebrews 11; 2 Peter 1:12-21).

Remember, David, a man after the Spiritual Living God's heart, who is closer than close in a personal relationship with the Spiritual Living God (Acts 13:22b), actually communicated and experienced the Spiritual Living God's leadership and blessing as a very young man. We need to remember 2 Peter 3 whenever we become confused in this generation. Nevertheless, when Lady Bathsheba arrived on the scene, things began to happen without an explanation. She knew David appeared on His balcony every day at a certain time. She used the power she had as a female to work on his weakness, which caused him to commit adultery. David was so out of control with the relationship he had with Bathsheba, he had her husband killed for not helping him cover up his sin against the Spiritual Living God. Bathsheba's husband had so much respect for David as a king, he refused to sleep with his wife while others were on the battlefield fighting for the king. When the Spiritual Living God provided a message by Nathan the prophet (2 Samuel 12:1-12), revealing David's sin without his being aware, David insisted the man be punished at the highest level of punishment, until Nathan told David, "You are the man." David's consequence was the sword would never depart from his family. He had other wives, but Bathsheba was the thorn in his side (yes, His grace is sufficient in times of trouble) (2 Corinthians 12).

The Spiritual Living God had mercy when David came to his senses and repented, restoring his relationship with

SHE REALLY SHOULD BE FEARED

with her plan after her daughter danced for Herod on his birthday. He promised the daughter she could have anything she wanted, including half of his kingdom. So, like a good daughter, she consulted her devious mother for a suggestion. Herodias told her to ask for the head of John the Baptist in a charger.

Herod appeared to be shocked, but his word could not be reversed; the evil mother still got her wish for John the Baptist's life.

Any males who think they can handle an evil and devious female can follow Solomon's words of wisdom (Proverbs 6:20-35). He really can take fire onto his chest without getting burned. Why do you think the Scripture states a woman will compass a man (Jeremiah 31:22)? Do you think it will be possible, because of her power to overwhelm the male gender, in his life of disobedience (Ecclesiastes 7:26)? Therefore, failure becomes his option without guidance from the Holy Spirit. Therefore, she will always be successful in her endeavors to lead, as he follows her leadership (Genesis 3:16; 1 Corinthians 11:3; Ephesians 5:22-33; 1 Timothy 2:12-15).

There are some cultures where the males allow the woman to experience everything that is within him. This can be a good thing, if she is led by the guidance of the Holy Spirit (Proverbs 31:10-31). She will always fear, honor, and respect her husband as the better half (Ephesians 5:22-33). Therefore, she will always fear the consequences from the Spiritual Living God. Nevertheless, if she does not have this kind of relationship with the Spiritual Living God, she will tear down and destroy everything that is not nailed down by faith (Ecclesiastes 7:26).

BECAUSE THE LORD IS YOUR SHEPHERD

Anytime a male allows the female to lead, they never fail to self-destruct. Just observe those males who pursued relationships without spiritual guidance in the past and current generations. They usually have a testimony that causes other males to think twice about walking in their shoes. It is very wrong to be blessed with a male child, only to allow a female to destroy your heritage. Fathers should demand their sons read the book of Proverbs 4-7, and provide answers to their questions, providing their children with prior knowledge so they might encounter life lessons better equipped to handle all situations. Otherwise, there is a female waiting to lead him like a sheep to a slaughter. Some mothers teach their daughter how to pursue relationships with males who have a substantial income, teaching them to be humble, but when she becomes deceitful, moms cannot be found. Surely, the male gender cannot battle two females who set out to deceive them. Anytime a female becomes successful in breaking your spirit (Ecclesiastes 7:26), learn from your mistakes and teach other males about your experience. Just like you were warned and fail miserably, maybe someone will listen in the future generations.

Just like the men in this generation, I bet Adam could not believe he allowed a woman to deceive him (Proverbs 3-4; 5:1-6), but some men are learning from past generations' mistakes. Do not use Adam's line, "The woman you gave me . . ." (Genesis 3:12). Chances are, you probably never sought the Spiritual Living God about the woman, with guidance from the Holy Spirit (Proverbs 9:13-18). This is the result anytime we desire relationships without spiritual help; this is why you are experiencing this heartache and pain.

SHE REALLY SHOULD BE FEARED

Some men are beginning to realize that some women are like eggs--the outer appearance can be deceiving regarding the contents found inside. Until you experience what is located on the inside of the shell, you really do not know what to expect. Take the time and crack a few eggs; you would be surprised how the yokes can vary. Sometimes the eggs will crack at the slightest touch, just like women, or they can be rotten, and you could not tell until you reached the insides. Otherwise, they can be delightful and very enjoyable; their character really should be dependent upon the guidance of the Holy Spirit.

Yes, men can have these characteristics (Proverbs 17;24). Also, anytime a female trains a son without the guidance of the Holy Spirit and without a God-fearing male's input, the son will observe and copy what has been introduced to him in training him up by the female. Look around in this generation. Some men have more female characteristics and material things (shoes, gadgets, cologne, and clothes) than women. Past generations before the twenty-first century never had to deal with males staying in the mirror longer than women. There is nothing wrong with a male taking care of his appearance, but when he becomes obsessed with his appearance, it can become a weakness, therefore, hindering his spiritual strength needed to make the right decisions about all things, including spiritual things (1 Corinthians 2). The Spiritual Living God knows your heart, and if your relationship with Him is more important than your physical appearance (Proverbs 3:5-6; Matthew 6:25-33), if you are spending more time reading the Holy Bible and living according to the plans and purposes the

BECAUSE THE LORD IS YOUR SHEPHERD

Spiritual Living God has for your life, **then, the message is not for you; pass it on to someone who needs to hear what is being said about spending time feeding the flesh and not the Spirit (John 4:23-24; Romans 8; Ephesians 4:14-32; Galatians 5:16-26).**

Why Would Any Male Access an Evil Spirit?

I really do not think this is something males choose to do, intentionally setting out to experience this activity in his lifetime (Proverbs 12; 16-17; 22-24). There is so much emotional baggage tied with being evil; they can actually become overwhelmed, but must keep going without the guidance of the Holy Spirit (Acts 19:11-19; 1 John 4:1-6). Women are equipped emotionally so they can carry a lot of baggage without revealing it. Nevertheless, anytime you cross them, and they decide to get even with you (Proverbs 31:3; Ecclesiastes 7:26), only the guidance of the Holy Spirit protects us from evil spirits. It is possible you will never experience those other spirits, which can show themselves when they are least expected, whenever we follow the guidance of the Holy Spirit.

Women also need to stop thinking every male they meet will fill the shoes of the positive male they have experienced so far in this life.

Nevertheless, males who choose to ignore the original plans and purposes the Spiritual Living God has for the male gender (Proverbs 4-7) will allow other spirits to reside within them (1 John 4:1-6; Acts 19:15-20), instead of the guidance of the Holy Spirit (John 14-16; Acts 2; 1 Corinthians 2). There were actually males before this generation with this problem, before you were born, according to the Scriptures found

BECAUSE THE LORD IS YOUR SHEPHERD

in the Holy Bible. The very first male to hold the position of a king, to lead the people of the Spiritual Living God (1 Samuel 9-10) allowed his pride to interfere with the purpose and plans the Spiritual Living God had for his life here on Earth (1 Samuel 13:8-14; 15).

We know why the Spiritual Living God allowed the evil spirit to reside in Saul (1 Samuel 16:14-23; 19:9; 22:6-23; 28:3-25). He actually sought an evil spirit when he could not hear from the Spirit of the Spiritual Living God. If males do not learn anything else in this life, they should recognize evil spirits are real, and they do exist among us in this generation (Proverbs 1-3; 1 John 4:1-6). Exactly what level of intelligence allows a male who is a human to think he is capable of controlling an evil spirit? If the most intelligent man the Spiritual Living God has ever allowed to lead His people provided words of wisdom (1 Kings 3:3-15) before Jesus' arrival as His only begotten Son (Matthew 12:40-45; Hebrews 1), sought the Spiritual Living God, how did you as a mere human gain this wisdom, knowledge, and understanding without the guidance of the Holy Spirit, provided by accepting the Spiritual Living God's only begotten Son, Jesus Christ (Matthew 12:42; John 1:1-18, 3:16-21; Galatians 5:16-25; Ephesians 1-2: all, 3:4-21, 4:3-6)? Solomon tried to warn you, as a male, to steer clear of evil males and females (Proverbs 4; Matthew 12:33-37; Luke 6:45). How did you acquire this knowledge without the guidance of the Holy Spirit, thinking being evil has its benefits?

The evil spirits always provide enough rope to allow you to think you are in control (Matthew 12:43-45). Then, the rope is jerked, and you find you have hung yourself with spiritual warfare (Romans 7:14-25; 2 Corinthians 10:3-6; Ephesians

WHY WOULD ANY MALE ACCESS AN EVIL SPIRIT?

6:10-20; 1 Timothy 6:11-13). This evil spirit will continue to control you, and you cannot be released without the Holy Spirit (John 14-16; Acts 2; Romans 8; 1 Corinthians 2; Hebrews 1; 8). The Spiritual Living God has provided inspired words to help those whose hearts are not hardened (Hebrews 3:7-11) about His divinity as the Spiritual Living God (John 4:23-24). If we desire to know and experience Him, it must be through spiritual interactions. This spiritual life can only be experienced by accepting the only Person who is allowed to prepare us (Romans 8) for a spiritual relationship with the Spiritual Living God (John 1:1-18; 3:16-21; Hebrews 1). Jesus Christ is the only contact we have to interact with the Spiritual Living God (Romans 1:16-20; 9-10; 1 John 1-5).

Some of the men (males) in this generation are displaying evil spirits at work in their lives. They are destroying females, who are supposed to be the weaker gender (1 Peter 3:7), but they are not privy to this information without spiritual guidance. Why would you kill someone you should have the spiritual guidance to walk away from and never look back (1 Corinthians 9:5; Galatians 5:16-26)? Males are also stealing and sometimes killing their own heirs, which means they are planting evil seeds in their heritage. If they do not destroy all their heirs, they can look forward to this life cycle repeating itself without the guidance of the Holy Spirit (Galatians 6:6-10). Geez, surely these are not seeds planted by their ancestors, where some generations were passed over because of their fear and personal relationship with the Spiritual Living God.

Now, you finally have the generations that do not believe in the Gospel (Psalm 22; Isaiah 53; Romans 1:16-20; Ephesians 1:13; 1 Thessalonians 1:5-6; Hebrews 1; 1 Peter 1:12-25). Do you think they are reaping the consequences from past generations plus their own disobedience because they refuse to acknowledge the Spiritual Living God (Exodus 20:5-6; Galatians 6:7-9)? Remember, the promises are made available to those who believe the Gospel (Psalm 22; Isaiah 53; Romans 1:16-20; Ephesians 1:13; 1 Thessalonians 1:5-6; Hebrews 1) of Jesus Christ (Romans 8; 9:16-29; 10:9-21; 11:16-24; 15:7-21). This is really something to think about; without the guidance of the Holy Spirit, the human race is set up for defeat. How in the world did the males gain this deceptive characteristic in this generation? Yes, they are appearing as the incomplete gender in this day and time without the guidance of the Holy Spirit (1 Peter 3:7-12; James 1:12-15). Surely, women are not affecting them in a negative manner, but women have been powerful in past generations. Research the life of any male who has been successful in causing great destruction in this world. Look for information on the mother or any female encouraging him to seek revenge for something he experienced in life. I have mentioned on numerous occasions women are very powerful only by the guidance of the Holy Spirit; this power is controllable (Ecclesiastes 7:26). Otherwise, the world can experience this great evil provided by her influence upon any male not covered by the blood of Jesus. Even if you only find two, it is still two too many for the many lives that were lost during that time period.

We must remember, males and females are created in the image of the Spiritual Living God. We must make a choice as to which spirit will lead our lives here on Earth; the Spiritual Living God allows us to make a choice (Joshua 24:14-15). Joshua informed the people in his generation

WHY WOULD ANY MALE ACCESS AN EVIL SPIRIT?

of the advantage and disadvantages of not serving the Spiritual Living God. They did not have a chance to accept life in the Spirit (John 14-16; Acts 2, Romans 8); their disobedience only allowed them to experience physical death (Joshua 24:19-20). Surely, we can thank the Spiritual Living God for His darling Son, Jesus Christ, in this generation (Acts 28:24-31; Romans 1:16; 3:21-31; 2 Corinthians 3:3-6; 11:2-4). We really need to pay attention in this generation without the guidance of the Holy Spirit. The evil spirits will take up residence in your life without inquiring about your preference. They will take over your life, and you do not have a choice in the matter. They will reside because you do not have access to the Holy Spirit. Always remember, the evil spirits are more powerful than human beings (Ephesians 6:10-20).

There are quite a few humans in this generation allowing others in this generation to observe evil spirits in this day and time. Young men are taking their heirs' lives--gender is not important--and killing the little children under the age of seven. How can you kill, burn, or hurt a child who cannot harm you or would try to harm you as an adult? Males are killing females at a record number, sometimes including any female connected to her. Why can't people just walk away from relationships in this generation? They could start over without making the same mistakes as before, with the guidance of the Holy Spirit. It is very possible to arrive at this kind of understanding (Romans 1; 8; 2 Corinthians 3:2-6, 14-18; 1 John 1-5). Only an evil spirit has the power to control a human and cause that human to make decisions displeasing to the Spiritual Living God. If you are capable of taking the life of another human being who presents no threat to your

BECAUSE THE LORD IS YOUR SHEPHERD

well-being, Lord, have mercy; if it is a blood relative, and it does not affect your inner spirit, it will be obvious, the Holy Spirit has not enlightened you regarding spiritual things, according to the inspired words of the Spiritual Living God (John 1:1-18; 14-16; Acts 2; Romans 8-10; 1 Corinthians 2; Galatians 3:24-29). The promises we find in the Holy Bible are for the children of the Spiritual Living God, who accept the Gospel (Psalm 22; Isaiah 53; Romans 1:16-20; Ephesians 1:13; 1 Peter 1:13-25). Otherwise, we do not have access to the promises provided by the Spiritual Living God for His children (Romans 8; Galatians 3:24-29; Ephesians 4:14-32).

If David informed his son Solomon of the need to follow the instruction provided by the Spiritual Living God in his generation (1 Kings 3:11-14), exactly how did the males in this generation drop the ball regarding teaching their sons the inspired words of the Spiritual Living God (Proverbs 4; Joel 1:3)? Solomon was inspired by the Spiritual Living God to provide words of wisdom in Proverbs found in the Holy Bible, with instructions regarding life experiences and the right responses, mostly for the male gender. The males in this generation with the guidance of the Holy Spirit do not have a valid excuse for not seeking the Spiritual Living God, who resides in heaven as their Heavenly Father, whenever it comes to making any decisions about His plans and purposes for their lives while living here on Earth.

Seven Women to One Man

These statistics appear to be very true for the future generations, just like the Scripture states in Isaiah's generation (Isaiah 3-4:1). Do you think we are doing exactly what took place in Judah during Isaiah's generation (3:8-12)? Look at the statistics of the male population in the twenty-first century; things must turn around in a positive manner for the statistics not to come true in future generations (Isaiah 2:5-22). Surely, the males in this generation cannot identify with things said in Isaiah's generation.

The examples found in the Holy Bible are true (2 Timothy 3:14-17); we were provided with experiences from past generations about the male population failing whenever they chose not to live a life of obedience according to the plans and purposes of the Spiritual Living God. The instructions are for males, regarding how they could be successful after being warned of the destruction waiting for them for being disobedient. The Holy Bible helps those in each generation choose their path for living in this world. There are some men in past and current generations that appear to have very strong spiritual relationships with the Spiritual Living God. Nevertheless, they still manage to experience defeat or serious consequences for their decisions in life.

We are all warned about feeding the flesh instead of the Spirit, which is obvious grounds for defeat. Every male is set

BECAUSE THE LORD IS YOUR SHEPHERD

up for destruction without a spiritual relationship with the Heavenly Father, Son, and the guidance of the Holy Spirit (2 Timothy 3; Hebrews 12; 2 Peter 1-3).

Jesus has come to set those bound by sin free from sin (Romans 6). The Holy Spirit will empower us to make decisions that are pleasing to the Spiritual Living God, in the name of Jesus. There is not a weapon here on Earth that can form against you and prosper (Isaiah 54:17). We can look forward to an abundant life (John 10) with the blood of Jesus covering us, as you are being guided by the Holy Spirit (2 Corinthians 10:3-5; Galatians 5:16-26; Ephesians 6:10-20). Women who desire to have power must check the source of their strength by the Spirit--exactly where is she gaining her power (1 John 4:1-6; Acts 19:14-18)?

Some men have experienced hurt and pain from a relationship with a woman. If a male desires to share all that is within him with a woman, he needs the guidance of the Holy Spirit to lead in their relationship. The Spirit of the Spiritual Living God will never guide you in the wrong manner. There might be some things the Spiritual Living God is teaching you to trust Him with. What He provides is for you and only you until the Holy Spirit reveals the next step to you. Choosing to love a woman more than the Spiritual Living God can cause devastation in a relationship (Ephesians 5:22-33). We need to remember to put all our trust in the Spiritual Living God (Proverbs 3:5-6; Matthew 6:25-33). Then, He will direct our path to experience the things our heart desires in this life (Psalm 37).

Otherwise, the hurt and pain you experience in this life can cause you to seek out the same gender. Anytime a male allows a male with strong female characteristics to sooth him, or a female allows a female with male characteristics in times of trouble to comfort her, this will cause you more confusion than before (2 Corinthians 4). They are setting themselves up for defeat as long as they continue this activity. The Spiritual Living God never created a male in His image (Genesis 1:27-28; 5:2; Matthew 19:4-5) to seek another male for encouragement and restore the love he lost in a prior relationship with a female, deciding a male is a better choice. There are inspired words from the Spiritual Living God about interacting with males like womankind (Leviticus 18:22); the message was provided before your birth.

This distress will put you outside the will of the Spiritual Living God for those created in His image (Genesis 1:27-28; 5:2; Matthew 19:4-5). We must remember, He never makes mistakes, but spiritual warfare can lead you in the wrong direction (1 Samuel 17:47; 2 Corinthians 10:3-5; Ephesians 6:10-20).

We have been warned not to quench the Spirit (Holy Spirit) (1 Thessalonians 5:19). This is exactly what we do anytime we participate in sinful activities (Romans 13:8-10), displeasing to the Spiritual Living God. Then we drink alcohol to experience oblivion or take drugs to ease the heartache and pain provided by this world we live in. These are spirits that will take control of your life. They will become addictive, causing an exorbitant amount of additional pain and heartache to you and others associated with you in any way. The negative actions produced from this activity have consequences, when reality returns and your problems still exist. Heaven help you, if you were able to compound the problems, depending on your actions while

BECAUSE THE LORD IS YOUR SHEPHERD

being seduced by these spirits. Remember the warning about spirits (2 Corinthians 3; 1 John 4:1-6; Acts 19:15-18). The Spiritual Living God only communicates with Spirits (John 3:15-21; 4:23-24); therefore, you need the guidance from the Holy Spirit.

If and when you decide you would like to be released from those controlling spirits (1 Peter 3), just remember (Romans 10:9-13), only through Jesus Christ can you receive your help (John 14-16; Acts 2; 1 Corinthians 2). Then, you will receive the spiritual strength you need to fight with those other spirits (Galatians 5:16-20; Ephesians 6:10-20). The battle becomes the Spiritual Living God's (1 Samuel 17:47; 2 Chronicles 20:15); there will be no more chains holding you. It will be a blessing to be free (Romans 6). Praise the Spiritual Living God when you become free from this pain and heartache (1 Thessalonians 5:19, 22). Never forget to put on the whole armor of the Spiritual Living God in this generation (Ephesians 6:10-20); we really need to take a stand against spiritual darkness.

There is also a culture that is incarcerated without the freedom of experiencing life to the fullest. Only the Spiritual Living God knows why it is hard for a male to forgive and forget past experiences of his heritage. As long as he chooses to look back, it will be hard to go forward and build a life of faith, hope, and love. It is just so much easier to turn things over to your Heavenly Father, who resides in heaven. Yes, your earthly father failed to lead and provide the instructions needed to experience life in the Spirit; chances are, no one explained this life to him, also. Nevertheless, you do have a Heavenly Father that sits high and looks upon those who desire to become His children (Romans 8;

Galatians 3:24-29; Ephesians 4:14-32), who knows and sees all things. He has reminded us vengeance belongs to Him. He will repay those who deceitfully misuse and abuse His children (Romans 12).

The problem with this generation is we must learn to let go in order for the Spiritual Living God to handle the things we turn loose, in the name of Jesus. Otherwise, He allows us to handle the situation, and it gets worse before it gets better. Choosing not to remember the sins of past generations and use them as a stepping stone always allows the children of the Spiritual Living God to cross over to the other side of Jordan, just like past generations. We should choose to walk forward and never look back, remembering the hurt and pain of previous generations. Otherwise, when we choose to have a hard heart (Proverbs 23:7a; Hebrews 3:7-11), we are allowed to become stagnant. This position will never allow you to move forward to reach your potential goals, to accomplish the plans and purposes of the Spiritual Living God. He really spared our lives to continue to exist among the land of the living for a reason. Anytime we think we can make others pay for something we never really personally experienced, we will always set ourselves up for defeat in this generation. Whenever we choose to walk around with a millstone hanging around our neck, it holds us back from being successful. Always remember, you can have faith, or you can have fear. Choosing to fear someone makes them your god; surely, the Spiritual Living God is bigger than the one you allow to steal your joy and peace in this generation.

Do you think if past generations could speak to the current generations in this day and time, they would express their disappointment? I really think they would cry with a broken heart and ask: "Why were my living and experiences in vain? The suffering I experienced should have been enough for future generations to look to the hills for their help, which comes from the Spiritual Living God (Psalm 121). Your freedom came with a price from the Spiritual Living God's Son, Jesus Christ (Romans 6-8). My experiences of heartache, pain, and sometimes premature death were not to set you up for failure, but success. Nevertheless, is this all the gratitude I can receive from my heritage and culture? Surely, you could have received the education I missed out on receiving in my generation. The choice of becoming a menace to society is not the plans the Spiritual Living God has for His children (Romans 8; Ephesians 4:14-32). I was not able to receive the education that is available to you today or given a chance to vote. Because I really wanted my heritage to know my life had a purpose here on Earth, I wanted my vote to be counted as a citizen with full rights and privileges here in the United States of America. I personally think it breaks the heart of every person who lived and died in your heritage to see you incarcerated (locked up in prison)."

We also have those males in other cultures living in America who try to suppress and disrespect the female gender. Anytime you treat anyone in any manner you would not want them to treat you in (Job 4:17-21), it is **impossible** for you to have wisdom, knowledge, and understanding with the guidance of the Holy Spirit. We are reminded, whatever we sow, that we shall reap (Galatians 6:7-10). If you do not personally experience this defeat, remember, you have a heritage, which can experience the sins we sow without the guidance of the Holy Spirit (Exodus 20:5-6). We must

SEVEN WOMEN TO ONE MAN

choose to live a life of obedience (Romans 8; Ephesians 4:14-32), which is found in the Holy Bible, in order to receive the promises and blessings provided by the Spiritual Living God through His darling Son, Jesus Christ, with the guidance of the Holy Spirit (John 10).

Do you think these are the reasons for the male population's diminishing in the twenty-first century? Anytime you have been provided with instructions regarding how to have a successful life here on Earth, regardless of our excuses in this generation, we have been provided with inspired words according to the Spiritual Living God's plans and purpose found in the Holy Bible.

Nevertheless, some have decided our plans are better than the Spiritual Living God's plans, and refuse to learn from past generations' mistakes.

I think women can look forward to being like the women in Isaiah's generation (Isaiah 3:16-26). They will also share a man--seven women to one man--and be glad to have a piece of a man (Isaiah 4:1). Heaven help any man if the women do not fear, honor, and respect the Spiritual Living God (Ecclesiastes 7:26).

Yes, the Spiritual Living God said spiritually, there is no difference when it comes to the Holy Spirit revealing wisdom, knowledge, and understanding whenever it comes to His children (Romans 8; Galatians 3:24-29), those of the Spiritual Living God, but He will always have an order for us to follow (1 Corinthians 11:3; Ephesians 5:22-33). This really helps His children to be on one accord and stop the division among those who believe the report of the Gospel (Psalm 22; Isaiah 53; John 12:38-50; Romans 1:16-20; Ephesians 1:13-14; 1 Peter 1:13-25).

He Closes and Opens Wombs

In the beginning, the Spiritual Living God created males and females in His image (Genesis 5:1-3); He allowed them to produce a baby in their likeness.

The encounter was the beginning of creating humans to exist in a world established by the Spiritual Living God (Genesis 1:1-2; 2:26-28). This all took place without consulting any humans, in the past or present generations (John 1:1-18; Romans 9:18-24; Hebrews 1). He made this decision without needing man's assistance, since He had to create us to start His world. The problems with creating someone in your likeness is the possibility of the person deciding he or she is more intelligent than you are. We are currently seeing this take place in the current and past generations (Psalm 14; 53; Romans 1:21-32; 1 Corinthians 1:18-31).

The animals do not have this problem; they are very capable of following instructions provided on their level of intelligence. They never appear interested in questioning the One who originally designed them. They are capable of making a lot of decisions about survival and existing among other animals, but appear to be content with existing on the level the Spiritual Living God designed them, according to the Spiritual Living God's plans and purposes for their design here on Earth (1 Corinthians 15:38-58). Observe the children created in your likeness in this generation; if the truth be told, they would question everything that proceeds out of their parents' mouths (Exodus 20:12; Proverbs 30:11-17; Ephesians 6:1-4), making you question and doubt your level of intelligence in this current generation. *In other words, why do you exist? "I am here now; I can handle everything from this point on. OOPS! The material things you have, leave them, including your money. I am really not interested in starting from scratch."*

We must continually thank the Spiritual Living God for Jesus and the guidance of the Holy Spirit. Where would we be without the angels that encamp around us daily and Jesus interceding on our behalf to the Spiritual Living God to have mercy? Look at those created in the Spiritual Living God's image with a hardened heart (Hebrews 3:7-11) in this generation. They are experiencing heartache and pain, without understanding how to change their ways in this generation (Proverbs 30). In Moses' generations, the Spiritual Living God did not think twice about anybody who disagreed with His decisions as the Spiritual Living God, even if you decided to disagree with someone He called into obedience according to His plans and purpose.

The Spiritual Living God actually removed you from the land of the living (Genesis 19:1-29; Numbers 16; 21:4-9; Deuteronomy 13). How do humans in this generation challenge the Spiritual Living God and not die on the spot? Jesus is His name. "Bless that wonderful name of Jesus." There is power in that wonderful name of Jesus (Isaiah 7:14; 9:6-7; Matthew 1:23; 28:18-20; Luke 2:11; John 1:1-18; 3:16-21; Ephesians 1:17-23; 2:13; Hebrews 1; 8). We would not breathe hard in this generation if the Spiritual Living God responds to us like He did in Moses' generation. Anytime we do not have the guidance of the Holy Spirit, it is impossible to understand spiritual things, without giving up carnal things (Romans 8:4-10; 1 Corinthians 9:11; 15:35-58; 2 Corinthians 3).

In Moses' generation, their level of intelligence did not allow them to comprehend spiritual knowledge (Numbers 14; 16; Deuteronomy 9:29). Therefore, they would set out to cause mass confusion and discourse among those who observed the Spiritual Living God, as a cloud by day and a pillar of fire by night (Exodus 13:21-22, 40:34-38). We have been provided with the Spirit of the Spiritual Living God in this generation (Jeremiah 31:31-35; Joel 2:28-32; Romans 9; Hebrews 1; 8; 1 John 4:12-15). We just need Jesus, His only begotten Son, to provide the access by accepting the Gospel (Psalm 22; Isaiah 53; John 1:1-18; 3:16; 4:23-24; 10; Romans 8; 10; Ephesians 1:13; Hebrews 1), the birth, life, death, resurrection, and ascension of His only begotten Son, Jesus Christ, who provides our Helper, the guidance of the Holy Spirit (John 14-16; Acts 2; 1 Corinthians 2).

This enlightenment provides the wisdom, knowledge, and understanding regarding all things, especially spiritual things. We receive the power and strength to keep us from wavering or being discouraged in our faith in this generation (2 Corinthians 4; Hebrews 11). We would never have any faith or hope of receiving eternal life (1 John 1-5). If someone sowed some bad seeds in your heritage before your birth and decided not to leave this information for future generations (Joel 1:3), you have entered this world with a disadvantage, choosing not to live according to the purpose and plans of the Spiritual Living God. Anytime we choose not to accept His Son in order to gain spiritual

BECAUSE THE LORD IS YOUR SHEPHERD

knowledge, exactly why should the Spiritual Living God allow those in your heritage to multiply? Do you think we have enough evil and disobedience in this world already? Do you have any idea how many parents cry with a broken spirit? Regarding the children, they were allowed to conceive, and they turned their backs on the Spiritual Living God. It is very possible He is trying to spare you of the heartache and pain associated with disobedience.

I really believe, the pain of seeing a child shot and lying around like a dead animal is not an experience everyone can handle. Anytime a child is removed from the parents and experiences hurt, harm, or danger that can really hurt the parent, anytime a daughter or son experiences any kind of abuse by someone he or she trusted, it really hurts. Only the Spiritual Living God knows why this kind of pain is being experienced so heavily in this generation (Proverbs 30). We must remember the words found in Psalm 37. The people did not receive pain at this level in the nineteenth and early part of the twentieth century. The only difference I can recall is we have more gods than they had. We have been deceived about adultery and fornication being pleasing to the Spiritual Living God (Galatians 5:16-26; 6:7-10). Therefore, we are more disobedient and suffer consequences with great pain in this generation. We are reminded, whenever the children choose not to honor and respect the Spiritual Living God, sins from past generations can be experienced (Exodus 20:5-6) by them. Whenever we choose not to believe the Gospel regarding the Heavenly Father, Son, and the guidance of the Holy Spirit, we must experience consequences; otherwise, we would get worse before we become better. The world is providing more gods for future

HE CLOSES AND OPENS WOMBS

generations to acknowledge. Those in this generation will not be able to comprehend all the disobedience and the consequences they will face for choosing a life of disobedience (Romans 1:21-32; 1 Corinthians 1:18-31). This is just like the generations before this current generation-- they are not capable of comprehending our disobedience. When our generations are compared, they actually feared, honored, and respected the Spiritual Living God more than our generation.

An example is the cellular (cell) phone, the majority of people who have a personal relationship with the Spiritual Living God know they can depend upon Jesus to see them through in times of trouble, with the guidance of the Holy Spirit (2 Corinthians 4). We used to call on Jesus first and wait patiently for our guidance, just like Elijah did when he prayed for rain (1 Kings 18:41-45). Now, we call everybody in our cell phone, most of the time, becoming totally disappointed with their level of spiritual wisdom, knowledge, and understanding regarding what we are experiencing. Then, we might remember, "Lord have mercy, I should have called you first, and I put you last. Now I know why I have not received my help" (Isaiah 50).

The future generations will not be able to comprehend this level of spiritual guidance if they have all this technology (computer, GPS, robots, etc.) to get answers from man-made devices. Do you see the visual of electricity coming to a standstill and the generation going back to candlelight?

Do not think about generators or batteries; there will not be enough to go around. People who do not fear, honor, and respect the Spiritual Living God would probably take your life for these material things. They would take them in the twenty-first century without a second thought. Lord, have mercy, without future generations learning about You and Jesus with the guidance of the Holy Spirit, they are going to suffer consequences worse than those in this century who lose their lives daily over material things. Do you think this would help us remember who is responsible for man having access to the electricity they need to operate their technology in this day and time? In the news today, it is being said that a country is currently creating a robot for human companionship to meet all their personal needs. Electricity is only one example of the consequences we could suffer from the Spiritual Living God. Let us pray, He will not decide to reveal Himself to humans in future generations in this manner. Nevertheless, pray you are not experiencing health problems that require medical equipment that use electricity for staying here among those in the land of the living. We will find these things do not work without the Spiritual Living God's assistance.

What are we doing in this generation with our limited intelligence to displease Him (Psalm 53; Romans 1:21-32; 1 Corinthians 1:18-31)? The Spiritual Living God used Elijah to provide a visual for the people in his generation to observe His power (1 Kings 18:20-40). Surely, we can learn from others' mistakes and make the right decisions in this generation, with the guidance of the Holy Spirit (John 14-16; Acts 2; 1 Corinthians 2).

Anytime we choose to live a life of disobedience, refusing to acknowledge Jesus Christ as the Son of the Spiritual Living God (Hebrews 1), therefore, deciding we do not need help from the guidance of the Holy Spirit to turn away from sin (Psalm 19; Romans 6-8), so we might receive the wisdom,

HE CLOSES AND OPENS WOMBS

knowledge, and understanding needed to establish a spiritual personal relationship with the Spiritual Living God, **not a religion**, exactly why should the words spoken then not affect us today? Surely, we are intelligent enough to know, we will not escape the consequences for choosing these lifestyles (sexual activity without marriage, drugs, alcohol, adultery, homosexuality, etc.). Do you think we are the generation spoken about in Proverbs 30; Matthew 12:39; and 2 Peter 2:14, the adulterous generation, just like the Pharisees in Jesus' generation? They partially believe the things spoken regarding Jesus Christ (John 3:1-15; 12:38-50). They were actually blind regarding spiritual things.

The generations before our generation were not perfect, but adultery and fornication is more prevalent today, without any shame or remorse. Therefore, the consequences are experienced more heavily, drawing our attention to this sin. The children we intentionally conceive through adultery or fornication never requested to enter this world, to suffer from our disobedience. Nevertheless, it was said before our birth, we bring them here suffering consequences from our sins very often (Proverbs 30:11-17; 2 Peter 2:14). We also find excuses for the diseases we suffer in this generation or blame the Spiritual Living God for allowing us to make decisions that affect our health, after we were warned not to participate in this great evil. This is one sin that has such a domino effect, until the other sins just automatically follow you trying to cover the original problem we experienced with sinning against the Spiritual Living God. Remember, we cannot receive spiritual knowledge unless we have spiritual guidance. This guidance is only supplied by Jesus Christ, whom you chose not to accept as the only begotten Son

BECAUSE THE LORD IS YOUR SHEPHERD

of the Spiritual Living God (John 1:1-18; 3:16-21; Hebrews 1). Jesus provides the spiritual access to the Spiritual Living God (John 4:23-24; 14-16; Acts 2; Romans 8; 10:6-21; 1 Corinthians 2; Hebrews 8). Never forget, the Spiritual Living God has a way to deliver His children from all temptations (Ephesians 4:14-32; 2 Peter 2:9).

There really are reasons for things taking place the way they do without humans really understanding why in this day and time. We have been warned, without spiritual knowledge (1 Corinthians 1:18-31), it is impossible to understand spiritual things (1 Corinthians 2). If this is a part of the Spiritual Living God's plans and purpose for our lives here on earth at this time, because of our disobedience, the children of the Spiritual Living God can look forward to having a testimony, if you can pass the test; just try and keep man from interfering (Job 1:6-12). Only the Spiritual Living God knows which spirit (1 John 4:1-6) is encouraging you to change the original plans He has for your life here on Earth in this generation.

Some women have wombs that are available for conception without a prayer requesting this blessing from the Spiritual Living God, found in the Holy Bible: Eve, Hagar, Lot's daughters, Jacob's wives (handmaids) Jacob's sons, Joseph's wife, Judah's wife (Genesis 38), Tamar, Jochebed, Zipporah, David's wives, except Michal (2 Samuel 6:20-23), even Bathsheba, just to name a few.

Mary, the mother of Jesus, experienced His conception by spiritual interaction, which was actually because of the Spirit of the Spiritual Living God (Matthew 1:18-25; Luke 1:26-38) coming upon her (Psalm 53; 1 Corinthians 1:18-31).

There were many petitions for the Spiritual Living God to open the wombs of these women--Sarah, Rebekah, Leah,

HE CLOSES AND OPENS WOMBS

Rachel, Hannah, Samson's mother (Judges 13), and Elizabeth, the mother of John the Baptist (Luke 1:5-25). Someone prayed or the Spiritual Living God's plan and purpose for the child was ready to come to forth for His glory.

Hannah, Samuel's mother, prayed with the understanding the child would be given back to the Spiritual Living God for His plans and purpose for the child. Samson's mother never ceased with her petition for a child. She was given instructions about things she should not consume while carrying the child. She was also given certain instructions about training up the child. Elizabeth conceived a child in her old age, thinking the time had passed for conception of a child. This was the child needed to be the forerunner for the Spiritual Living God's only begotten Son (Malachi 4:5-6; Matthew 11:10-15; Luke 1:11-17; John 1:1-34). Some women were given the requirements they must be willing to meet in order to have a child. We need to ask the question in this generation "Is there anything too hard for the Spiritual Living God to accomplish (Genesis 18:14; Numbers 11:23; 2 Kings 4:14-37; Jeremiah 32:17, 27; Matthew 1:47-55; 19:26; Mark 10:27)?" Depending on your answer, your level of spiritual maturity will be exposed; it is really okay (Ephesians 3:14-21). Think about those who have no earthly idea what the answer should be.

Only the Spiritual Living God knows His reason for opening some wombs and closing others in this generation. It is the hidden things that cannot be seen that the Spiritual Living God allows to take place without humans' natural understanding, which totally confuses the humans' natural mind, challenging our level of intelligence in this generation (Hebrews 11). Therefore, He does things according to His purpose and plans for our lives here on Earth (Romans 4:13-25).

Sometimes we need to recall the heartache and pain parents experienced in past generations, who actually were in spiritual communication with the Spiritual Living God. Before Jesus Christ's arrival as His only begotten Son, He called others into obedience to lead His people. The Spiritual Living God actually provided His Spirit for each and every person He called. He communicated with some who were anointed with oil, but they all possessed His Spirit in order to communicate with Him, the Spiritual Living God.

Adam and Eve were blessed with two sons; then, one decided to kill the other because of offerings to the Spiritual Living God.

Isaac prayed and was blessed with two sons. Before their birth, their mother was told she was carrying two nations. The older would serve the younger, everything came to pass just like the Spirit revealed to their mother. After the younger son (Jacob) received his father's blessing, the older son became distraught because the first son should have received the blessings according to tradition. The oldest son (Esau) rebelled and took a wife among the people who did not acknowledge the Spiritual Living God (Genesis 25:21-34; 27; 28:1-9). Esau wanted to hurt his father for giving the blessing to Jacob (Romans 9:10-15).

Aaron was a Levite, the chosen tribe to come before the Spiritual Living God with any offerings for the people. He was blessed with four sons. Two of His sons forgot they were required to maintain a certain level of righteousness before they could come before the Spiritual Living God. Two of his sons died for disrespecting the Spiritual Living God (Leviticus

HE CLOSES AND OPENS WOMBS

10; Numbers 3:1-10). Aaron was told by Moses not to show any outward actions of grief because they sinned against the Spiritual Living God; otherwise, He would take his life and the other two sons (Leviticus 10:6-7).

Naomi was blessed with two sons, and they took wives from among the people of Moab, who did not worship the Spiritual Living God. The father and his sons died in this foreign land. Naomi only had her new daughters when she decided to return to the land that worshiped the Spiritual Living God. One daughter-in-law stayed in Moab, and the other daughter followed her mother-in law, and was later blessed abundantly by the Spiritual Living God (the book of Ruth).

Eli was a priest called into obedience to serve the Spiritual Living God. Nevertheless, his two sons did not know the Spiritual Living God and sinned greatly. They were sleeping with the women that came to worship; they were totally out of control according to the people. The Spiritual Living God warned Eli, He was going to cut off his seed and there would be no more males (1 Samuel 2:12-36) because of their evil ways.

Samuel was prayed for and promised to the Lord before he was conceived by his mother (1 Samuel 1:9-28). He was also blessed with two sons, who chose to sin against the Spiritual Living God (1 Samuel 8:1-3). Surely, you would think after observing Eli's sons, Samuel would have a better understanding about raising his sons. Nevertheless, they also died from being disobedient, when their father chose a life of obedience regarding the Spiritual Living God.

David's relationship with the Spiritual Living God was blessed with many sons, but one decided to lust after his

BECAUSE THE LORD IS YOUR SHEPHERD

sister and eventually raped her. The sister's brother decided to kill him for raping the sister. That same son decided to try and remove David as the king and tried to also kill him (2 Samuel 13; 15; 18).

Hezekiah had a strong relationship with the Spiritual Living God (2 Kings 18:1-8). He was told to get his house in order because it was time for him to leave this world (2 Kings 19-20). He prayed, and the Spiritual Living God provided an additional fifteen years on his life. Nevertheless, he entertained the king of Babylon, which was displeasing to the Spiritual Living God. He also conceived a son during these fifteen years who caused a lot of devastation for others. His son Manasseh was totally evil and did a lot of things displeasing to the Spiritual Living God (2 Kings 21:1-18). Surely, this is one son Hezekiah did not need to conceive; he actually provoked anger from the Spiritual Living God (21:6).

Since I have your attention regarding the children of parents who walk closely with the Spiritual Living God that terrorized others or just died for being disobedient, stop and sincerely reflect on your desire to bring forth a child into this world in this day and time (Proverbs 30). It is time to pray and ask the Spiritual Living God, "Do You need me to bring forth a child in my likeness to glorify, worship, and praise You?" If you are not willing to conceive this child and train him or her up according to the Spiritual Living God's plans and purposes, you might think a little harder about conceiving a child in this generation. Their peers are influencing their lives heavily in this generation, especially when they can convince each other taking their parent's life is okay while they sleep. Only by the guidance of the

HE CLOSES AND OPENS WOMBS

Holy Spirit will your child fear the Spiritual Living God and not take your life as you lie down to sleep in this generation. Start surveying parents and ask how many actually lock their bedroom doors in this generation. Their grandparents and parents never locked their bedroom doors, fearing them in their generation, because their generations feared, honored, and respected the Spiritual Living God more than the twenty-first century generation.

Those who are barren in this generation need to make sure they are not fulfilling the Scriptures found in Deuteronomy (27:11-26).

If our hearts are hardened (Hebrews 3:7-11) with being inpatient with the Spiritual Living God's timing, conception will only take longer or never be accomplished according to His plans for your life (1 Samuel 16:7; Job 34:21-37). So, try surrendering your life to the Heavenly Father, Son, and accept the guidance of the Holy Spirit. Repent and ask for forgiveness for things you thought, said, or did that were displeasing to the Spiritual Living God. He already knows your heart, and if you are being sincere (1 Samuel 16:7; Psalm 7:9; 139:23-24; Jeremiah 17:9-10; Romans 2:5-9; Revelation 2:22-24).

So, do not start until you are sincerely ready without any doubt about accepting the Gospel (Psalm 22; Isaiah 53; Romans 1:16-20; 10:8-21; 2 Corinthians 10:3-18; Ephesians 1:13-14) of Jesus Christ. We can deceive man, but the Spiritual Living God formed each of us in our mother's womb (Job 31:15; Isaiah 49:1-6; Jeremiah 1:5; Galatians 1:15). If the Spiritual Living God decided to open Sarah's womb at the age of ninety to conceive the promised son, Isaac, do you think we are forcing the hand of the Spiritual Living

BECAUSE THE LORD IS YOUR SHEPHERD

God by using man's devices to help women conceive in this generation? It really does make you wonder what kinds of problems we are creating by assisting the Spiritual Living God with helping women conceive in this day and time. Just think, if technology existed in Abraham's generation, we would be in trouble trying to learn how to step out in faith (Hebrews 11) and trust the Spiritual Living God's inspired words, which are totally true (John 5:39-47; 2 Timothy 3:16; 1 Peter 1:24-25; 2 Peter 1:12-21).

This is exactly what is going to happen in future generations if we do not stop and teach our heirs, reminding them to teach their future generations (book of Joel). The Spiritual Living God will return with a devastating vengeance, just like He demolished Sodom and Gomorrah. They could possibly be the next generation to experience a great devastation, provided by the Spiritual Living God's hand of heaviness. We really do have a responsibility to teach future generations the Truth (John 16:13; Philippians 4:6-9). The world is creating many things to provide answers to questions in this day and time. Just think about how confused the future generations will become with technology leading their decision making regarding the Spiritual Living God's plans and purposes for our lives here on Earth. I recall watching a program on television about a couple trying to conceive with man's help about eleven times before they thought they were successful--only to find the babies came into this world with a desire to be the opposite gender they were born as. The little boy never felt right as a male, and the little girl was confused also. These children were on elementary levels with this confusion. Anytime we assist the Spiritual Living God, we need to have ways to solve the confusion we cause others to experience.

HE CLOSES AND OPENS WOMBS

Hopefully, others will observe this confusion and think twice about helping the Spiritual Living God with females trying to conceive a baby. Whenever He closes a womb, it should not be opened until the Spiritual Living God decides to open the womb. The consequences will always be devastating to all those involved because of their disobedience. We were warned in Leviticus 20 of things displeasing to the Spiritual Living God, which can have consequences. If Isaac had to pray for Rebekah's womb to be opened and waited, Jacob prayed and waited for Rachel's womb to be opened, and Hannah prayed and waited on the Lord for her womb to be opened also, what are we doing in the twenty-first century assisting the Spiritual Living God with His plans and purposes for human life here on Earth in this generation? Whenever we stop and really think about or witness the life that enters this world as a baby, man cannot take any credit for this miracle taking place; new life has been provided by the Spiritual Living God. We are tremendously blessed to have this baby with all of his or her extremities in place without man's assistance (Ecclesiastes 11:4-6). Just because a male and female came together in an intimate way does not always bring forth these results. We must always give the Spiritual Living God the glory for allowing this creation in our likeness to take place.

If the people were warned in Jeremiah's generations about sin being a consequence of being childless, exactly how are we exempt from these consequences in this generation (Jeremiah 31:15)? The steps taken by man in this day and time to allow embryos to develop outside the womb, then replant them, trying to recreate the Spiritual Living God's design for development of human life.

BECAUSE THE LORD IS YOUR SHEPHERD

This method of technology really inflates man's pride in the medical field; without spiritual guidance, they develop godlike complexes here on Earth. Nevertheless, they fail at being able to heal all the problems (Psalm 103) they create from their interference with the Spiritual Living God's plans and purpose for a person's life. We must never forget to give man credit for the confusion they cause other humans. Being confused about your gender, health, and life in general can be a possible consequence we eventually suffer for helping the Spiritual Living God.

Recently, I heard about a program where women were paying women in India money to carry their baby. Whenever we think about different cultures and their beliefs, which could greatly affect the child you are carrying, this becomes very scary (Luke 1:39-45). Only the Spiritual Living God knows what gods, prayers, and promises were made about this child. You have my sincere regrets for the Spiritual Living God's decision not to open your womb (Luke 23:28-29). Nevertheless, only the Spiritual Living God knows if we can handle the problems we create here on earth for future generations. Hosea had to warn the people in his generation about the days of judgment for being disobedient. He also stated the women would have miscarrying wombs (Hosea 9). Isaiah reminded the people, according to the Lord GOD, those that were alone without husbands were more fruitful than those with husbands (Isaiah 54:1). Do you think we can learn anything from past generations' experiences in this day and time?

Nevertheless, there were probably other things you needed to ask forgiveness for in the past and forgot (Psalm 19). We are holy people set aside for the Holy, Awesome, Wonderful, and Spiritual Living God (1 Peter 2:9-17). Only by

HE CLOSES AND OPENS WOMBS

the guidance of the Holy Spirit will we have the power to follow and be successful in serving the Holy, Spiritual Living God (Deuteronomy 7:7-11; 1 Corinthians 2; 1 Peter 2) in this generation. Then, we can receive His blessings for our obedience to Him. Look at all the promises He made to the Israelites, to love them, bless the fruit of their womb, take away sickness, males and females would not be barren, and they would not experience the diseases of Egypt. They would be blessed above all people (Deuteronomy 7:12-26). Jesus is the key in this generation to receive the promises from the Spiritual Living God (Ephesians 1:3-2:22). Why are we forgetting the promises made before our birth and written for our benefit in the twenty-first century (Hebrews 1; 8; 10-11)?

Only the Spiritual Living God Knows the Plans He Has for You

Sometimes we struggle with trying to work out things without knowing the plans and purpose the Spiritual Living God has for each one of His children. It is a blessing from the Spiritual Living God, if parents are able nurture, teach, and train their children without showing favoritism among them. Before we were born, the Spiritual Living God provided an example of things that would take place between two brothers. This information was provided while their mother (Rebekah) was carrying the twin boys in her womb (Genesis 25:19-28). Isaac favored Esau because of his interest in things he liked. Rebekah favored Jacob, and I guess we label him a mama's boy. We would probably like to give Rebekah credit for the deceit in fooling Isaac for the blessings that belonged to the oldest son, Esau (Genesis 25:29-34), according to tradition. Nevertheless, the truth about the boy's future was spoken before they entered into this world (Genesis 25:23). Jacob actually feared any activity associated with deceiving his father, wondering if this would cause him to be cursed (Genesis 27:11-46). Rebekah received a promise about the boys while carrying them in her womb (Genesis 25:23-27). It is possible she remembered the promise, so she felt justified in her actions to deceive her husband. We will give man credit, when the glory really belongs to the Spiritual Living God.

BECAUSE THE LORD IS YOUR SHEPHERD

If the truth be told, many of us are only following the Spiritual Living God's original plans and purpose for our lives here on Earth. The experiences we have participated in from the beginning of birth until today have been a lesson. Somewhere in life, we can look forward to recalling something we did not understand then, but it makes sense now (Psalm 145). Sometimes our plans are not the Spiritual Living God's plans, so we struggle to proceed according to our own plans. This is one battle we cannot win, but we can struggle until we get tired. Eventually, some of us choose to surrender to the Spiritual Living God's plans and purpose for our lives here on Earth. Otherwise, the consequences for choosing not to surrender are so great, it is like experiencing death, but you are still living. Always remember as humans, there are two different lives and deaths that we can experience while living here on Earth (John 1:1-18; 3:16-21; 10; 14-16; Acts 2; Ephesians 5:16-26; Galatians 6:10-20). Nicodemus was a Pharisee (blind to spiritual things); he came to Jesus in the night, fearing others might see him (John 3).

Jesus explains the difference in the births to him and future generations. Many have confirmed the truth for those who believed the report of the Gospel (Psalm 22; Isaiah 53; John 12:38-41; Romans 1:16; 9-10; Ephesians 1:13-14; 1 John 1-5). The Spiritual Living God has provided His Spirit to everyone created in His image (Genesis 1:27-28; 2:7; 5:2; Matthew 19:4-5; Jeremiah 31:31-34; Joel 2:28-32). Jesus Christ, His only begotten Son, supplies access for the children of the Spiritual Living God to be enlightened by the guidance of the Holy Spirit (John 14-16; Acts 2; Romans 8; 1 Corinthians 2; Ephesians 2-3; 4:14-32; 6:10-20; Hebrews

ONLY THE SPIRITUAL LIVING GOD KNOWS...

1; 8; 10-11; 1 John 1-3). The children of the Spiritual Living God have been provided with wisdom, knowledge, and understanding regarding spiritual things. Those here on Earth without the guidance of the Holy Spirit are spiritually dead (Psalm 14; 53; Romans 1:21-32; 1 Corinthians 1:18-31). We are actually living in darkness without knowledge about the Light (John 1:1-18; 3:16-21; 5:17-47; 6:31-71; 8:12-30; 10; 12:28-50; Ephesians 5:1-21; Hebrews 1). We are absolutely ignorant about the constant battle that exists between the Spirit and the flesh daily (Romans 1:21-32; 6-8; 1 Corinthians 15; Galatians 3-4:1-6; 5; Hebrews 2; 10; 1 John 4:1-6; 5). The children of the Spiritual Living God, with the guidance of the Holy Spirit, have enough intelligence to repeat the Scriptures by Jesus and Michael the archangel without being stressed in this generation (Matthew 4:1-11; Jude 9). Anytime others challenge you spiritually, we have been provided with the response needed to set the record straight. They have already informed us a long conversation was not necessary in order to make a point regarding Light and darkness; they will never be on one accord.

Those in darkness start recalling Murphy's Laws and giving credit to the wrong source for what is taking place in their life in this generation. Spiritual growth (Galatians 3:24-29; Ephesians 3:14-21) allows the children of the Spiritual Living God to connect to their Source of strength, totally committing to His plans and purposes (John 16:13; Philippians 4:6-9, 13; 1 Timothy 4:1). It is amazing how many people have testimonies about their fight to flee the Spiritual Living God's call into obedience (Jonah 1-4). They actually can encourage others to never choose to battle, advising them, they would lose and still do things according to the Spiritual

BECAUSE THE LORD IS YOUR SHEPHERD

Living God's plans. There is nothing like a good testimony to encourage others in their spiritual growth (Romans 8; Galatians 5:16-26; Ephesians 4:14-32; 6:10-20). We might detour for a little while, but I guarantee you, if the seeds of faith (Hebrews 11) have been planted, you are coming back this way again.

Does anyone ever consider his actions could be repeated by those conceived in his likeness (Exodus 20:5; Galatians 6:4-10)?

Let us think about this: Your egg or sperm was used in order to conceive this child. So, whatever genes, characteristics, obedience, disobedience, or good or bad habits associated with you will be passing to this child. Lord, have mercy; everything I did before submitting my life to Jesus Christ for a complete overhaul could be experienced by my future heirs. That is correct, if they choose not to have a spiritual personal relationship with the Heavenly Father, Son, and allow the Holy Spirit to guide them in this world (Jeremiah 32:16-27). Do you think it is time to tell the future generations about the seeds that were planted, and you are praying they would not take root in their generation? Encourage them to always teach future generations about the benefits of living their lives in obedience to the inspired words found in the Holy Bible (Genesis 18:19-21; Exodus 20:5-6; Deuteronomy 4:9-14; 11:18-25; John 15:1-16; 1 Corinthians 15:58; Hebrews 8-12; 1 John 1-5). Otherwise, the disobedient generations will suffer greatly for choosing to live without the wisdom, knowledge, and understanding about spiritual things. We have inspired words found in the Holy Bible regarding the guidance of the Holy Spirit, who is only accessible through a relationship with Jesus Christ.

ONLY THE SPIRITUAL LIVING GOD KNOWS...

We can observe this taking place before our birth (Genesis 12:11-13; 26:7-9; Deuteronomy 7:1-5; 8:11-20). Abraham and Isaac both had beautiful wives, but they feared another male would harm them to gain her. In different generations, they lied to save their lives, only to have the Spiritual Living God intercede on their behalf.

We need to remember these situations and trust the Spiritual Living God to come through for us in times of need. He promises to take care of those who sincerely belong to Him (Proverbs 3:5-8; Matthew 6:25-33; Romans 8; Ephesians 4:14-32). Plotting and planning are not necessary if we are going to learn how to trust the Spiritual Living God. How can He receive His glory if we can take the credit in this generation?

The Spiritual Living God has decided according to Scriptures, males will lead in relationships, according to His plans and purposes, while living here on Earth (Genesis 3:16; 1 Corinthians 11:3; Ephesians 5:22-33; 2 John 2:13-17; Philippians 2:5-11). Who told those in this generation operating in darkness without spiritual guidance, they could reset the moral standards (Proverbs 30; Romans 1:21-32; 9; 1 Corinthians 5-6; 2 Peter 2:14; book of Jude) provided by the Spiritual Living God? The inspired words found in the Holy Bible were written by inspiration before their birth (Matthew 5:17-20; John 12:32; Romans 14-15; Hebrews 1; 2 Peter 1:12-21; 1 John 5).

Regardless of the generation that is now in existence, the Truth (John 4:23-24) will not change to benefit whatever is taking place in your generation (Hebrews 13:8; 1 Peter 1-2). If the men have a continence of a stone, they will stand and refuse to be suppressed by women, with the guidance

BECAUSE THE LORD IS YOUR SHEPHERD

of the Holy Spirit. If the men are like sand, they will move with the wind, like a sheep being led to slaughter. Nevertheless, we have been warned, the inspired words of the Spiritual Living God will stand forever (Isaiah 40:7-8; John 1:1-18; 1 Peter 1:13-25).

Fathers here on earth who encourage their sons to participate in sexual activities before finding their soul mate are setting those males up for failure, if not death, in this day and time. According to the Scriptures, anytime a male has sexual contact with a female, he is bonding with her (1 Corinthians 6:15-20). All these females have become a part of you. Lord, have mercy, when she has an evil spirit connecting with you as a believer, who is guided by the Holy Spirit (1 Thessalonians 5:19-23). Anytime a man thinks he needs experience outside the Spiritual Living God's plans and purpose, He is stating, the Holy Spirit is not capable of taking care of his need to please his wife. We do not have an excuse for choosing to participate in things that are displeasing to the Spiritual Living God, if we are His children (John 10; Romans 8; Galatians 3:24-29; Ephesians 4:14-32; Hebrews 2:16-18; 2 Peter 2:9). This is a reason to run, not walk, when it comes to finding a soul mate without the guidance of the Holy Spirit (Proverbs 9; Ecclesiastes 7:26). Satan knows everything you are looking for in a relationship and will set you up according to your desires and a little extra to draw you away from the Spiritual Living God. If he tried to tempt Jesus Christ (Matthew 4:1-11; Mark 1:11-13; Luke 4:1-15), exactly why should he leave you alone without any temptations (1 Corinthians 10:6-13; Hebrews 2; 2 Peter 2:9)? We should be thanking the Spiritual Living God for His only begotten Son, Jesus' experiences here on Earth. They

ONLY THE SPIRITUAL LIVING GOD KNOWS...

actually encourage the children of the Heavenly Father to tie a knot and hold on to our faith in times of trouble (Romans 1:16-20; 2 Corinthians 4; Hebrews 11; 1 John 5).

Jesus has provided our Helper, the guidance of the Holy Spirit (John 14-16; Acts 2; 1 Corinthians 2; Philippians 4:6-9, 13, 19) to help us make the right decisions in this day and time.

Only the Spiritual Living God knows how these relationships impact your mental state, which causes you to work hard and not smart. This generation has so many STDs (sexual contact diseases) without a cure; therefore, your life among the living can be shortened (Romans 1:21-32).

Sometimes males are dealing with the law for rape or a relationship with an underage female, who set them up with deception (Ecclesiastes 7:26; Romans 1:21-32). There is a warning for those who commit adultery regarding their prayer life being hindered (1 Peter 3:7). Anytime our hearts are hardened (Hebrews 3:7-11) regarding being obedient to the Spiritual Living God's inspired words, and we decide to conceive a child in our disobedience, we are committing a terrible tragedy and can look forward to the problems in life associated with this sin (Luke 12:42-48; 2 Peter 2:14). Always remember, children are a blessing; it is our disobedience that causes this generation to think, *Life is trying to beat the life out of me.*

What we call cruel and unusual punishment will only make you strong if you repent and ask for forgiveness in the name of Jesus (1 John 1-2). We will be provided with an abundant life because of our obedience not to intentionally sin against the Spiritual Living God (Psalm 19; Luke 12:48; John 10; 1 Corinthians 10:6-13; Hebrews 10). Surely, there

BECAUSE THE LORD IS YOUR SHEPHERD

is not a relationship in this world worth these experiences. Nevertheless, some males will have to experience this heartache and pain because of their decision to be disobedient. Whenever they are ready to receive the inspired words of wisdom they will find only by developing a spiritual personal relationship with the Heavenly Father, Son, and the guidance of the Holy Spirit, males will be sustained until they are connected with their soul mate (1 John 1-5), therefore, experiencing a fulfilled relationship with the opposite gender according to the Spiritual Living God's plans and purpose for their lives here on Earth (1 Corinthians 6:15-20; Ephesians 5:22-33; 1 Peter 3:1-12).

Nevertheless, if you fail at being obedient, receive your lemons in life and make the best possible lemonade available. Always repent and ask for forgiveness in the name of Jesus. Try to be a living testimony about your mistakes, hoping those in the next generation will learn from your mistakes. They will be strengthened and encouraged by your experiences (Proverbs 4-7; Ecclesiastes 7:26).

During Moses' generation, they could plead ignorance, and it was really true (Leviticus 4:1-2, 22, 27). They could not have a spiritual personal relationship with the Spiritual Living God (Isaiah 54:13; Jeremiah 31:31-34; Joel 2:28-32; John 6:44-65; 1 Corinthians 2; Hebrews 10:16-18; 1 John 1:20-29). Only through Jesus Christ, the Son of the Spiritual Living God, are we allowed to have access to the guidance of the Holy Spirit (John 14-16; Acts 2; Hebrews 1). We have a choice in the twenty-first century to receive or reject the Gospel of Jesus Christ (Psalm 22; Isaiah 53; John 1:1-18; 3; 4:23-24; 6:44-65; 10; Romans 1:16-20; 8; Ephesians 1:13-14; Hebrews 1; or Psalm 53; Romans 1:21-32; 1 Corinthians

ONLY THE SPIRITUAL LIVING GOD KNOWS...

1:18-31), the Spiritual Living God's only begotten Son, who provides His children (Romans 8; Ephesians 4:14-32) with a Helper (John 1:1-18; 3:16; 14-16; Galatians 4:4-7). We must accept the Gospel (Psalm 22; Isaiah 53; Romans 1:16-20; Ephesians 1:13; 6:10-20; Hebrews 1; 8; 10; 11), which entails the birth, life, death, resurrection, and ascension of Jesus Christ. Otherwise, a spiritual personal relationship with the Spiritual Living God is off limits to those operating in the human flesh (John 3; 10; Romans 8; Galatians 3:24-29). The Spiritual Living God is a Spirit and only communicates with the Spirit and accepts the Truth (John 4:23-24), according to the inspired words found in the Holy Bible. As humans, we have a natural and spiritual body; the one we decide to feed will experience growth (1 Corinthians 2:9-15; 15:39-50). It is totally impossible to have wisdom, knowledge, and understanding regarding spiritual things without guidance from the Holy Spirit. We must receive life in the Spirit (Romans 8; Ephesians 4:14-32) to have spiritual communication. Anytime the world is interested in challenging your spiritual guidance, be sure and remember the words Jesus spoke to the devil: "It is written, that man shall not live by bread alone, but by every word of God" (Luke 4:4, it is written, is sufficient). Even Michael the archangel refuses to entertain a conversation with Satan (Jude 9). "The Lord rebukes thee"--that was very short and sweet, not a very long debate. Exactly what are we doing (Psalm 14; 53; Romans 1:21-32; 1 Corinthians 1:18-31) debating and entertaining questions from those who refuse to accept the Gospel (Psalm 22; Isaiah 53; 1 Corinthians 1:16-21; Ephesians 1:13-14) in this generation (2 Timothy 3:14-17; 2 Peter 2:20-21)? We have been told the Spiritual Living God will draw us

BECAUSE THE LORD IS YOUR SHEPHERD

unto Himself (John 6:44-65). Just like the Holy Spirit provided wisdom, knowledge, and understanding for your personal spiritual growth (1 Corinthians 2:9-16), everyone the Spiritual Living God decides to grant this blessing to can receive it (Hebrews 8:6-13; 10:1-17). He is no respecter of persons (Deuteronomy 10:17; Acts 10:34; Romans 2:11; Ephesians 6:9), but a hardened heart (Hebrews 3:7-11) will keep us from receiving guidance from the Holy Spirit. Do you think this generation received knowledge higher than Solomon (Matthew 12:42), Jesus (Hebrews 1), and Michael the archangel (Jude 9)? Remember, pride can always get us in trouble; we will lose our focus (Proverbs 3:5-6; Matthew 6:25-33). We should always live by faith (Hebrews 11); "remember, your faith has nothing to do with the wisdom of men," but stands according to the power of the Spiritual Living God (1 Corinthians 2).

They Meant It for Evil, but the Spiritual Living God Used It for His Glory

Exactly what has the Spiritual Living God revealed to you for the good of all men, but someone tried to use it for evil (Acts 7:7-18)? Remember, Joseph had a dream (Genesis 37) about the future. He ran to tell others, who did not understand his dream.

Joseph's brothers hardened their hearts because of the favoritism their father paid to Joseph and the dream he shared (Genesis 37:3-11). They decided to try and control Joseph's future by selling him into slavery, choosing to grieve their father of the son he loved the most (Genesis 37:34-36).

Remember, the Spiritual Living God's plans were established before our birth; we are just following things that were already planned whenever we choose a life of obedience according to His plans and purpose for our lives here on Earth. Joseph's brothers sold him into slavery being evil, but in the dream, he had revealed the things for the future. This situation will eventually be used for the Spiritual Living God's glory (Genesis 40-48). We must always remember, when the Spiritual Living God provides a vision for His children (Romans 8; Galatians 3:24-29), it can be a seed for future use; sometimes family cannot receive what the Spiritual Living God is providing for you. Just remember, disillusion and frustrations come from trying to help others

BECAUSE THE LORD IS YOUR SHEPHERD

see your spiritual vision (1 Corinthians 1:18-31); "it is for you" (1 Corinthians 2). Remember to be still; in time the Spiritual Living God will allow His plans to come forth for His glory (Psalms 46-50).

So, You Think You Do Not Need Jesus

There is no excuse for people living after Jesus Christ's generation choosing not to serve the Spiritual Living God. There is a promise for anyone regardless of your nationality or speech (Isaiah 56:3-8; Revelation 5:8-10; Matthew 25:31-45; Luke 2:32; 24:46-47; Acts 20:28; Romans 3:24-25). The Spiritual Living God observes our hearts and knows if we have accepted the blood His Son shed on Calvary's cross (1 Samuel 16:7; Psalm 7:9; 139:23-24; Jeremiah 17:9-10; 2 Corinthians 3:2-6, 14-18; Colossians 1:20-22; Revelation 2:22-24). It is the blood of Jesus that allows us to experience eternal life with the Spiritual Living God (1 John 5). Those who have access to the Holy Bible, rejoice; you can read the inspired words of the Spiritual Living God for yourself, with the guidance of the Holy Spirit. Those without the Holy Bible will need to believe within your hearts the words you heard about the Gospel (Psalm 22; Isaiah 53; Romans 1:16-20; Ephesians 1:13-14; Hebrews 1), spoken about the blood, are totally true (John 12:38-50; 1 John 1-2).

According to Revelation, they are drafted in because of the promise (5:9); let no one deceive you regarding the inspired words spoken before their birth here on Earth. If the Spiritual Living God took the time to demolish a nation of people before your birth to reveal His displeasure in man's disobedience (2 Peter 2:6), He also decided to wipe the old world off the map and started over with Noah and his family only (Hebrews 11:7; 2 Peter 2:5). The Spiritual Living God was also upset with the humans created in His image during Moses' generation again (Exodus 32:7-18; Deuteronomy 9:6-29). He was ready to kill everyone and start over with a new nation of people, but Moses was able to intercede on their behalf to the Spiritual Living God. We need to stop listening to people in this day and time when they state everybody is going to heaven, unless they are speaking about Judgment Day (Matthew 7:21-23; 25:41-46). This is foolishness (Psalm 14; 53; Romans 1:21-32; 1 Corinthians 1:18-31) to forget the past generations' experiences with the Spiritual Living God. We should state everyone will be given a chance to go to heaven (Romans 1:16-20; 10:9-21; 1 John 1-5) before Jesus returns, in this generation, if they do not harden their hearts (Hebrews 3:7-11). You have got to admire how the Spiritual Living God never had a problem with demolishing and starting over with people. Anytime we think we can rise above Him and decide we do not need Him, it is not long before we experience His holiness.

We will find He desires to interact with certain people when it comes to humans and angels (2 Peter 2:4); He is capable of removing all obstacles. Just think about how many people could have made a better decision, but they listened to the deceiver with the wrong report (Psalm 22; Isaiah 53; Hosea 4; Romans 1:16-20; 10:9-21; 2 Corinthians 6:4-18; Titus 1:10-16; 2 John 7-11). The humans in this day and time who think the Spiritual Living God will not judge the human race after He has provided His only begotten Son (Psalms 46-50; John 1:1-18; 3:16-21; 10; 1 John 1-5), think again; there is a day coming when we will not have

SO, YOU THINK YOU DO NOT NEED JESUS

a choice, in order for us to choose a life of obedience to Him as the Spiritual Living God. We need to remember, it is only a matter of time before those who refuse to accept the blood that has been provided by His Son (Acts 2:21; Colossians 1:14-29; Hebrews 1) will perish. Many in this generation will perish for their lack of knowledge (Psalm 1:6; 37; 14; 53; Hosea 4:5-7; Romans 1:21-32; 1 Corinthians 1:18-31) because they fail to receive spiritual enlightenment the Spiritual Living God provides for His children (Romans 8; Galatians 3:24-29; Ephesians 4:14-32), who are the only people here on Earth in each generation with spiritual guidance to comprehend spiritual things (1 Corinthians 2; Hebrews 1). The others will finally realize the inspired words were really the Truth (John 4:23-24) and they needed to have a spiritual personal relationship with the Spiritual Living God, **not a religion**. We can look forward to His return with a force of vengeance and judgment for those humans that refuse the blood of His only begotten Son (Matthew 11:20-30; 24; Colossians 1:14-29; Hebrews 1; 1 John 1-5). This is one of the reasons as humans, we choose to disrespect the Spiritual Living God, because we do not really know Him spiritually; therefore, we do not fear Him out of respect. Nevertheless, we fear someone who looks just like us except for their culture, and they only have the power you allow them to have regarding your life, without the guidance of the Holy Spirit. Whenever Jesus returns to judge the Spiritual Living God's world (John 5:17-47; 9:39; Romans 14:9-12; Hebrews 1; 9:27-28), it will be too late for you to call on the name of Jesus and ask Him to mediate (Romans 8:34) with the Spiritual Living God. Take the time and reflect on you being in a position to help someone in need. You offered

BECAUSE THE LORD IS YOUR SHEPHERD

the person something that holds a special meaning to you personally. Then you realized he rejected your offering, allowing it to sit among things he has no use for, especially if it is something near and dear to you.

Exactly how would you feel? (My point exactly!)

The promise was made in Jeremiah's generation (Jeremiah 31:31-40; Joel 2:28-32; Hebrews 1; 8:6-13; 10:16-17). Only through Jesus Christ (John 1:1-18; 3:16-21) will we have access to the guidance of the Holy Spirit (John 14-16; Acts 2; 1 Corinthians 2). The Spiritual Living God only communicates spiritually (John 4:23-24). Remember, Jesus Christ is superior to all, including Moses (Hebrews 3-5).

The people thought they did not need Moses in his generation also. They were excited about the miracles performed by the Spiritual Living God against the people of Egypt. The parting of the Red Sea was even more breathtaking than anything they could recall (Exodus 14:14-15:21). Moses actually stretched out his rod, and the Spiritual Living God parted the waters to allow them to pass. Then, He closed the waters and drowned Pharaoh and his army. The people became impatient with Moses and his progress to the Promised Land by the Spiritual Living God. They decided to forget the Spiritual Living God's promise and started being disobedient (Deuteronomy 8:11-20). Anytime the Spiritual Living God calls His children to follow Him, we must reflect on past generations and any current miracles He has performed (Exodus 16). They actually forgot in this very short time span about all the Spiritual Living God had accomplished for them as His people. They actually received bread from heaven (Exodus 16:15); we sing about bread of heaven in the twenty-first century, asking the Lord

SO, YOU THINK YOU DO NOT NEED JESUS

to allow it to fall down from heaven and praising Him, for He is our Spiritual Living God in this generation.

What a confirmation to actually receive bread from heaven because He is the Spiritual Living God. We are reminded of Jesus' being the Bread of Life in this generation (John 6:31-65). Moses' generation was not satisfied with bread being supplied; they complained about eating the same food every day. They remembered the different things they had to eat, but left them behind in Egypt (Numbers 11; 14; Deuteronomy 9:6-29). They could not recall the Spiritual Living God had kept His promise to deliver them out of bondage. They were not able to recall, before they spoke words others could hear, the Spiritual Living God already knew their thoughts. They complained about the food until the Spiritual Living God provided fiery serpents to bite them. Many lost their lives for this disobedience against the Spiritual Living God. He actually did not stop the fiery serpents until Moses placed one on a pole. Everyone who could remember to look up in his distress was saved from the poison of the fiery serpents (Numbers 21:4-9). Now we know why the medical field has a serpent on a pole for its medical emblem, even if they choose not to acknowledge the reason being associated with a biblical reference. This actually took place before their birth and was passed on to the next generation. Pride causes some doctors to take the credit for saving lives in this generation. If anyone is sick in this generation, we need to follow the inspired words found in the Holy Bible (John 12:28-50; James 5:13-16).

As long as we can be identified as a child (Romans 8) of the Spiritual Living God, who resides in heaven as our Heavenly Father, this generation must remember, just like

BECAUSE THE LORD IS YOUR SHEPHERD

they had to look up in Moses' generation in order to be healed, we need to look up at the Savior, Jesus Christ, who was put on Calvary's cross to shed His blood for all humans regardless of your nationality, if we desire to be identified as the children (Isaiah 56:3-8; John 3; Romans 8; 1 John 1-2) of the Spiritual Living God. Jesus Christ is the only One with the power to heal in this generation, but you must believe within your heart, without a doubt, before you will be healed, providing this is the will of the Spiritual Living God in this generation, because He already knows if you will give Him His glory or the doctor (Matthew 4:23-25; 9:35; Luke 9:1-6; John 12:29-50; Acts 10:38; 1 Corinthians 12:9; Philippians 2:26-30) who stands before you.

Do not forget, when Hezekiah was sick and told to get his house in order because he was going to die, he sought the Spiritual Living God. The relationship he had with the Spiritual Living God allowed him to pray, and he was granted an additional fifteen years to exist among the land of the living in his generation (2 Kings 20:1-11). Jesus also reminded the children of the Spiritual Living God, all sickness is not unto death in His generation (John 11:3-5). Just in case we forget and try to give up our hope in this generation, the Holy Spirit interprets our utterance to the Spiritual Living God (Romans 8:26-27), as long as you can be identified as His child.

It really is amazing, when the Spiritual Living God uses a doctor in this generation by providing healing hands, this doctor has to be a child of the Spiritual Living God (Romans 8; Ephesians 4:14-32) to receive this power from Jesus. Many can testify, when the doctors could not find their way, they called on the name of Jesus, and He provided wonder-working powers in this generation.

SO, YOU THINK YOU DO NOT NEED JESUS

Nevertheless, one day every knee will bow and tongue confess (Isaiah 45:18-25; Acts 2:21; Philippians 2:10-11) that Jesus is the Way, the Truth, and the Light; no one can have a spiritual relationship with the Spiritual Living God unless he or she accepts Him as the only begotten Son (John 1:1-18; 5:17-47; 8:12-59; 10; 14-16). **This is why we need to teach the next generation about the Spiritual Living God** (Deuteronomy 30; Joel 1:3). He should always be feared, honored, and respected as the Spiritual Living God (John 4:23-24). Otherwise, those in the next generation will not fall down with their hands lifted up and their hearts filled with praise, worshiping Him. Nevertheless, He is an awesome, wonderful, marvelous, powerful, and the Spiritual Living God; He is absolutely worthy to be praised in this generation.

The Israelites became so disobedient in their generation until they eventually stressed Moses, who knew for a fact He had spoken with the Spiritual Living God and had been given instruction and directions regarding leading the Israelites. Regardless of Moses' experiences, he still allowed the people to frustrate him in his generation. When the Spiritual Living God told Moses to speak to the rock in front of the people so they could observe the miracle and power, He was providing them water to drink, Moses was so frustrated with the people, he hit the rock with force and caused the Spiritual Living God to become displeased with his actions (Numbers 20:8-13). Okay, what was that again about you not needing Jesus in this generation, and you interact with people daily? This action will cause Moses to look upon the Promised Land, but he will not be allowed to enter.

The Spiritual Living God also provided him with insight about the people and their disobedience in the future

BECAUSE THE LORD IS YOUR SHEPHERD

(Deuteronomy 31:16-29). Moses reminded the people in his generation, their sin would find them out (Numbers 32:23). The disobedience of the people caused those living over the age of nineteen, except for Caleb and Joshua, to die in the wilderness (Numbers 14). Their disobedience caused them to wander around in the wilderness until everyone had died. Now, we have some insight as to why the people had to wander around in the wilderness for forty years without finding the exit. They appeared as sheep without a shepherd; no one was able to interfere with the Spiritual Living God's destroying all the people over the age of nineteen, except for Caleb and Joshua. Before Moses died, he was reminded of his disobedience (Deuteronomy 32:48-52). After commissioning Joshua to lead the people of the Spiritual Living God (Deuteronomy 31), Joshua warned the Israelites before his death of the consequences for not serving the Spiritual Living God (Joshua 24:19-20).

He reminded them of the Spiritual Living God's holiness, and He is a jealous Spiritual Living God. During Joshua's generation, they were not forgiven for sinning against the Spiritual Living God. If they served other gods, they would experience His wrath. This action in most cases was immediate removal of life from among the living because He is holy and righteous. Just think of the different gods we serve in this generation; who or what receives the majority of your thought, concentration, and time is considered your god (a person, television, computer, phone, electronics, etc.). Exactly which one of these things can you call on in times of sincere need and deliverance from the storms (health, family, job, finances) that are occurring in your life (2 Corinthians 1:3-11; 12). Whenever life becomes really

SO, YOU THINK YOU DO NOT NEED JESUS

overwhelming, causing you to think there is no hope for your future, this is an opportunity to surrender your life to Jesus Christ (1 John 1-2), allowing the Holy Spirit to lead you (Hebrews 1; John 14-16; Romans 10; 1 John 5) as a child of the Spiritual Living God (Romans 8; Ephesians 4:14-32), in this generation.

The Spiritual Living God realized regardless of whomever He sent to lead His people (priest, prophets, judges, kings, seers), the people would choose obedience, then decide to be disobedient. This was like the experience of riding a roller coaster, the up and down activity continually.

Finally, the Spiritual Living God came as an example, as foretold in the book of Psalms by David and Isaiah (Psalm 22; Isaiah 53)--the life His Son (Jesus Christ) experienced here on Earth and the blood that was shed on Calvary's cross for our sins (Hebrews 1; 9:11-10:18; 1 John 1-5). Jesus provides an example of what it would take for humans to have a spiritual relationship with the Spiritual Living God (John 1:1-18, 3:16-35, 4:23-24, 5:17-47, 10; 12:28-50; 14-16; Acts 2; 1 Corinthians 2). We must remember in this generation, just like the Israelites had to look up at the fiery serpent on the pole to be healed in Moses' generation, we need to look up at the cross for our healing Source in this generation (John 3:14-21; 8:27-30; 12:28-50), which comes from the Spiritual Living God's only begotten Son, Jesus Christ (Isaiah 53:5; Matthew 4:23-24; 9:35; Luke 6:17-19; 8:26-56; Acts 3; 5:14-16; 14:9; Hebrews 1; 1 Peter 2:24). We can become successful in pleasing the Spiritual Living God if we choose to live like Christ (Galatians 5:16-26; Ephesians 5:1-21; 6:10-20).

Exactly who can live in this day and time without becoming stressed out and confused when they are interacting with the human race, knowing all kinds of spirits exist in this day and time (Acts 19:11-19; 1 John 4:1-6).

We even have discourse among those who believe the report of the Gospel (Psalm 22; Isaiah 53; Romans 8; Galatians 5:16-26; Ephesians 1:13-14; 4:14-32; Hebrews 1), and we are supposed to be on one accord with the guidance of the Holy Spirit (Philippians 2:1-11).

Jesus lived, walked, taught, and empowered His disciples with guidance from the Holy Spirit (Matthew 10:5-42; John 14-16; Acts 2).

Before ascending into heaven to reside at the right hand of the Heavenly Father (Luke 24:49-53; Acts 2:32-34; Romans 8:34; Hebrews 1), the relationship Jesus had with Peter confirms even in our weakness, He understands (John 16:13; Philippians 4:13).

We do not have the strength to say and do the right things (Philippians 4:6-9, 13) without guidance from the Holy Spirit. Peter's actions were provided as encouragement for future generations. Just when we think our sins are too great to be forgiven, we must remember the experience Jesus had with Peter denying Him when he was needed to speak up (Matthew 26:69-75). No one in this generation was actually physically close to Jesus like Peter, in his generation. Exactly how do we refuse to accept Jesus' love in this generation? After all, Peter did; before Jesus ascended, He reminded Peter to feed His sheep (John 21:15-19). We really hurt Jesus when we choose to intentionally sin and not grow spiritually (Ephesians 3:14-21; Hebrews 10; 1 John 1-5), choosing to allow sin to defeat us (Romans 5-7).

Just like Moses reminded the people that sinned against the Spiritual Living God, "Your sin will find you out," heaven

SO, YOU THINK YOU DO NOT NEED JESUS

help us in this generation, thinking we can sin and find ways to hide it. We serve a Spiritual Living God that never slumbers or sleeps (Psalm 121). He actually knew we were going to fail at being obedient before we were born. He is an Awesome, Wonderful, Loving, Spiritual Living God; with spiritual guidance, we can be acknowledged as His children (Romans 8; Galatians 3:24-29; Ephesians 4:14-32). His children are equipped spiritually to make decisions that are pleasing to Him.

Nevertheless, we must work harder at being obedient, allowing the Holy Spirit to lead in our decisions here on Earth (Galatians 5:16-26; Ephesians 6:10-20) in this generation. Jesus still loves us and intercedes on our behalf, when we repent and ask for forgiveness for our sins in this generation (1 John 1-2). The children of the Spiritual Living God should always remember, Jesus is our Mediator (Romans 8:34; 1 Timothy 2:4-6; Hebrews 1) in this generation. He is constantly asking His Heavenly Father to have mercy on us, showing us He loves us in our weakness. He really helps those with a desire to grow in grace and spiritually. We need to realize, only by the guidance of the Holy Spirit, this will be accomplished. Then, we can take a stand in this generation for what was spoken in Philippians (4:6-9), even those who make mistakes in this generation, who are the Spiritual Living God's children (Romans 8; Galatians 3:24-29; Ephesians 4:14-32). We need to remember, we are forgiven just like Peter, in Jesus' generation, when we repent for our sins. Nevertheless, let us not forget, there have to be consequences; otherwise, we would never learn from our mistakes in life.

Thanks be to the Spiritual Living God for Jesus, who intercedes daily, asking the Heavenly Father to have mercy on His children. Therefore, we do not experience the Heavenly Father's hand of heaviness in this generation.

We really would not exist in this generation without Jesus Christ. We would have left here a long time ago for being disobedient and choosing not to keep the Spiritual Living God's commandments (Matthew 22:34-40, which covers the Ten Commandments; Exodus 20:1-17). We should never cease from praising and worshiping the Spiritual Living God, thanking Him continually for His darling Son, Jesus Christ.

How Should I Receive Death?

Jesus came into the world with the understanding, one day, He would leave this world (John 16:25-33). If we desire to be like Jesus, we can also be provided with the guidance of the Holy Spirit, therefore, understanding it is a blessing to be here on Earth, among the land of the living. The Spiritual Living God has a plan and purpose for each life He created in His image (Genesis 1:26-28). As long as the Spiritual Living God needs His children (Romans 8; Ephesians 4:14-32), we will be here, but when He calls us to come on in and rest, we really need to be grateful for the time He has provided because many left here a long time ago (2 Corinthians 5). They never had a chance to experience all the blessings you have lived to experience here on Earth.

It was said before our birth, there are inequalities of life here on Earth (Ecclesiastes 8:6-17); surely, we are not complaining in this generation. When we choose to receive the Helper (Philippians 2:1-11) provided by Jesus (John 14-16; Acts 2; 1 Corinthians 2), we will be provided with wisdom, knowledge, and understanding about spiritual things (1 Corinthians 2:9-16). Then, we will have the strength to be like Jesus (John 16:13; Philippians 4:13; Colossians 1:3-29). As spiritually mature Christians, we should never grieve like those without hope (1 Thessalonians 4:13) if we believe the Gospel is the Truth and Jesus will return (Romans 1:16-20;

BECAUSE THE LORD IS YOUR SHEPHERD

1 Thessalonians 4:14-18) for the children of His Heavenly Father (1 John 5).

As a mature Christian who can accept meat and no longer drinks milk (1 Corinthians 1:1-3; Hebrews 5:11-14; 1 Peter 2:1-3), these inspired words strengthen us in times of need. We should rejoice about the spiritual guidance (1 Corinthians 2) being provided as we experience life here on Earth, even when we fail at being obedient (2 Corinthians 3-5), realizing without the blood of Jesus, we could have left here a long time ago (Romans 5). Anytime someone receives the spiritual call to come on home to his or her heavenly resting place, spiritual maturity allows us to be thankful for the time the Spiritual Living God allowed the person to live here on Earth. Just think of those who never had an opportunity to experience all that you experienced with this person before he or she left this world. We should take the time to become grateful, grateful for the Spiritual Living God's grace and mercies in this generation. The wisdom, knowledge, and understanding provided by the guidance of the Holy Spirit should help us learn to let go and allow others to rest in peace, especially if they have been suffering but are willing to hold on until you come to a spiritual understanding of their need and desire to depart from this world.

Children (Romans 8; Galatians 3:24-29; Ephesians 4:14-32) of the Spiritual Living God must be grounded in their faith and belief (John 15:16-18; Ephesians 3:16-20; Colossians 1:23-29; 2 Peter 1:12-21). They know without a doubt everything will be all right because of our spiritual relationship with the Spiritual Living God's Son, Jesus Christ.

If we remember to do all we can, when we can, while someone is living here on Earth, the transition of leaving here will become a celebration of the person's life experiences here on Earth, instead of the grief of never seeing him or her again (1 John 5).

Nevertheless, the children (Romans 8; 2 Corinthians 5; Galatians 3:24-29; Ephesians 4:14-32) of the Spiritual Living God accept the fact, this person has moved to a new house (spiritual body). He or she does not need the old house (natural body) the person resided in here on Earth. The children of the Spiritual Living God never grieve as though they have no hope of seeing that person again (2 Corinthians 5; 1 Thessalonians 4:13-18; Titus 1:2; 3:7; 1 Peter 3:15). They will always have a much shorter time frame of grief than those left behind without spiritual knowledge of the Heavenly Father, Son, and the guidance of the Holy Spirit. We will look forward to seeing the person again, when Jesus returns for the children (Romans 8; Ephesians 4:14-32) of the Spiritual Living God (1 John 5).

Those without this knowledge of the Gospel will experience 2 Corinthians 6:14-18 and 2 Thessalonians 2. Jesus Christ took the time to reveal He was human, just as we are, yet without a sinful nature (1 Timothy 3:16; Hebrews 1-2) before His ascension into heaven to reside at His Heavenly Father's right hand (Luke 22:37). He allowed us to view Him as a human with the knowledge of experiencing pain (Luke 19:41-44; John 11:32-36) and what the future held for Him (Matthew 26:36-46; Luke 22:39-46). Peter being a person like many of us, ready to defend without spiritual guidance, cut off the ear of one of those who came for Jesus (Luke 22:51-54; John 18:10-11). Jesus had to restore the man's ear and told Peter to put up the sword. In other words, if Jesus wanted to be rescued, He could have called for more than twelve Legion of Angels (Matthew 26:51-56). Jesus knew the Scriptures had to be fulfilled, as they were written before His arrival as the only begotten Son of the Spiritual Living God (Psalm 22; Isaiah 53; John 1:1-18; Hebrews 1).

For those who sometimes forget the Spiritual Living God is holy, righteous, and a Spirit (John 4:23-24), never forget past generations' experiences without the guidance of the Holy Spirit (Deuteronomy 7; 11:1-7). We must also remember to worship Him in Spirit and truth (John 4:23-24), in this generation. Those who came to arrest Jesus were reminded when they decided to touch Him, He was not like any other human (Philippians 2:6-11; 1 John 5:18-20). We are reminded by the inspired words found in the Holy Bible before our birth here on Earth. The Scriptures remind us before Jesus' arrival, "Touch not Mine anointed"--do not touch those that belong to the Spiritual Living God (Psalm 105:14-15; 1 John 5:18). If the Spiritual Living God stated before Jesus Christ's arrival as His only begotten Son, "Touch not My anointed," who told those in Jesus' generation they had permission to arrest Him by just walking upon the only begotten Son of the Spiritual Living God without permission (John 18:4-7)? We need to remember in this generation, even Satan had to ask permission from the Spiritual Living God to interfere in Job's life (Job 1:6-12). Exactly how can a mere human being touch His only begotten Son without permission (Psalm 45:7; 1 John 5:18)? This is why they had to fall down (John 18:6) and wait until the Spiritual Living God decided it was okay for them to touch His holy, righteous, and spiritual Son, Jesus Christ (Matthew 3:13-17; Mark 1:9-11), that Scriptures might be fulfilled (John 18:7-9).

Those who came to arrest Jesus Christ found themselves

getting up off the ground for not acknowledging the holiness of Jesus Christ (John 18:5-11). Jesus provided us with details of the things we could accomplish with the guidance of the Holy Spirit (John 14-16; Acts 2; Philippians 4:13). He showed us He would be a friend that sticks closer than a brother (Proverbs 18:24). A man that lays down his life for a friend provides an example of the greatest love (John 15:1-17).

I'm reminded of a story about two men who were friends and worked in a high-rise building. One of the men was confined to a wheelchair, and the other man had the ability to move as he was pleased. America was provided with an opportunity to observe the Spirit of the Spiritual Living God in this generation. These men were trapped in a burning building, but they provide an example of living the Christian life with the guidance of the Holy Spirit, according to the teachings of Jesus Christ. They provided a testimony of living life in the Spirit (Romans 8). They called their respective families and told them how they were above the fire in the building and the possibilities of making it out of the building alive did not look promising.

The one not bound by the wheelchair probably could have tried to make it out of the building, but decided to stick closer than a brother, just like Jesus provided in His examples while living here on Earth. I believe they had time to talk to Jesus before they left this world. What they accomplished as friends helps those with the guidance of the Holy Spirit accept it as a testimony, exemplifying the life of Jesus Christ. They actually displayed the teachings of Jesus for this generation to observe as a visual in the twenty-first century. As children of the Spiritual Living God, we have a big brother named Jesus, who gave up His life for His sisters and brothers, the

BECAUSE THE LORD IS YOUR SHEPHERD

heirs of His Heavenly Father (Romans 8; Galatians 3:24-29; Ephesians 4:14-32; Hebrews 1).

In life-and-death situations, with spiritual guidance, we can make the right decisions and be at peace with them. I believe they knew where they were going after experiencing physical death (Ecclesiastes 12:7; 1 John 1-5). We need to accept the facts; the world is a temporary place for living. As children of the Spiritual Living God, we have been enlightened about our heavenly home, a place of resting, where we will eventually experience eternal life. We realize our body is a shell, just like a peanut is found in a shell. When the time comes to leave this Earth, our soul returns to the Spiritual Living God (Genesis 2:7; 35:18; Ezekiel 18:3-4). Our Spirit returns to the Spiritual Living God (Jeremiah 31:31-34; Joel 2:28-32; Ecclesiastes 3:21; Acts 5:10; 1 John 4:12-14). The body returns to dust (Genesis 3:19; Job 21:26; Ecclesiastes 3:20; 12:7). Nevertheless, there is a day coming when we shall all be judged by Jesus Christ regarding experiencing eternal life (1 Corinthians 15:35-58; 2 Corinthians 5; 2 Thessalonians 2; 1 John 5). He promised to return for those who belong to the Spiritual Living God as His children (John 14). Therefore, remember to be like Paul (Galatians 5:16-26; Philippians 1:11-26). If I live, I will be with Jesus Christ, or if I die, I am still blessed to be in His presence, waiting for eternal life to take place. To live or die is being with Christ. The guidance of the Holy Spirit will always provide peace for those who have a spiritual relationship with the Heavenly Father and Son. This is why we are reminded at the home going (celebration of life) of loved ones not to weep like those without hope (1 Thessalonians 4:13-18; Titus 1:2; 3:7; 1 Peter 3:15).

Which Do You Have, Faith or Fear?

Vengeance belongs to the Spiritual Living God (Romans 12). We need to observe the life of Joseph after he experiences slavery, almost raped by his master's wife, and prison. He chose not to be discouraged. Remember, this all started because of his brothers' jealousy (dad's favorite child, coat of many colors, and his dreams), but the Spiritual Living God (Genesis 37:2-5, 26-36) is always on time. He might not come when we want Him, but He is always on time, according to His time. Joseph's brothers' plans were for evil, but the Spiritual Living God used them for good (Genesis 45:4-8), when Joseph wanted to get even. He was reminded in Genesis (39:20-23; 42:16-18; 43:22-30) of his relationship with the Spiritual Living God.

We should observe the life of Joseph and remember, the Spiritual Living God never slumbers or sleeps (Psalm 121). We need to allow Him to handle the storms that occur in our life here on Earth. He will provide an anchor in the name of Jesus. Your anchor will hold when you are tossed and driven. Just remember, Jesus has the power to make the waves behave (Matthew 8:23-27; Mark 4:35-41).

During Joseph's testing of his brothers, he requested the youngest brother be brought into his presence. Israel (Genesis 32:26-30), Joseph's father, was put in a position to release his last son, so others would live (Genesis 43:8-14).

BECAUSE THE LORD IS YOUR SHEPHERD

He said, "If I am bereaved then let me be bereaved." He had to trust the Spiritual Living God with someone he did not want to depart from him. Never think someone in this world can harm a child (Romans 8; Ephesians 4:14-32) that belongs to the Spiritual Living God without permission from Him (Isaiah 54:17; Job 1-2:8).

The problem with this generation is we love our children more than the Spiritual Living God (Matthew 22:37-40). He already knows our hearts (Jeremiah 17:9-10); therefore, we experience great heartache and pain for putting them before Him. They do not have the protection of angels watching over them daily or being covered with the blood of Jesus. Anytime we cannot be identified as children (Romans 8; Galatians 3:24-29; Ephesians 4:14-32; Hebrews 1) of the Spiritual Living God, we become responsible for watching over our children, and we cannot always protect them like we should in the flesh. We have been warned before our birth about the disadvantage of choosing to be disobedient (Proverbs 30; 2 Peter 2:14), according to the Spiritual Living God's inspired words found in the Holy Bible.

Anytime children experienced death before Jesus' arrival as the only begotten Son, it was because of their disobedience regardless of their parents' relationship with the Spiritual Living God. We have been warned on many occasions before and after the arrival of Jesus Christ, the parents have been given the responsibility of training up their child, according to the inspired words found in the Holy Bible (Proverbs 16:20-22; 19:18; 20:11, 20; 22:6, 14-15; 23:13-16; Ephesians 6:1-4). Nevertheless, when we are disobedient and the children decide to become disobedient, or sometimes

WHICH DO YOU HAVE, FAITH OR FEAR?

we are obedient and the children are disobedient, the children of the Spiritual Living God are able to pray for their children, with Jesus mediating on our behalf (Hebrews 1). Depending on how hard their heart is (Hebrews 3:7-11), their life can be spared, or they might experience physical or spiritual death. Regardless of the consequences, we have an example of Aaron and his sons, Eli and his sons, and Samuel and his sons (Leviticus 10; 1 Samuel 3; 8:1-5)-- the parents were obedient, and the children chose to be disobedient.

We all have a part of the Spiritual Living God within us, His Spirit (Jeremiah 31:31-34; Joel 2:28-32; 1 Corinthians 2; Ephesians 1:13; Hebrews 1; 8; 1 John 4:12-14). Even when we choose to ignore the Spiritual Living God, His Spirit will always instruct us not to touch those who belong to Him (Genesis 31:24; Psalm 105:12-15). Otherwise, we can look forward to observing the angels He has watching over His children. Your obedience to the Heavenly Father, Son, and Holy Spirit allows us to be His children and to be protected at all times (Romans 8; Ephesians 4:14-32).

The Spiritual Living God provides situations in past generations where He spoke to those trying to harm those under His guidance (Genesis 12:14-20; 20; 26:6-16; 28:15; 31:24; 39:21; Exodus 1:16-21; 2:2; 15:14-18; 1 Chronicles 16:19-27; Jeremiah 39:11-14; 1 Peter 3:10-22).

Satan (the devil) had to ask permission to test Job's faith and belief (Job 1:6-2:8); it was granted with conditions.

Sometimes the children of the Spiritual Living God will use the world's cliché "Murphy's Law" (man's intelligence) to justify spiritual testing. Those who take the time and grow spiritually (Ephesians 3:14-21) already realize, the Spiritual

BECAUSE THE LORD IS YOUR SHEPHERD

Living God will be glorified, and they will experience spiritual growth with a testimony when this trial is over. The Spiritual Living God promised the Israelites, He would be an enemy to their enemies.

If they would choose to live a life of obedience, according to the words spoken to Moses during his generations (Exodus 23:22-33; Deuteronomy 8:11-20), He told them they would always have bread and water; He would remove sickness away from them.

He would take care of their babies, and women would not be barren (closed womb). Those outside His will would be fearful and become confused in every nation they encountered. He would protect the Israelites from all hurt, harm, and danger as they acquired the land He has placed before them.

The Spiritual Living God also informed the Israelites, they could not associate with the enemy (Deuteronomy 7:1-5). Those who dishonored, disrespected, and disqualified His inspired words were not His people. Those who belonged to Him regardless of the generation could not make any covenants with those He considered His enemies. They could not worship, honor, or respect their gods (hello, America!). These people were strong enough to turn their hearts away from Him, the Spiritual Living God (Numbers 33:50-56).

Does this mean the United States of America has people available to pray and turn from their wicked ways in this generation? Therefore, our land can be healed and blessed in this generation. The Spiritual Living God can provide all our needs; we do not need to be in foreign countries buying their products and trying to protect them because they choose not to believe in this generation. They have gods;

WHICH DO YOU HAVE, FAITH OR FEAR?

why can't they protect their own land? Some of the other nations have more gods than America's one Spiritual Living God. If the United States of America is going to change the Spiritual Living God's expectation of those created in His image because of their decision to be disobedient (Romans 1:21-32; 1 Corinthians 1:18-31), they should be on the front line of all battles with their gods leading them. Let's see if they return to the Spiritual Living God's nation He established for His people in this generation (Isaiah 49:1-6). It is obvious in this generation, the people have hardened their hearts (Isaiah 56:3-8; Hebrews 3:7-11) regarding the inspired words of the Spiritual Living God. They are so powerful with the spirit of deception, those who believe and are grounded in their faith can become confused anytime they take their eyes off Jesus Christ without the guidance of the Holy Spirit (Proverbs 3:5-6; Matthew 6:25-33).

All the Israelites had to do was listen, pay attention, and follow the Spiritual Living God's instructions. They had already been warned about their enemies and the strength they possessed. It was obvious they would only be successful with the Spiritual Living God's instructions.

We are commanded to read about the past generations' mistakes in this century and make better decisions. Once we accept Jesus Christ as the Spiritual Living God's only begotten Son (Hebrews 1), those who can be identified as His children (Romans 8; Ephesians 4:14-32) in this generation know we receive our help from the Holy Spirit, who provides wisdom, knowledge, and understanding about all things, especially spiritual things (John 14-16; Acts 2; 1 Corinthians 2). The guidance of the Holy Spirit informs the children of the Spiritual Living God when enemies are approaching on

BECAUSE THE LORD IS YOUR SHEPHERD

every side (Ephesians 6:10-20). You know them, so there is no fear of those that are your enemies (Psalm 53; Romans 1:22-31; 1 Corinthians 1:18-31). You'll realize you cannot acknowledge their gods at all. The enemy might appear as a stronghold, but you realize Philippians 4:13 was written for your benefit. Others observe your life and see the blessings and favor of the Spiritual Living God. Everything you touch brings forth Light in this world of darkness (John 8:12-30). The children of the Spiritual Living God who choose to grow spiritually will never be defeated by their enemies (Romans 8; Ephesians 4:14-32). We should reflect on all the promises the Spiritual Living God made in Moses' generation (Exodus 6:1-13), acknowledging as children of the Spiritual Living God due to our spiritual (Romans 15:7-13; Titus 1:1-3; Hebrews 1) relationship with His Son, Jesus Christ, we have access to all the promises the Spiritual Living God stated before and after His Son's arrival here on Earth, as flesh and blood (Romans 4:13-25; 8; 10; 15:3-21; Hebrews 6:12-20; 10-11).

Always remember, without the guidance of the Holy Spirit, it is impossible to comprehend spiritual things (1 Corinthians 2; Ephesians 1:3-23; 1 John 5). The world is confused about the Truth in this generation (Psalm 53; Romans 1:21-32; 1 Corinthians 1:18-31). They have no idea what is right, fair, and how to be honest (John 16:13; Philippians 4:6-9). Anytime human beings make rules as they live their lives, it only causes mass confusion, without the guidance of the Holy Spirit. As children of the Spiritual Living God, the guidance of the Holy Spirit will always provide wisdom, knowledge, and understanding for His children (Romans 8; Ephesians 4:14-32). We must remember to always reference the original Source before our birth here on Earth. The inspired words found in the Holy Bible are the original source, through spiritual enlightenment (John 1:1-18; 3:16-21; 4:23-24; 5:17-47; 10; 14-16; Acts 2; Hebrews 1; 8; 1 John 1-5). The natural mind cannot comprehend anything spiritual (Psalm 14; 53; Romans 1:21-32; 1 Corinthians 1:18-31) the Spiritual Living God has spoken before or after the arrival of His only begotten Son, Jesus Christ (Hebrews 1). Our Lord and Savior, Jesus Christ, is our only Redeemer in this generation, just like Isaiah spoke to those in his generation about the Lord GOD (Isaiah 43-44).

Anytime we fail to teach the next generation, we are providing a disservice, and they will suffer greatly, out of ignorance (Joel 1:3). They will be like those in Psalms 14 and 53; Romans 1:21-32; and 1 Corinthians 1:18-31. Just think of the blessings you missed out on because of disobedience. You experienced many consequences that caused you much pain and heartache in your generation, without spiritual knowledge. Try and bless someone with a testimony about the Spiritual Living God's mercy and grace, you have experienced while living here on Earth.

We should always thank the Spiritual Living God for allowing us to make decisions in this generation (2 Timothy 1:8-17). Our personal experiences with fear and faith will be a testimony to those who doubt the report in this generation (Psalm 22; Isaiah 53; John 12:38-50; Romans 10:16-21; Hebrews 1). The Scriptures still hold true for those who believe (Psalm 56; Proverbs 3) the Heavenly Father, Son, and the Holy Spirit, these three, agree in one (1 John 5). We will always have faith (Hebrews 11; 2 Corinthians 4-5), looking forward to eternal life without fear. "Blessed is the man that totally fears the Lord GOD" (Psalm 112) in this generation.

PRIDE, Pride, Pride, Pride

The characteristic of pride must diminish with spiritual growth (Ephesians 3:14-21). We should never take the Spiritual Living God's glory; otherwise, the consequences will cause us great pain and sorrow, just like those in past generations. They had to humble themselves and pray, turning from their wicked ways, in order to hear from heaven (Proverbs 16; James 2; 1 Peter 5:5-8). Remember, **"skills can take you, where only character will allow you to stay."**

There were generations before we were born (1 Samuel 15; Daniel 2:26-5:30; Romans 12; Hebrews 10:30-39) who suffered greatly for their mistakes. This road has been traveled and has very deep tracks, reminding us, others have been there and done that. It really does not matter what career or profession we choose. There is a constant battle for us to think more highly of ourselves than we ought to (Jeremiah 13:12-27; Romans 7:13-25; 8:1-17; 9:14-24; 12; 2 Timothy 2:14-26). Anytime we are blessed to accomplish anything in this life, we need to focus on the Source of our strength (Proverbs 3:5-6; Matthew 6:25-33; Philippians 2; 4). Whenever we decide to be still (John 16:13; Philippians 4:13, 19; Psalms 46-50), the Holy Spirit will always reveal the wisdom, knowledge, and understanding we need to work smart and not hard (1 Corinthians 2). The knowledge of the Spiritual Living God is man's glory (Psalms 8-10; Jeremiah

BECAUSE THE LORD IS YOUR SHEPHERD

9:23-26). Whenever we choose to take the Spiritual Living God's glory (Acts 12:21-24; 2 Corinthians 10), we eventually give up things to Satan's devices because he will encourage us in acknowledging (10:12) it was because of me, myself, and I.

If the Heavenly Father, Son, and the Holy Spirit decide to draw you back into obedience, according to the Spiritual Living God's plans and purposes, your testimony of "Heavenly Father, I stretch my hand to Thee; no other help I know" will be a constant reminder for you in your daily walk with Jesus, "just a closer walk with Thee; Heavenly Father, grant it, if You please; I am weak, but You are strong" (Galatians 5:16-26). Remember, the Spiritual Living God is a jealous God and refuses to share His glory (Exodus 20:5, 18-21; Deuteronomy 4:15-40). Your testimony will benefit many who chose to forget (Deuteronomy 8:11-20) the Spiritual Living God has commanded these inspired words. Do not think, *That was then; this is now.*

A song penned before our birth says, "Oh what needless pain we bear, all because we refuse to take things to the Spiritual Living God in prayer."

Our testimony allows others to observe our pain and heartache, helping them to realize the inspired words in the Holy Bible must really be the Truth (John 4:23-24; 2 Timothy 3:16; 2 Peter 1:12-21). The Spiritual Living God will not change His inspired words to please each of the future generations (Isaiah 40:7-8; John 12:34-36; Hebrews 13:8). We can look forward to experiencing the Spiritual Living God's consequences. Hopefully, it will not require a lot of pain to draw us back into obedience, according to the original plans and purposes the Spiritual Living God has for

PRIDE, PRIDE, PRIDE, PRIDE

His children (Romans 8; Ephesians 4:14-32). Surely, you know at least one person with a testimony about experiencing consequences for being prideful. Hopefully, you can learn from their mistakes, so you will not experience the exact same consequences.

Anytime the Spiritual Living God is trying to move you to the next level spiritually, you need to let go of whatever He is trying to remove from your life. This is like trying to take candy from a two-year-old who refuses to let go. Therefore, you pry open the child's fingers to get the candy. Lord, have mercy, do You hear the loud crying? Will it ever stop? This is exactly how we respond to the Spiritual Living God when we are being told we need to let go. Only by the guidance of the Holy Spirit will we have the strength to release whatever we are holding on to. We will acknowledge these tears are just temporary, and one day, we will not have to cry anymore (Psalm 30:5).

Anyone or anything we put before the Spiritual Living God will always hinder our spiritual growth (Matthew 10:34-39; Luke 14:25-27). It becomes very easy for Satan to use anything and everything to interfere with our spiritual personal relationship with the Heavenly Father, Son, and the guidance of the Holy Spirit. If we do not do exactly what the Scripture states, that nothing should come before the Spiritual Living God to hinder our spiritual relationship (Matthew 22:37; Mark 12:30), we will observe the power of the Spiritual Living God removing all obstacles interfering with His plans and purpose for our lives. The Holy Spirit will always provide the guidance needed for those desiring our love and concern about all things (Romans 8; Ephesians 4:14-32). We can look forward to stumbling as we grow,

BECAUSE THE LORD IS YOUR SHEPHERD

but remember, the Spiritual Living God will never allow you to fall (Jude 24-25) in your spiritual growth. Nevertheless, if you have a hardened heart (Hebrews 3:7-11) and refuse to follow the guidance of the Holy Spirit, sometimes we must fall down before we can look up in order to get up, reaching for the hand stretched out to you. We must remember the promises of the Spiritual Living God found in the Holy Bible are for His children (Romans 8; Ephesians 4:14-32). With this knowledge, including the fact He is not a man, so He has no reason to lie to us, we really can trust Him (Numbers 23:19; Malachi 3:6; Titus 1:2; James 1:16-18; 1 Peter 1:13-25).

How do you think Abraham was able to offer his only son, who was promised to him on the altar, before the Spiritual Living God (Genesis 22)? Be still and listen (Psalms 46-50; John 16:13; Philippians 4:13, 19); only by spiritual communication was he able to recall the promise made to him by the Spiritual Living God, in his generation (Hebrews 11). We are provided with wisdom, knowledge, and understanding to comprehend all things according to the Spiritual Living God (1 Corinthians 2). Anytime we can be identified as the children (Romans 8; Ephesians 4:14-32) of the Spiritual Living God, we will be informed of the plans and purposes He has for His children here on Earth with the guidance of the Holy Spirit, in this generation. If the Spiritual Living God promised (Galatians 3) you something and decides to remove it, accept this removal as a test. Some way or somehow, He will restore His promise, but He must search your heart (1 Samuel 16:7; Psalm 7:9; 139:23-24; Jeremiah 17:9-10; 20:11-12; Revelation 2:22-24) and see if the promises mean more to you than He does.

Abraham passed the test because he remembered if the Spiritual Living God removed his son, Isaac, He would

PRIDE, PRIDE, PRIDE, PRIDE

eventually provide another son based on the promise He made (Genesis 17:19). We must be able to stand on the promises of the Spiritual Living God (Romans 8; Ephesians 4:14-32). Otherwise, we will be like a ship that is tossed and driven during the storms of life (Matthew 8:23-27; Galatians 3). Peter was reminded about being able to focus on Jesus Christ, in his generation. When Peter observed the Lord's walking on water, he asked the Lord, "Can I come to You?" and He said come (Matthew 14:22-33). As long as he kept his eyes on Jesus Christ, he was able to walk on water by faith. The minute he realized he was out of the boat, taking his eyes off Jesus, he began to sink. Do you ever consider how many blessings we have passed up because of our inability to focus on the promises of the Spiritual Living God (Proverbs 3:5-8; Matthew 6:25-33)? Sometimes we choose to look everywhere except to the hills for our help, which comes from the Lord (Psalms 46-50), where we find promises of the Spiritual Living God.

David knew where to go in his times of need and allows us to reflect on who provided his strength and helped him, in his generation (Psalm 121).

When we remove our eyes from our help, we can experience sinking situations (James 1; 2 Peter 2:9). We will eventually fall on our knees or lay on the floor, level with the ground. Sometimes we need to be put in a position of calling on the name of Jesus, asking the Heavenly Father, who resides in heaven, to have mercy on us. We need to state this pain is more than I can bear; just recall a James Cleveland song, "I know He will come through with a blessing for me; oh Lord, set my soul free."

We are not exempt in this day and time because of our faith and belief in the Gospel (Psalm 22; Isaiah 53; Ephesians

BECAUSE THE LORD IS YOUR SHEPHERD

1:13-14; Hebrews 1; 1 John 1-5). If you are not careful in this generation, man will lift you up and cause you to forget about your spiritual relationship with the Spiritual Living God (James 2). We are actually observing situations where a man has ways to lift you up, making you an icon (Proverbs 8; James 4) in this generation. This action will always cause heartache and pain (Psalm 124). It will be impossible for us to remember, "If it had not been for the Lord, who was on my side, tell me, where would I be?" Always remember, the Spiritual Living God has a way to deliver His children out of temptation (2 Peter 2:9); therefore, our mouths will continuously be filled with praise. Whenever we forget we need a heart of thanksgiving for the blessings from the Spiritual Living God, we can look forward to experiencing consequences for being disobedient in this generation.

Pride is one of the deadly sins found in Proverbs 6:16-19. Other warnings are found in Psalm 10:4; Proverbs 13:9-10; 26:10-13; 29:23-27; 30; Jeremiah 49:15-16; Daniel 5:20-23; and Hosea 7:9-10. We have been warned so many times, pride is not a characteristic of Jesus Christ. Therefore, the Spiritual Living God has no patience available for those who choose to indulge for a little while (Hebrews 10; Revelation 3:15-17).

Take the time and read the book of Job with the guidance of the Holy Spirit. This man had a heart to do what was right, according to the Spiritual Living God, but while being blessed, he forgot, just like the current children (Romans 8; Ephesians 4:14-32) of the Spiritual Living God, in this generation--Job actually forgot where the blessings were coming from (Job 38-40). The Spiritual Living God allowed Satan to remind him one day, with very strict

PRIDE, PRIDE, PRIDE, PRIDE

instructions (Job 1:6-2:8). How many of us can handle the Spiritual Living God's allowing Satan to test us in this generation? Be careful what you speak; He knows our mind before we speak (Jeremiah 1:4-9). Remember, Satan had to ask for permission before he could interfere with Job's life. I guarantee you, this test will make you stronger in your faith, or you will find your faith needs to be strengthened (Hebrews 11). After the negative comments from his wife and friends during their counseling, Job continued to hold on to his faith. Sometimes others can encourage you in a negative way; we must be grounded enough in our faith to encourage ourselves (1 Samuel 30:6; 2 Peter 1:12-21). Always remember, some friends are seasonal; they move on just like the yearly seasons change with time.

Just be sure and reference the Scriptures found in 1 John 1-5. We are given friendly reminders, all thanks are to Jesus, our Mediator (Romans 8:34; Galatians 3:19-29; 1 Timothy 2:4-6; Hebrews 1). He actually provided the help for the children of the Spiritual Living God who have decided to grow spiritually, remembering to make better decisions with the guidance of the Holy Spirit. Anytime we forget and think it is about us and not about Jesus, get ready for the trials, tribulations, and storms coming your way as a reminder (Matthew 8:21-29; Mark 4:35-41; Luke 8:22). Whenever we humble ourselves and pray, asking for forgiveness in Jesus' name, things can turn around in a positive manner.

We really need to consider the life the disciples lived and the help they received with the guidance of the Holy Spirit (Mark 16:15-18; John 14-16; Acts 2). We will be allowed to come to the conclusion, we really can do all things through Jesus Christ. He provides the strength for

BECAUSE THE LORD IS YOUR SHEPHERD

the Spiritual Living God's children to be successful in this generation (Romans 16:25-27; John 16:13; Philippians 4:6-9, 13). Reflect on the promises found in the Holy Bible, which are available to the Spiritual Living God's children. The day we accept the Spiritual Living God is not a man, that He will not lie about anything to us (Numbers 23:19; 1 Samuel 15:29; James 1:16-18; Malachi 3:6; Titus 1:2), this will be the day we will soar in our faith and trust in the Spiritual Living God (1 Corinthians 2; Hebrews 11). Just like eagles, when danger approaches, they go higher up in the atmosphere, which causes the enemy to turn back (Isaiah 40:29-31). Choosing a relationship with Jesus allows us to have access to the guidance of the Holy Spirit, which allows us to lay our problems at the feet of Jesus, choosing not to access them again, and allowing someone else to lead, and you to follow His leadership. This process can really relieve a lot of stress, which causes many of the health problems in this day and time. You must believe He can take care of all the situations you experience in this life better than you can, in order for you to let go. Try taking small steps until you are strong enough in your faith to let go; He will not let you fall (1 John 1:5-2:17; Jude 24-25). Increase your steps as you continue to grow spiritually (Romans 8; Ephesians 3:14-21). We will eventually come to a spiritual understanding, we can trust the inspired words of the Spiritual Living God, and they are very true, just like the Holy Bible stated (John 5:39-47; Romans 15:1-6; 2 Timothy 3:15-17; 2 Peter 1:20-21).

Eventually, you will be confident enough to walk by faith and not by sight (John 20:27-31; 2 Corinthians 5:7; Galatians 5:16-26; Hebrews 11).

This is the same progress babies make when they are

PRIDE, PRIDE, PRIDE, PRIDE

learning to walk. They hold on to their parent's hand until they trust themselves to stay balanced on their own two feet. They must fully trust their parents when they are starting out without any knowledge about how their feet actually move. Anytime they reach for you and fall, it will take them a while to reach for your hand, but eventually, they will reach out for your hand again. Remember, you always hear, "I will not let you fall." It is the trust and confidence babies have in parents that encourages them to let go.

We also have to trust our Heavenly Father, who resides in heaven, even when we fail at being obedient, according to His words. We should cry with brokenness (Psalm 51), because we fail at receiving the hand available to us--the one He provided to help us overcome things that would easily set us back when we are trying to go forward (John 14-16). Choosing a life of obedience regarding the Heavenly Father, Son, and the guidance of the Holy Spirit allows us to have some needed peace. Whenever others are confused and disillusioned about the Spiritual Living God (Psalm 53; Romans 1:21-32; 1 Corinthians 1:18-31), His children need to be still (Psalms 46-50).

Observe the things taking place around you, which man cannot take the credit for in this generation. This means, the Spiritual Living God is still in control of His world. Those without a spiritual personal relationship (Romans 8) with the Spiritual Living God's Son (1 Corinthians 2) are killing themselves slowly. Remember, we have been given the Spirit of the Spiritual Living God in this generation (Jeremiah 31:31-35; Joel 2:28-32); spiritual access comes from His only begotten Son, Jesus Christ (John 1:1-18; 3:16-21; 4:23-24, 5:17-47; 10; 14-16; Acts 2; 1 Corinthians 2; Hebrews 1). The choice is ours,

BECAUSE THE LORD IS YOUR SHEPHERD

if we really would like to know Him for ourselves (Hebrews 8). The Heavenly Father has children (Romans 8; Ephesians 4:14-32) living right here on Earth, in this generation.

They provide a visual of the Spiritual Living God's discipline (Proverbs 3:11-26) for others to learn it is possible to work smart without working hard (Galatians 5:16-26; Ephesians 6:10-20). It is very obvious, they receive their help, the guidance of the Holy Spirit. They always remember to give the Spiritual Living God glory for allowing them to be successful in all things (Proverbs 3:5-6; Isaiah 40:25-31; Matthew 6:25-33).

Are You Caught in Sin and You "Can't" Get Loose?

If this is your insight regarding sin that has a hold and will not let you go, STOP! Ask yourself this question, because I had to: Do I still have a desire, regardless of how small, to be connected in some way?

Allow your heart, not your mind, to answer. This is the only way the truth will come forth (1 Samuel 16:7; Psalm 7:9, 139:23-24; Jeremiah 17:9-10; Revelation 2:22-24). Yes, I thought the same thing until the Holy Spirit revealed the area I was not ready to release. So, until we are ready to surrender everything to the Spiritual Living God, we must continue to be a road lizard, doing the same thing the same way, expecting different results.

Remember, the Spiritual Living God is patient with those who pray in Jesus' name with a broken spirit (Psalm 51). The blessings from the Spiritual Living God do not flow in disobedience, so you can stop expecting that miracle and the impossible (Proverbs 15:29). Whenever we become tired and brokenhearted, it will be time to sincerely go to the Heavenly Father, in Jesus' name. We need to have a humble and sincere heart, stating we are finally ready to surrender our lives to His will and way (Proverbs 3:5-6; Matthew 6:25-33). We need to confess and state, we are tired of this wilderness (maze), so He can point us to the exit (Romans 6; 1 John 1-2). Otherwise, the walls will become taller, your ears will become duller, and your sight will become dimmer (Isaiah 6:8-10; Jeremiah 5:19-31; Ezekiel 12:2; Matthew 13:13-15; Mark 4:11-29; Luke 8:10-15; John 12:38-50; Acts 28:24-29; Romans 11:7-10). Whenever we choose to keep company with those who choose to participate in things displeasing to the Spiritual Living God (1 Corinthians 5), we can lose sight of our directions, according to His plans and purpose for our lives here on Earth. This is why we have Scriptures stating the Spiritual Living God's moral standards for His children in this generation (Proverbs 3:5-8; Matthew 6:25-33; Mark 7:6-23; Romans 8; Galatians 1-3; 5:16-26; Ephesians 4:14-32; 6:10-20). We really do not have an excuse for not serving the Spiritual Living God, in this generation of the twenty-first century.

If we are not careful, we will be in darkness, never realizing the light went out without our knowledge. Sin has a way of causing the light to grow dimmer each time you participate, so you become immune to what is taking place (Hebrews 10). You no longer have the small voice trying to encourage you to make a better decision, because you have actually hardened your heart (Hebrews 3:7-11) regarding this sin.

Remember, the Spiritual Living God sent His Son so we might live a life of obedience to do His will (Hebrews 1; 1 John 1-5). We are given a choice when it comes to having a spiritual personal relationship with the Spiritual Living God (John 4:23-24). He is known to His children (Romans 8; Ephesians 4:14-32) as their Heavenly Father, who has one begotten Son (Hebrews 1), Jesus Christ, who provides access to spiritual enlightenment (John 14-16; Acts 2; 1 Corinthians 2) through the Holy Spirit. Now, we are allowed to communicate in the Spirit with the Spiritual Living God, who resides in heaven. Sometimes we like to give credit to past generations for our disobedience in this day and time. This is possible considering the Scripture states, "Whatever we plant can be harvested" (Galatians 6:7-10). Anytime we have a generation that refuses to accept the Gospel (Psalm 22; Isaiah 53; Romans 1:16-20; Ephesians 1:13-14; Hebrews 1) and chooses a life of disobedience regarding the inspired words provided by the Heavenly Father, Son, and our Helper, the guidance of the Holy Spirit (1 John 1-5), we can look forward to the past generations' experiences before Jesus Christ's arrival as the only begotten Son.

In Deuteronomy 24:16; 2 Chronicles 25:4; 2 Kings 14:6; and Ezekiel 18:1-20, we are reminded, "The Father shall not die for the children, neither shall the children die for the fathers, but every man shall die for his own sin." Sometimes children observe the sins of their parents. These actions cause the children to think the Spiritual Living God does not provide consequences for sin and their sin becomes more grievous than their parents' original sin, they observed in the past.

We must remember, there are two kinds of sins we commit in this day and time--unintentional and intentional sin (Psalm 19)--anytime we use our limited intelligence to make decisions that are displeasing to the Spiritual Living God, due to ignorance. In others words, we thought we were making the right decision; He observes our heart and knows without a doubt, this sin was unintentional. He also observes our heart and knows if we are being defiant and rebellious without a doubt. In other words, you know this is displeasing to Him, but it is all about you and what you what. You have hardened your heart and refuse to allow the guidance of the Holy Spirit to lead you spiritually.

BECAUSE THE LORD IS YOUR SHEPHERD

Therefore, you are intentionally sinning against the Spiritual Living God without any remorse or shame.

Whenever we choose not to accept the Spiritual Living God's grace and mercy for our sins, refusing to accept the blood shed by His Son, Jesus Christ, provided to cleanse us from sin and unrighteousness (Luke 24:45-47; Romans 3:21-25; 5:1-11; Ephesians 1:7; Hebrews 1; 1 John 1-2), according to the Spiritual Living God's inspired words found in the Holy Bible.

We are choosing to live our current life without experiencing eternal life (1 John 5). The promises were made to the children (Romans 8; Ephesians 4:14-32) of the Spiritual Living God before our birth here on Earth. Second Peter 2 reveals insight about past generations' experiences with the Spiritual Living God. The problems present themselves when you desire access to the Holy, Righteous, Spiritual, and Living God without the Mediator, His Son, Jesus Christ (Mark 16:19; Romans 8; Colossians 3:1; Hebrews 1; 7:25). We have the Spirit of the Spiritual Living God (Jeremiah 31:31-35; Joel 2:28-32; 1 John 4:12-14) within us. He is just dormant until we have spiritual access through Jesus Christ; we are enlightened regarding spiritual things with the guidance of the Holy Spirit (John 3; 14-16; Acts 2; 1 Corinthians 2; Ephesians 1:13).

Sometimes we choose to forget, according to the Scriptures, the Spirit communicates with the Spirit, and the flesh communicates with the flesh (John 3:5-6; Romans 8; Galatians 5:16-26; Ephesians 4:14-32).

There is a difference in the guidance the Holy Spirit provides to communicate with the children whose Heavenly Father resides in Heaven (1 John 4:1-6; Acts 19:12-20) and the evil spirits. The Spiritual Living God does not allow evil spirits to have access to those who can be identified as His children (Romans 8; Ephesians 4:14-32). Anyone that is not His child, without an interest or desire to be obedient to His will (Joshua 23:15-16; Judges 9:23; Isaiah 19:14; 2 Chronicles 18:20-22; 1 John 4:1-6), can look forward to those other spirits taking up residence within you. Exactly what is the Spiritual Living God's will for our lives (Jeremiah 29:11-14)? Try reading John (1:1-18; 3:16-21; 4:23-24; 6:44-71; 10; 14-16; Acts 2; Romans 1:16-20; 8-10; 1 Corinthians 2; Ephesians 1:11-13; 3:11; 4:14-32; 2 Timothy 1:19; 3:10; Hebrews 1; 8; 10-11; 1 John 1-5).

Pray an honest and sincere prayer to the Heavenly Father in Jesus' name, seeking the Spiritual Living God, who resides in heaven, in the name of Jesus, asking the Spiritual Living God to reveal His Holy Spirit to you (John 6:44-65; 1 Corinthians 2), so you might receive wisdom, knowledge, and understanding in holy, righteous, and spiritual things (2:12-16), according to His will and ways for your life while living here on Earth (Ephesians 1:15-23; 3-4).

We should always remember, children observe everything their parents do. Whenever we choose to be disobedient, according to the will of the Holy, Righteous, Spiritual, and Living God, it is very possible they will double, if not triple, their parents' life of disobedience regarding the Spiritual Living God. So, we only plant seeds that continue to grow in the lives of our children (Galatians 6:7-10). The Spiritual Living God blesses us with children for His glory and to do His will (Galatians 4:1-7; Colossians 1:9-29).

Regardless of the good or bad growth, it will always be observed by others they will see you in their lives for

BECAUSE THE LORD IS YOUR SHEPHERD

continuous generations. There is a promise for those who have trained up a child according to inspired words found in the Holy Bible (Genesis 18:19-21; Deuteronomy 4:10, 11:19-20; Proverbs 4: all, 13:24, 22:6).

If the seeds are bad, each generation will be given a chance for a different life (Proverbs 30) while living here on Earth by observing the Light (John 8:12-30) of others the Spiritual Living God has here on Earth who are His children, according to His inspired words (Romans 8:5-16; Ephesians 4:14-32). Anytime we choose to have a spiritual personal relationship with the Spiritual Living God through Jesus Christ, this is the only experience (John 6:44-65) that allows each generation to change from their life of disobedience. We can look forward to the blessings in future generations, but as soon as those in the next generation take their eyes off Jesus, they will always go back to a life of being disobedient, just like the past generations. Only by the guidance of the Holy Spirit (John 14-16; Acts 2; 1 Corinthians 2) will they be able to accept these blessings (Romans 16:25-27; Philippians 4:13).

There were many before you who chose to be disobedient regarding the Spiritual Living God's inspired words. They lost their lives for choosing to sin against the Holy, Righteous, and Spiritual Living God, who resides in heaven. They did not have the guidance of the Holy Spirit before Jesus Christ's arrival here as the Spiritual Living God's Son (John 1:1-18; 3:16-21; Hebrews 1). The Spiritual Living God removed them from among the land of the living; they died instantly (Deuteronomy 7:3-5; 11:6-7; Joshua 24:14-15, 19-20; 2 Peter 2:4-9). Whose report will you believe (Psalm 22; Isaiah 53; John 12:38-50; Romans 1:16-20; 9-10)? We have the guidance of

ARE YOU CAUGHT IN SIN AND YOU "CAN'T" GET LOOSE?

the Holy Spirit available to us in this generation (Jeremiah 31:31-34; Joel 2:28-32; Romans 8; 1 Corinthians 2; Ephesians 1:11-13; 2:18; Hebrews 1; 8; 10-11). Nevertheless, when we choose to sin and think there will not be consequences in this generation (Romans 6-7; Hebrews 10), this is a sign of still drinking milk and not being able to accept meat (1 Corinthians 3:1-3; Hebrews 5:11-14; 1 Peter 2:1-3). Thank the Spiritual Living God for His Son, Jesus Christ. The Spiritual Living God's love, compassion, mercy, and grace have been made available to His children (1 John 4:7-21). Those who choose to live without acknowledging the Heavenly Father, Son, and Holy Spirit, there is a day coming when you will not have a choice (Isaiah 45:23; Philippians 2:5-11; 1 John 4:15). The Spirit within you will cause you to speak of the Holy, Righteous, Spiritual, and Living God, acknowledging His Son, Jesus Christ, just like Paul did in his generation, on the Damascus road (Acts 9).

The experience had him speaking (Acts 9:3-7) without receiving the guidance of the Holy Spirit (Acts 9:17-18). There will come a day when every knee will bow and tongue confess (Romans 14:11; Philippians 2:9-11; 1 John 5:6-21).

We will not have a choice, just like Paul; the Spirit that is within you will speak the Truth (Jeremiah 31:31-34; Joel 2:28-32; 1 Corinthians 2; 1 John 4:13-15). Then, we will cry with a broken spirit (Psalm 51), saying, "Lord, I did not know" (Matthew 21:33-44); hopefully, it will not be too late to experience (1 John 1-5) eternal life.

The Spiritual Living God Uses Ordinary People

When the Spiritual Living God calls us into obedience and provides a vision (Romans 8:28-39; Ephesians 2:18; 1 Thessalonians 2:3-16; 4:7-8), we really need to answer the call (Matthew 20:1-16); this will be the best career choice you could make in this life (1 Thessalonians 4:7-9). Anytime we decide to enter a Bible college to strengthen our foundation about the Heavenly Father, Son, and the guidance of the Holy Spirit, this decision allows us to pursue the only degree available to everyone on equal footing that actually allows you to reference your prior knowledge without the fear of it being outdated (Hebrews 13:8; 1 Peter 1:13-25; 2 Peter 1:12-21). There is a possibility of your being misinformed about the Scriptures without the guidance of the Holy Spirit, but at least you were somewhat familiar with what was being taught. You actually enjoy going to school without having surprises sprung on you. Your prior knowledge with a lifetime of training and experiences can be used. This knowledge really helps to keep us grounded in the expectation of things being taught because everything is centered on the inspired words found in the Holy Bible.

If you do not have a degree and desire to have one, consider studying at a Bible college of higher learning that believes in the guidance of the Holy Spirit's leadership. The

BECAUSE THE LORD IS YOUR SHEPHERD

guidance of the Holy Spirit will move you to a whole new level of learning; you will be impressed with your ability to excel in spiritual academics (John 14:26; 1 Corinthians 2). You will not receive this power in any college of other studies. Remember, most degrees we pursue, we are trying to excel in something that we have little or no prior knowledge about. When I graduated from college with a computer science degree, ten years later, it was considered outdated. This is being very generous with time. The degree I received from the Bible college will last until Jesus returns. The Holy Spirit will continue to enlighten me, but the knowledge I received will never be outdated by man's standards of knowledge.

Those who have tried until they are being spiritually drained to help others acknowledge the Gospel (Psalm 22; Isaiah 53; Romans 1:16; Ephesians 1:13; 1 Thessalonians 1:5-6; Hebrews 1) because you have been spiritually enlightened by the Holy Spirit, feel free to take a break and accept the fact that you have planted the seed. Someone else will do the watering in order for them to grow spiritually (1 Corinthians 3:5-10); the Spiritual Living God must provide the increase.

This is like, the Holy Spirit revealed to me, I needed to surrender my life, and my response was, "I did that a long time ago." The small voice did not argue, just said, "This is different." It was not until I spoke the words I was asked to speak, I began to experience something different within me like I had just made a big commitment. For those who feel like I did originally, I have been in church faithfully every Sunday and work very hard at being obedient, but fail quite often also. Why do I need to attend Bible college for a formal education about spiritual things (Acts 18:24-

THE SPIRITUAL LIVING GOD USES ORDINARY PEOPLE

28)? It was not until Apollos came in contact with Aquila and Priscilla, he was able to acknowledge his words were not totally lining up with the teachings of Jesus Christ.

Paul was also a strong persecutor (1 Timothy 1:12-16) for teachings according to his formal education, leaving out the Gospel (Psalm 22; Isaiah 53; Romans 1:16-20; Ephesians 1:13; 1 Thessalonians 1:5-6; Hebrews 1), without the guidance of the Holy Spirit. It was his Damascus road experience with Jesus Christ (Acts 9) that caused him to experience the discipleship training needed for teaching, according to the Gospel (Psalm 22; Isaiah 53; Romans 1:16-20; Ephesians 1:13; 1 Thessalonians 1:5-6; Hebrews 1), by the guidance of the Holy Spirit. We can also be eloquent in speech, when we speak with the guidance of the Holy Spirit (John 14:26) and biblical training.

It really did seem strange at first, but the small things that everybody does are no longer easy for you to participate in. The Holy Spirit begins to enlighten you regarding spiritual things, and as children of the Spiritual Living God, your decision to be obedient becomes a little bit easier (2 Peter 2:9). Teaching you small things really does matter in the eyes of the Spiritual Living God. The Holy Spirit begins to gently remind us, He is taking control of our lives, so we can make better decisions about all things. You are actually being convicted by the Holy Spirit right away about situations being displeasing to the Spiritual Living God. Once the Bible training has been acquired, we need to be careful not to think more highly of ourselves than we ought to (Deuteronomy 1:17-18; Romans 12; James 2).

Choosing a profession or career about spiritual things without the guidance of the Holy Spirit is not a good decision (Acts19:11-19; 1 John 4:1-6). It is best to wait until the Spiritual Living God calls us into obedience to do His will (Romans 8:28-39; 1 Corinthians 2; Ephesians 2:18; 4; 1 Thessalonians 2:3-16; 1 Timothy 3; 2 Timothy 4; 2 Peter 2; 1 John 1-2). We really need to be equipped with spiritual guidance in order for sin not to beset us in this generation. Anytime we choose not to accept Jesus as the Spiritual Living God's only begotten Son, with the guidance of the Holy Spirit (1 Thessalonians 4:7-8; Hebrews 1), we become like those in Acts 23:8; they are SAD-U-CEE. Paul was told by Jesus to open the eyes of the Gentiles and turn them from darkness to Light (Acts 26:18), informing them of the hold, the power Satan has over them. Teach them forgiveness of sin is provided by the Spiritual Living God, in the name of Jesus (Luke 24:45-47; 1 John 1-2).

As spiritually mature children of the Spiritual Living God in the name of Jesus, we have the responsibility to always inform anyone and everyone when they sin; it actually quenches their Spirit within them (Ephesians 4:29-32; 5:1-21). We are commanded to love the people, but we cannot accept their sin, as the Spiritual Living God's children (Romans 8; Ephesians 4:14-32). This is why it is absolutely necessary, we prepare but wait for the call into obedience because the Spiritual Living God's expectations are higher for those He called (Matthew 7:13-14, 21-23; 9:36-38; Luke 12:41-48; 1 Corinthians 9; 2 Corinthians 2-5; Galatians 1:6-24; Colossians 1:3-29, 3-4:5-6). We are not allowed to provide excuses for being disobedient as preachers and teachers (2 Peter 2:9) who are called into obedience. Whenever we refuse to rise to His level of Spiritual expectation as leaders, it will be impossible to speak regarding the teaching of

THE SPIRITUAL LIVING GOD USES ORDINARY PEOPLE

Jesus (Matthew 7:1-6) if we are going to be disobedient. We cannot encourage others to make a better decision about sinning against the Spiritual Living God when we will not allow the Holy Spirit to lead in our decisions. Therefore, they might receive the inheritance available for those who are sanctified by faith in Him (Hebrews 1; 8-11; 1 John 5). We have been given instructions by Paul and others regarding the Gospel (Psalm 22; Isaiah 53; Romans 1:16-20; Ephesians 1:13; 1 Thessalonians 1:5-6; Hebrews 1) of Jesus Christ being the power of the Spiritual Living God (Romans 1:16-20; 10:6-21) for those who desire strength to live according to the purpose and plans of the Spiritual Living God (John 16:13; Philippians 4:6-9, 13).

Anytime we are called into obedience and decide to step outside of the will of the Spiritual Living God without the guidance of the Holy Spirit, we are reminded of the consequences in Jeremiah's generation (Jeremiah 23; Romans 2:2-3). It is not an easy job to be Light in a dark world (Romans 2:8-9). Only by the guidance of the Holy Spirit will you be provided with spiritual strength (1 Corinthians 6:19-27; Philippians 3:14-21; 4:13, 19) to make the right decisions in this world. Exactly why would anyone choose to involve himself or herself in spiritual things without spiritual guidance when we were warned before our birth about those other spirits that exist (Acts 19:11-19; 1 John 4:1-6)? The consequences for those without spiritual guidance can be very devastating (1 Corinthians 9:11-18).

Paul reminds us (2 Corinthians 3), the Spirit of the Spiritual Living God speaks to our hearts in order for us to trust Him. We must always acknowledge the Spiritual Living God is a Spirit (John 4:23-24), and He only deals with Spirit and Truth.

BECAUSE THE LORD IS YOUR SHEPHERD

We must decide to live our lives in the Spirit in order to communicate with the Spiritual Living God (Romans 8; 2 Corinthians 3:17-18). We have a natural body and a spiritual body (1 Corinthians 15:35-58) that provides insight about our spiritual bodies. There is a difference in the body of humans and animals also. The Spiritual Living God provided bodies according to His desire for us. Our relationship with Jesus Christ allows us to receive the guidance of the Holy Spirit, revealing spiritual things (John 14-16; Acts 2; 1 Corinthians 2). Then, we can worship the Spiritual Living God in Spirit and Truth; His original standards for those who sincerely belong to Him, as His children (Romans 8; Ephesians 4:14-32), will be spiritually revealed. We must understand that flesh and blood will not be allowed to inherit the kingdom of the Spiritual Living God (John 3:1-15). Only with the guidance of the Holy Spirit will we gain the freedom to be free from sins, which usually causes stress because there are things we cannot change in this world (Romans 6).

We must live by faith in this generation, trusting every inspired word found in the Holy Bible as the Truth (Hebrews 11). Nevertheless, we must be enlightened by the Holy Spirit to have wisdom, knowledge, and understanding about spiritual things (John 14-16; Acts 2; 1 Corinthians 2; 2 Corinthians 4:7-18). Always remember, the flesh cannot sustain you when you have trouble on every side, causing you to become stressed out (Matthew 7:15-29). Never reach for a man's medicinal methods to handle life's twists and turns; remember, those who have a spiritual personal relationship with the Spiritual Living God, your strength is renewed day by day (Romans 16:25-27; 2 Corinthians 4:10-16). Walking by faith and not by sight allows us to grow

THE SPIRITUAL LIVING GOD USES ORDINARY PEOPLE

spiritually (2 Corinthians 5:5-10; Galatians 5:16-26; Ephesians 1:3-6). Paul reminds us to live or die: "He will experience life with Jesus Christ" (Philippians 1:11-30). Anytime we have to give an account of things we do to our body, which does not belong to us (1 Corinthians 12:12-31; 2 Corinthians 5:10), it is very important for us to take care of what belongs to the Spiritual Living God (1 Corinthians 3:16-20).

We have been given the power to become Light in a dark world (2 Corinthians 5:17-21; 6:11-18).

Others will observe your life, and they always need to see Jesus' leadership and guidance by the Holy Spirit; no excuse is acceptable when we become spiritually mature enough to lead others (John 16:13; Philippians 4; 1 Corinthians 9:11-14). Those who are babes spiritually become defeated when they observe those called into obedience are not capable of leading with the guidance of the Holy Spirit (2 Corinthians 6; 7:1; Galatians 5:16-26; Ephesians 4:14-32; 6:10-20; 2 Peter 2:9). It is impossible for Light and darkness to be on one accord (2 Corinthians 6:14; 1 Peter 2:9-10; 1 John 5).

Sometimes we think we can associate with those who choose to live their lives outside of the Spiritual Living God's will. Nevertheless, we have been reminded in several Scriptures (Deuteronomy 7:2-3; 1 Samuel 5:2-5; 1 Kings 18:21; 1 Corinthians 5:4-13; Ephesians 5:1-21; 2 Corinthians 6:14-18), be not unequally yoked with unbelievers; we do not have things in common.

It is easier to pull someone down, than to help him or her up to your level. Try standing on a chair and pulling someone up, then allow the person to pull you down. Wow! That was fast . . . something to think about.

BECAUSE THE LORD IS YOUR SHEPHERD

The world will always try and convince everyone, "Can't we all just learn to get along serving our own gods?" Children of the Spiritual Living God with the guidance of the Holy Spirit know without a doubt, they must take a stand for righteousness in this generation. Light and darkness will never get along; Jesus is the Light, and we are commanded to follow the Light (John 1:1-18; 3:16-21; 4:23-24; 5:17-47; 6:31-65; 8:12-30; 10; 12:27-50; 14-16). Therefore, it is impossible for Light and darkness to be on one accord (Matthew 7:13-29; Romans 12:3-21; Galatians 5:16-26). Jesus Christ always steps in to mediate with the guidance of the Holy Spirit; otherwise, we would be in trouble (Matthew 10:16-42; Galatians 3:19-29; 1 Timothy 2:5) for being deceived by those other spirits (1 John 4:1-6).

Anytime the Spiritual Living God provides a vision, be careful who you share it with because until He gets you ready to handle the vision, others could cause you to doubt your ability to bring it to fruition. Been there, done that; skip it if you can. It is not a warm, fuzzy feeling (1 John 4:1-6; Acts 19:15-19). Listening to negative feedback from those who you thought could relate to your vision really can plant seeds of doubt; listen to the words being sung today, "What the Spiritual Living God, has for you, it is for you," until further notice.

The visions in this day and time are usually a message to the people in that generation, or past generations' experiences reappearing in the current generation. Anytime we appear to be confused about the Spiritual Living God's inspired words found in the Holy Bible, we really need to reference the inspired words found in Psalm 53; Romans 1:21-32; 2:8-9; and 1 Corinthians 1:18-31; it is very possible you thought you were His child (John 14-16; Acts 2; Romans 1:16-20; 8; 1 Corinthians 2; Ephesians 4:14-32). Who would have ever thought the twenty-first century would be the generations to participate in the same things? The Spiritual Living God wiped Sodom and Gomorrah off the face of the Earth for participating in homosexual lifestyles and totally ignoring the Spiritual Living God's laws (commandments) (Genesis 18:20; 2 Peter 2:6; Jude 7). They were being disobedient, according to His commandments in their generation. He provided consequences for their disobedience; it cost everybody that had breath in their bodies, their lives in those cities and all the plains during Abraham's generation (Genesis 19:24-25).

I wonder if they could have made excuses like the people in the twenty-first century. Just like it did not work then, it will not work in this generation. We can be labeled the confused, weak generations that thought the Spiritual Living God finally accepts the homosexual lifestyles (sin) (2 Peter 2:9). Nevertheless, if we forget, we have been warned the Spiritual Living God knows how to deliver His children from temptation. The question is, do we want to be delivered? (Good question.) When it appears everyone is receptive to a sin, it can easily disillusion even a strong, spiritually led Christian (Jeremiah 3:20-25; Acts 19:24-30; James 3:15-18). Sometimes we need to remove ourselves from everyone and allow the Holy Spirit to speak to our Spirit (Romans 8; Ephesians 4:14-32). Then, the Light comes on and the Truth can reappear, so we can see the spirit of deception was very elusive. Some sins just work themselves right in as a part of everyday living, all levels of the media participating (visual, print, and audio). Anyway, we are the ones who choose to

BECAUSE THE LORD IS YOUR SHEPHERD

receive information about the world (Isaiah 26:2-4; Romans 12:1-2; 2 Corinthians 10:4-6); we need to always protect our minds. There is a great possibility of becoming blind without spiritual insight (Romans 1:21-32; 1 Corinthians 1:18-31; 2 Corinthians 10:4-6). Whenever we continue in sin without regrets or asking for forgiveness in the name of Jesus, our Lights become dim, then dull until they are dark without our realizing we are in darkness (Isaiah 5-6; Acts 28:26-29; Romans 11:8).

We are no longer in a position to recognize sin has taken control of our lives (Matthew 13; John 9:31). This can easily cause a spiritual communication breakdown. Your prayers are no longer getting through because the Spiritual Living God refuses to deal with sin (John 4:23-24; Ephesians 2; Hebrews 10).

These actions play with your mind, deciding to feed your mind, "Everybody is doing it or accepting it; do not rock the boat." Just like Jesus went in and turned over the tables in His generation when He found the people were misusing and abusing the purpose of the Spiritual Living God's house (Matthew 21:12-16), Jesus Christ had to take a stand in His generation for righteousness; He reacted accordingly due to His relationship with His Heavenly Father.

I am willing to take a stand for what is right, according to the inspired words found in the Holy Bible, in this generation. So, move while I tip the boat over regarding the words inspired by the Holy, Righteous, Spiritual, and Living God. Thank Him, He did not call you for this message because I have decided to follow Jesus; there is no turning back. In Ezekiel 33 and Isaiah 51, we are reminded of our responsibility to teach the Spiritual Living God's people. There we will find,

THE SPIRITUAL LIVING GOD USES ORDINARY PEOPLE

if we choose, to be obedient (Acts 5:29), speaking the Truth provided by the Spiritual Living God regarding His people. We can look forward to His blessings for being obedient to His calling (1 Corinthians 1:16-21; 2; Romans 2:8-9; 1 Peter 1:3-2).

Whenever warnings come and the people refuse to accept the Spiritual Living God's inspired words of wisdom from those called into obedience, the consequences will be applied to them and not the person called to deliver the message, for they chose to ignore His warning. Anytime we receive a vision from the Spiritual Living God regarding the people being blinded by sin, the person with the vision has a great responsibility to inform the people of the inspired words provided by divine guidance (Jeremiah 1:4-3:25). We will be held accountable for refusing to follow the guidance of the Holy Spirit. Ezekiel spoke of the warnings and consequences in his generation (33:7-9). DO YOU THINK WE CAN IGNORE THE WARNINGS AND CONSEQUENCES IN THIS GENERATION?

Jesus has come so we might be forgiven for our sins and choose a life of obedience to live abundantly (John 10; Hebrews 1-2; 8; 10-11). We are given a chance to make a decision; the choice really belongs to us, along with the consequences. Those called into obedience must be grounded spiritually (Galatians 5:16-26; Ephesians 6:10-20; Colossians 1:9; 2 Peter 1:12-21). Spiritual training through life experiences really helps a person mature spiritually; anytime we experience the Spiritual Living God personally, we are not able to doubt Him. We can stand for what is right, according to the inspired words found in the Holy Bible. Otherwise, those who question or would like to know right from wrong, we have the Spirit of the Spiritual Living God within each and every human created in His image (Jeremiah 31:31-35; Joel 2:28-32; 1 John 4:12-14). We need spiritual access from His only begotten Son (John 14-16; Acts 2; 1 Corinthians 2), Jesus Christ, to receive spiritual enlightenment from the Holy Spirit. This is the only way we will be able to comprehend spiritual things in this generation.

The standards can be found in the Holy Bible, His inspired words, which are provided for those who can be identified as His children (John 16:13; 2 Timothy 3:16; Philippians 4:6-9), in this generation. You no longer need to guess; the Holy Spirit is always willing to reveal the Truth (Luke 12:12; John 14:26; 1 Corinthians 2; 1 Thessalonians 2:4; 4:7-8; 1 Timothy 4:1). We must ask ourselves this question: Am I ready to receive the Truth with spiritual guidance? (Good question.) You can have the highest level of education respected by the world or a third-grade education according to the world. The Spiritual Living God is no respecter of persons; as His children (Romans 8; Ephesians 4:14-32), we are enlightened by the Holy Spirit. We receive wisdom, knowledge, and understanding regarding all things because we are the Spiritual Living God's children (Deuteronomy 1:17-18; 10:17; John 14-16; Acts 2; 10:34; Romans 2:10-16; 8; 1 Corinthians 2). It is usually those highly ED-U-CAT-ED that are so spiritually IG-NO-RANT (Psalm 14; 53; Romans 1:21-32; 1 Corinthians 1:18-31).

Why do you think the Scriptures warn us regarding the Spiritual Living God, commanding us not to be a respecter of persons (Deuteronomy 10:17; Job 34:19; Proverbs 24:23; Acts 10:34; Romans 2:10-16; Ephesians 6:9; James 2), owe no man anything? The reminder helps us remember it is hard to

THE SPIRITUAL LIVING GOD USES ORDINARY PEOPLE

be fair (John 16:13; Philippians 4:6-9) when we owe someone a favor. We will have to answer to the Spiritual Living God for not allowing the Holy Spirit to lead in our decisions. It really is impossible to be educated according to the world's standards and try to comprehend spiritual knowledge (Romans 1:16-20; 1 Corinthians 2:9-16; Ephesians 1:16-23; 6:10-20; 2 Peter 1:12-21); we can become disillusioned (2 Thessalonians 2:1-12). This activity could possibly find you being detained in a mental facility for going stir crazy (1 John 4:1-6; Acts 19:11-19). We have been warned to test the spirits by the Spirit; only by the guidance of the Holy Spirit will we be given power to withstand evil spirits. There are many that have been there and done that, challenging the inspired words of the Spiritual Living God without positive results (Romans 1:21-32; 1 Corinthians 1:18-31). I realize some of us have the Thomas syndrome (John 20:24-31).

If you really like to experience things for yourself, take my advice and skip this lesson. Otherwise, take the time and visit a mental facility, bringing up the Holy Bible. I am sure you will walk away as a believer regarding spiritual warfare and comprehension without spiritual guidance being powerful enough to make a person delusional. Some people actually have PHDs (poor heart defeated), the highest form of education, according to the world's standards. We really need to reflect on past generations' mistakes when they refused to follow the guidance of the Holy Spirit and those other spirits took up residence in their minds (1 Samuel 16:14-23; Isaiah 66:3-5; 2 Thessalonians 2:10-12).

Let us start with the (Hebrews) Israelites. The Spiritual Living God heard their groaning and remembered His promise to Abraham (Exodus 2:24-25; 6:1-13; Acts 7:1-53). The Spiritual

BECAUSE THE LORD IS YOUR SHEPHERD

Living God provided a deliverer, Moses. Nevertheless, while he was trying to increase the Israelites' faith and show them the power of the Spiritual Living God because of Pharaoh's hardened heart, Pharaoh's men made life worse for the Israelites, causing them to tell Moses to go away (Exodus 5:20-23). Moses even began to question if he misunderstood what the Spiritual Living God said about the people. The people were actually supposed to observe the miracles of the Spiritual Living God (Hebrews 3). Learning of His power and ability to accomplish all these things, Moses pronounced upon Egypt, without the Israelites being affected in a negative way. Nevertheless, the Israelites' disobedience allowed them to make an eleven-day journey in forty years (Deuteronomy 1:1-8).

Our generation is supposed to learn from past generations' mistakes (Hebrews 4) and the consequences they experienced for being disobedient. We have the guidance of the Holy Spirit in this generation, as children of the Spiritual Living God, to make better decisions in the name of Jesus (1 Peter 1:3-25). We need to rejoice in the blessings of being able to receive wisdom, knowledge, and understanding about spiritual things (John 14-16; Romans 8; 1 Corinthians 2), which allows us to stay focused, so we can do all things (Proverbs 3:5-6; Matthew 6:25-33; Philippians 4:6-9, 13) according to the plans and purpose of the Spiritual Living God, in the name of Jesus.

Whenever the Spiritual Living God is leading and His people are following in the name of Jesus with the guidance of the Holy Spirit, we can understand the inspired words provided by Moses for the Israelites, whenever they chose to follow Moses' leadership provided by the Spiritual

THE SPIRITUAL LIVING GOD USES ORDINARY PEOPLE

Living God's messenger in that generation (Deuteronomy 1:21; Hebrews 4:7). The message is still the same in this generation: promises for those who accept the Spiritual Living God's Son, Jesus Christ (Jeremiah 31:31-35; Joel 2:28-32; 1 Corinthians 2; Galatians 3; Hebrews 1). We must be acknowledged as children of the Spiritual Living God in this generation (John 14-16; Romans 8; Hebrews 1; 8; 10-11). A relationship with Jesus Christ is the only way this generation will receive the guidance of the Holy Spirit, so our hearts will not be hardened in this generation (Hebrews 3:7-11).

When the Israelites forgot to focus on Moses and followed another man (Deuteronomy 1:26-33), they experienced great consequences, sometimes the loss of life.

The Spiritual Living God provided reminders for the people, He is still the Spiritual Living God (Deuteronomy 1:34-40). Moses actually tried to warn the people in his generation (Deuteronomy 1:41-45). They failed to receive the words and suffered greatly for being disobedient.

David's generation under Saul's leadership also received a reminder from the Spiritual Living God (1 Samuel 12:10-25) about being obedient to Him. We need to thank the Spiritual Living God for His darling Son, Jesus Christ, who provides a spiritual connection, mediating between the Heavenly Father and His children in this generation. He has mercy on us whenever we fail at choosing a life of obedience according to His plans and purpose for our lives here on Earth (Acts 5:17-42), whenever we sin and think it is not necessary to repent and ask for forgiveness in Jesus' name (Hebrews 1; 1 John 1-2).

We need to reflect on David's relationship with the Spiritual Living God; it was closer than close (Acts 13:22), which means it was very special and stronger than anything we experience in relationships with each other in this generation. Nevertheless, when David sinned against the Spiritual Living God, he received consequences for his sins, also. The relationship he had with Bathsheba caused a sword to run through his family; the sin did not only affect him (2 Samuel 12), but his children also. David repented and asked for forgiveness with a broken spirit (Psalm 51), but the consequences were still experienced for his sin. A son was born from his adulterous relationship with Bathsheba; the child was born ill from the beginning of his birth. David seriously fasted and prayed for the Spiritual Living God to have mercy. When the child died, he did not become angry with the Spiritual Living God. Just think, how many of us would challenge the Spiritual Living God if David's first child would have lived?

    He actually understood the Spiritual Living God's actions being a consequence for his sin. How many of us actually have the guidance of the Holy Spirit providing us wisdom in times of need? When we sin and accept the consequences without hindering our spiritual growth, we will only become stronger in our faith. We should always reference David's situation and draw strength from his experience with sin and the consequences. We need to understand, we will never escape consequences from sin. If you do not think the consequences were bad, think again. Others will observe your actions and follow in your footsteps without the guidance of the Holy Spirit, especially that child you love more than the time you spend growing spiritually. So, look forward to this heartache and pain if you think you made it out without a scratch. The Spiritual Living God will always provide a way of escape from temptation for those

THE SPIRITUAL LIVING GOD USES ORDINARY PEOPLE

who are His children (2 Peter 2:9); just remember, you must have a desire to escape.

This generation is totally confused, thinking we can sin without consequences in the twenty-first century. Anytime the Spiritual Living God was teaching from Abraham's to Paul's generations, the lessons were for the future generations' benefit, also. We are just blessed to have a Mediator, His Son, Jesus Christ (Romans 8:34; Galatians 5:16-26; 6:7-10; Ephesians 1:3-13; Hebrews 1). We need to stop thinking we can sin because He will keep us from experiencing consequences. Surely, we are intelligent enough to understand, He has already paid the price with His life and blood, He experienced on Calvary's cross (John 19:16-20, 23; 1 John 1-5). Why should we continue to act as though we do not have a Helper to deliver us from the temptation to sin (John 14-16; Acts 2; Romans 6)?

As long as we choose to accept the Heavenly Father, Son, and the guidance of the Holy Spirit, we will never be easily beset by sin (Proverbs 3:5-6; Matthew 6:25-33). Just think, without Jesus Christ, we would have left here a long time ago. Moses' generations experienced this when they chose to live in disobedience against the Spiritual Living God. This cost many their lives right then and there. The Spiritual Living God was all action and had no patience for sins (Numbers 3:1-10; 16), and they were Levites. They were the chosen tribe for priesthood to lead the people of the Spiritual Living God, according to His guidance. They were responsible for communicating and presenting offerings for His people. During Joshua's generation, they were given instructions from the Spiritual Living God regarding the battle of Ai (Joshua 6:27-7:26). Anyone that was related to Achan experienced the hand of heaviness from the Spiritual Living God, even if you had no idea he was planning on stealing something from the battle (Joshua 7:19-26). We must always remember the Lord has mercy on His children, and we need to remember to THANK HIM FOR JESUS CHRIST, HIS DARLING SON.

This generation needs to understand the Spiritual Living God is too Holy, Righteous, and Spiritual to interact with humans, without the guidance of the Holy Spirit, provided by Jesus Christ. We must be free from sins (Romans 6; Hebrews 10), which easily beset us; otherwise, we have interference in our spiritual life (Romans 8; 1 Corinthians 2). Jesus has come to set those in bondage by sin free because the Spiritual Living God will help those who are His children (2 Peter 2:9). Psalm 53; Romans 1:21-32; and 1 Corinthians 1:18-31 have a message used in the past that still holds true today in this generation. Hopefully, Psalm 33 and 1 Corinthians 2 have positive insight and expectations for those created in the Spiritual Living God's image, for this generation and the future generations (Ephesians 1:13; Hebrews 1).

Whenever we choose to live in the flesh like Israel's generation, we are reminded not everyone called into obedience accepts the call or is called into obedience (2 Chronicles 7:14; Proverbs 1:20-33; Matthew 20:16; 1 Corinthians 1:18-27; Ephesians 1:17-23; 4:1-13; 2 Timothy 1:9-14; 2 Peter 1:5-21).

The flesh will never allow us to choose a life of obedience regarding the Heavenly Father, Son, and the guidance of the Holy Spirit (Romans 9; Galatians 5:16-26). Do you remember the story of Esau and Jacob (Romans 9:11-13)? "Jacob have I loved, but Esau have I hated"--those are

THE SPIRITUAL LIVING GOD USES ORDINARY PEOPLE

some very strong words. Nevertheless, He is the Spiritual Living God, and we love to question Him and challenge Him in the twenty-first century, without the guidance of the Holy Spirit. Wow! He will have compassion on whom He decides to have compassion on. Be very sure you are choosing a life of obedience and can be identified as His child (Romans 8; Ephesians 4:14-32) before you decide to communicate with the Spiritual Living God. It is possible you can have a living testimony for others to be encouraged in their faith. Anytime others challenge your faith regarding the Spiritual Living God (Matthew 10:16-42), remember, the foolishness of the Spiritual Living God is wiser than men. The weakness of the Spiritual Living God is stronger than men (1 Corinthians 1:18-31). The Spiritual Living God has revealed things by His Spirit, for the Spirit searched all things, yes, the deep things of the Spiritual Living God (1 Corinthians 2:4-16). Never forget to try the spirits by the Spirit (1 John 4:1-6).

Only by the guidance of the Holy Spirit, provided by Jesus Christ (John 14-16; Acts 2), can our Spirit from the Spiritual Living God be enlightened, in this generation (Jeremiah 31:13-35; Joel 2:28-32; 1 Corinthians 2; Ephesians 1:13; Hebrews 1; 1 Thessalonians 4:7-8; 1 John 4:12-14).

A New Heart and New Spirit

When Israel decided to sin against the Spiritual Living God, He provided wisdom through Ezekiel (36:15-38). Ezekiel told them the Spiritual Living God was very displeased with their disobedience. The Spiritual Living God reminded them of all the things they had done (36:18-20). He told them how others observed their disrespecting His holy name.

The Spiritual Living God told the people of Israel, He would reveal to those outside His will His name is holy and will be greatly praised by Israel (36:23-25). Ezekiel told Israel they would be cleansed and gathered from among other countries. Jesus has made this provision for His children in this generation (Hebrews 1; 1 John 1-2). Then, the Spiritual Living God would give them a new heart and new Spirit (2 Thessalonians 3:2-5; Hebrews 8) within them. He would remove their heart of stone from their flesh.

The new Spirit He provided (Jeremiah 31:31-34; Joel 2:28-32) would cause them to follow Him and maintain His judgments. They would be blessed according to the promises He made with Abraham, Isaac, and Jacob. The guidance of the new Spirit would cause His children (Romans 8; Ephesians 4:14-32) to be convicted of disobedience and seek Him (Ephesians 1-2) so the blessings He had in store for them could be received as His children. Then, others would

BECAUSE THE LORD IS YOUR SHEPHERD

observe the life of His children's obedience to Him as the Spiritual Living God, in each generation.

Everyone will acknowledge, He is the Lord, the Spiritual Living God, and He is worthy to be praised. If the Spiritual Living God provided His guidance to His leaders (priests, prophets, seers, judges, kings) before Jesus Christ's arrival as His only begotten Son (Jeremiah 31:31-35; Joel 2:28-32, 1 John 4:12-14), He was trying to gain a relationship with Israel, only to find out later they still had problems with being obedient. How is it that in this current generation with the acceptance of His Son, Jesus, providing the guidance of the Holy Spirit (John 1:1-18; 3:16-21; 4:23-24; 14-16; 1 Thessalonians 4:7-8; Hebrews 1), we are not being successful also? As children (Romans 8; Ephesians 4:14-32) of the Spiritual Living God, we still feel like disrespecting Him when we know without a doubt, He is the Holy, Righteous, and the Spiritual Living God in this generation, the Heavenly Father, who resides in heaven. Nevertheless, we desire to sin and make excuses for choosing a life of disobedience in this day and time (Ephesians 2:1-10; 4:14-32). Remember, the promises were provided for His children, but a life of disobedience does not allow us to claim the promises made before our birth here on Earth. The Spiritual Living God observes our heart and knows right away if we really enjoy sinning against Him (1 Samuel 16:7; Psalm 7:9; 139:23-24; Proverbs 3:5-6; 23:7a; Jeremiah 17:9-10; Revelation 2:22-24). He really has the power to deliver those who sincerely belong to Him as His children, removing them from all temptations (Matthew 6:25-33; 2 Peter 2:9).

The Spiritual Living God told us during Ezekiel's generation, we must be cleansed to receive a new heart and new Spirit. We

A NEW HEART AND NEW SPIRIT

are reminded in this generation, we must also have a method of cleansing before we can interact with the Spiritual Living God (Hebrews 1; John 1-2). Then, we would have the wisdom to make the right decision regarding life here on Earth (Romans 8; 1 Corinthians 2). We really do not have a valid excuse in this generation for sinning against the Holy, Righteous, and Spiritual Living God. Therefore, any consequences received are justified, in order for us to learn from our mistakes and begin to grow spiritually (Ephesians 2:17-18; 3:14-20; 4:1-10). This reminder should help in future situations regarding the Spiritual Living God's expectations for His children here on Earth. If we have not accepted Jesus as the Son of the Spiritual Living God who now resides in heaven with His Heavenly Father (Mark 16:19-20; John 12:28-50; Romans 8:34; Colossians 3:1; Hebrews 1; 7:25), we really are without the guidance of the Holy Spirit (John 3:16-21; 8:12-59; 14-16). Therefore, sin will always overtake those with great intentions; they work hard but never have spiritual insight regarding how to work smart (Luke 12:11-12; John 14:26). They will not be able to understand spiritual things (1 Corinthians 2), words inspired by the Spiritual Living God that are found in the Holy Bible regarding obedience and the promises for His children (Romans 8; Ephesians 4:14-32). These instructions inform us how to have an abundant life (Proverbs 3:5-6; Matthew 6:25-33; John 10) while living here on Earth (Philippians 4:4-13, 19).

False Teaching and Consequences

We were reminded in Isaiah 30:7-26, there is a generation that refused to accept the inspired words of the Spiritual Living God as the Truth (30:9). The teachers of the Spiritual Living God's inspired words gave them what they wanted to hear. They asked the leaders to bypass the Truth and speak of deceits. They were reminded of despising the Spiritual Living God's inspired words. They enjoyed oppression and perverseness (Romans 1:21-32) during their generation. Do you think we are experiencing these same things in the twenty-first century (Psalm 1:1-6; 119:9-16, 33-40; Proverbs 30)?

Many leaders of churches in this generation speak to the people without the guidance of the Holy Spirit. They enjoy coming out to worship about being successful without surrendering their lives to Jesus Christ (Matthew 7:15-29; Colossians 2:4-23; 2 Timothy 4:1-5). They will be like tares and wheat in times of trouble (Matthew 13:1-30, 36-43). They will not be grounded spiritually in times of trouble (2 Corinthians 4). They will be like a ship without a sail, just wavering back and forth, without any directions to their destination (John 8:47; 10; Ephesians 3:14-21; Colossians 1:23). The Spiritual Living God promises those who teach others without spiritual guidance "will be held accountable to Him" (Jeremiah 10:21; 11:3-4; 23; 1 Corinthians 9:7-27). We really should think

BECAUSE THE LORD IS YOUR SHEPHERD

twice about misguiding those who really desire to know the Truth (1 Corinthians 9:11-14). According to the inspired words of the Spiritual Living God, which are found in the Holy Bible (John 5:39-47; Romans 15:4; 2 Timothy 3:16; 2 Peter 1:20), we are reminded to always remember only by the guidance of the Holy Spirit will we be provided with spiritual insight (John 14-16; Acts 2; 1 Corinthians 2; Hebrews 8).

If you are not being enlightened like others who are preaching and teaching the inspired words of the Spiritual Living God, check Romans 8; 1 Corinthians 12; and Ephesians 4:14-32--"Are you there yet?" Then read Deuteronomy 29:29 and be still (Psalms 46-50). He is the Spiritual Living God all by Himself; He decides who, what, and when things will take place (Romans 9) in His world, in this generation.

We Need a Relationship, Not Religion

Whenever life in general is not working, there is a great possibility you do not have a spiritual personal relationship with the Spiritual Living God (Jeremiah 31:31-35; Joel 2:28-32; John 3; 4:23-24; 5:17-47; 6:44-65; 10; 14-16; Acts 2; Romans 8; 1 Corinthians 2; Ephesians 1:13; Hebrews 1; 1 John 1-5). Chances are you have a **religion,** and there are so many man-made **religions**, until you have become confused and disillusioned about the Spiritual Living God. Nevertheless, there were others before you were born in Elijah's generation that had the same problems we have today about the Spiritual Living God's Deity (1 Kings 18:20-40). They had their gods made of wood, stubble, and so on (1 Corinthians 3:11-23) and **religions** back then also. I will repeat what Elijah told those who did not need or desire any knowledge about the Spiritual Living God, in his generation. The Spiritual Living God through His prophet with spiritual guidance told them, "If your god be god, serve him; if the Spiritual Living God is your God, serve Him." It is time to stop trying to convince human beings who the Spiritual Living God really is (Jeremiah 31:31-35; Joel 2:28-32; 1 Thessalonians 4:7-8; Hebrews 1; 8). The Scriptures state Jesus will not return until everyone has had a chance to hear the report, which is the Gospel (Psalm 22; Isaiah 53; Romans 1:16-20; Ephesians 1:13; 1 Thessalonians 1:5-6; Hebrews 1;

BECAUSE THE LORD IS YOUR SHEPHERD

Mark 13:10) regarding Jesus Christ being the Spiritual Living God's only begotten Son. The Scriptures did not state we had to accept Jesus in order for Him to return; all Scriptures have to be fulfilled (Mark 13:10) to keep man from saying, "I did not know."

Regardless of the god you acknowledge, the next showdown will be too late for excuses to be accepted by Jesus to mediate on our behalf to the Spiritual Living God (Hebrews 1; 8:6-13; Revelation 21:1-8). Stop whatever you are doing, and repent for your sins, accepting the blood provided to cleanse us so we might have a spiritual relationship with the Spiritual Living God (Isaiah 56:3-8; 66:18-20, 23; 1 John 1-5). Every human being created in the image of the Spiritual Living God needs to be able to say for himself he has tried Him. Nevertheless, He knows if we really would like to get to know Him personally with a sincere heart and bypass the spirit of deception (Jeremiah 9; Matthew 24:4-31; 1 Corinthians 6:9; Ephesians 4:14-32) in this generation. Many are deceived by others not teaching the Gospel or those spirits we were told exist among us in this day and time (1 John 4:1-6; Acts 19:11-19).

If Satan has enough intelligence to acknowledge the presence of the Spiritual Living God (Job 1:6-12; Matthew 8:28-34; Mark 1:23-25, 34; 3:11; Luke 4:6-15, 33-35, 41) and he was an angel kicked out of heaven (Acts 26:18; 2 Peter 2:4), who told this generation you could have spiritual access without His only begotten Son, Jesus Christ, in this generation? Just like those who believed the Gospel were drawn into obedience by the Spiritual Living God (John 3:16-21; 4:23-24; 6:31-69; 10; Romans 8; Acts 2; 1 Corinthians 2), anyone whose heart is not hardened regarding spiritual things (Hebrews 3:7-11) can have the exact same spiritual relationship with the Spiritual Living God by accepting the Gospel (Psalm 22; Isaiah 53; Romans 1:16-20; Ephesians 1:13; 1 Thessalonians 1:5-6; Hebrews 1). ***Otherwise, when the ship comes in, and you are left standing on the dock, remember, you missed the boat earlier, also (John 8:12-30).***

The people in Elijah's generation who were seeking other gods made the decision not to believe in the power of the Spiritual Living God. They did not have the guidance of the Holy Spirit in his generation, so they seriously wavered in their knowledge about the Spiritual Living God before He spoke through Elijah. The showdown was provided for their generations as well as future generations with hardened hearts (Hebrews 3:7-11); the Spiritual Living God provided His power for those who doubted Him (Romans 16:25-27).

Just observe all the **religions** that exist in this generation; anytime man cannot find one that satisfies their need, they start another **religion** (James 1:27-28). Just think, you could start a **religion** yourself, but the Spiritual Living God would hold you accountable for misleading the people, created in His image (Jeremiah 23; Matthew 7:15-23). Ask someone born before the twenty-first century about a man named Jim Jones. He was able to lead many Americans to their death because they took their eyes off Jesus Christ (Proverbs 3:5-6; Matthew 6:25-33). The guidance of the Holy Spirit will never allow those who choose a life of obedience to become deceived by man. Nevertheless, when we worship a man, he becomes more powerful, and the spirit of deception will help you believe in a human just like you. It appears he was probably called into obedience but forgot to follow the teaching of Paul regarding Jesus (1

BECAUSE THE LORD IS YOUR SHEPHERD

Corinthians 9:11-13). He destroyed many who did not have a spiritual personal relationship with the Spiritual Living God (Psalm 53; Romans 1:21-32; 1 Corinthians 1:18-31), through Jesus Christ with the guidance of the Holy Spirit. Surely, that one experience should be enough visual experience to help any intelligent person realize, it is not good to follow men or women without spiritual guidance provided by the Holy Spirit, especially when we have been told the Spiritual Living God communicates spiritually with all His children (Romans 8; 1 Corinthians 11:3, 11-12; Galatians 3:26-28; Ephesians 4:14-32) without there being a difference in wisdom, knowledge, and understanding. The Holy Spirit communicates with the Spirit within us, according to Jesus (Luke 12:12; John 14:26).

You never have to wonder if the Spiritual Living God actually said something that was said by man and not Him (Luke 12:12; John 14:26; 1 Corinthians 2). The people were warned before you were born, the Spiritual Living God is not pleased with this action (Psalm 14; 53; Romans 1:21-32; 1 Corinthians 1:18-31). Paul tried to help the Ephesian elders in his generation to always allow the Holy Spirit to lead their decisions, according to the Gospel (Psalm 22; Isaiah 53; Romans 1:16-20; Ephesians 1:13; 1 Thessalonians 1:5-6; Hebrews 1), reminding them the Lord Jesus Christ said, "It is more blessed to give than to receive" (Acts 20:35; Ephesians 4:28-32). This should help those following a **religion** in this generation who are being deceived by their leaders about giving to them to expand their personal greed. Remember, if our hearts are not hardened (Hebrews 3:7-11) regarding the Heavenly Father, Son, and the guidance of the Holy Spirit, there is no reason for the Holy Spirit not to reveal

WE NEED A RELATIONSHIP, NOT RELIGION

spiritual things to the children of the Spiritual Living God (1 Corinthians 2). We have been reminded, all the Spiritual Living God's children (Romans 8; Ephesians 4:14-32) have access to receive the same guidance from the Holy Spirit about spiritual things (Galatians 3:28; Ephesians 5). Exactly why would a person guided by the Holy Spirit mislead the children of the Spiritual Living God (Matthew 7:15-23)? Nevertheless, we have been told to try the spirits by the Spirit (1 John 4:1-6). Only the Spiritual Living God knows which spirit is being used to deceive His children (Romans 8), when their leaders are constantly asking their followers to give up all things to them for personal use (Acts 19:11-19).

Nevertheless, it is still taking place in the twenty-first century; some **religions** are so perverted they are harming little children. Jesus warned us in His generation these actions will cost people greatly (Matthew 18:6-10; 19:13-15; Mark 9:42-50; Luke 17:1-2). We must acknowledge the Spiritual Living God is a Spirit (John 4:23-24; Galatians 4:1-7) and has provided a spiritual connection for those who desire to know Him personally (Jeremiah 31:31-35; Joel 2:28-32; 1 Thessalonians 4:7-8; 1 John 4:12-14). When the Spirit of the Living God draws us into obedience (John 6:44-65) to accept His only begotten Son, Jesus Christ (John 1:1-18; 3:16-21; 5:17-47; 10; 14-16; Hebrews 1), we must receive the inspired words by the Spiritual Living God with a childlike faith (Matthew 18:1-5), totally putting all of our trust in the promises spoken before our existence as humans here on Earth (Romans 8; 9; 10:9-21; 14:11; 15:1-13). Life is so much easier when we take the time and develop a spiritual personal relationship with the Spiritual Living God, as the

BECAUSE THE LORD IS YOUR SHEPHERD

Heavenly Father, who resides in heaven--accepting the Gospel (birth, life, death, resurrection, and ascension) of His only begotten Son, Jesus Christ (Psalm 22; Isaiah 53; John 1:1-18; Hebrews 1), receiving the Helper, the guidance of the Holy Spirit provided for those who sincerely believe (John 14-16; Acts 2; Galatians 5) with the faith of a little child (Matthew 18:6-14). We are His children (Romans 8; Ephesians 4:14-32), according to His inspired words (1 John 1-3). We are given a chance to make a decision to accept the inspired words of Truth provided by the Spiritual Living God (John 4:23-24), with the guidance of the Holy Spirit. Choosing not to accept His inspired words allows us to recall a promise made by the Spiritual Living God (Psalm 14; 53; Romans 1:21-32; 1 Corinthians 1:18-31; Galatians 3): "I will destroy the wisdom of the wise and will bring nothing to the understanding of the prudent." The Spiritual Living God provided His inspired words to those He enlightened before our arrival here on Earth (Romans 15:1-13; 2 Timothy 3:14-17; 2 Peter 2:21; 1 John 5).

The Holy Bible is the blueprint for each and every human created in the image of the Spiritual Living God (Genesis 1:27-28; 2:7; 5:2; Matthew 19:4-5). We begin to experience problems without solutions, because we choose not to follow the blueprint of our design. The Holy Bible can be read by anyone who is capable of reading any book. Nevertheless, wisdom, knowledge, and understanding about spiritual things come from the Spiritual Living God through Jesus Christ (John 14-16; Acts 2; Hebrews 1), who provides guidance through the Holy Spirit to comprehend spiritual things (1 Corinthians 2-3). The Spiritual Living God tried to have a relationship with His people by providing

WE NEED A RELATIONSHIP, NOT RELIGION

guidance through priests, prophets, judges, seers, and kings. He was never able to have a continuous positive relationship with the people until He sent His only begotten Son (Luke 1-4:21; Hebrews 1), Jesus, as an example for the people to observe with a spiritual connection (John 3:16-21; 4:23-24; 5:17-47; 6:44-65; 10; 14-16; Acts 2; Romans 8; Ephesians 1:13) to Him, as their Heavenly Father, who resides in heaven as the Spiritual Living God (1 John 1-5).

Choosing to live a life of obedience to the Heavenly Father, Son, and the guidance of the Holy Spirit allows us to totally depend upon the Spiritual Living God (Proverbs 3:5-6; Matthew 6:25-33; Romans 8; 1 Corinthians 2). Whenever we follow the plans and purposes the Spiritual Living God has for His children's (Romans 8; Ephesians 4:14-32) lives here on Earth, we can look forward to our blessings for choosing to be obedient.

We should be willing to please the Spiritual Living God before considering relationships with others we know and commune with daily here on Earth who we really, sincerely care about (Matthew 10:34-39). We should not have any relationship here on Earth more powerful than your spiritual relationship with the Spiritual Living God. Whenever we are not successful in pleasing the Spiritual Living God, we have a big brother, Jesus Christ, mediating (Romans 8:34; Hebrews 1) on our behalf to our Heavenly Father to have mercy. You are struggling, but in your heart you really desire to please Him (Psalm 139). Anytime we try to deceive the Spiritual Living God, this is definitely a sign of ignorance; He already knows if we are being honest. Remember, He has access to our hearts (1 Samuel 16:7; Psalm 7:9; 139:23-24; Jeremiah 17:9-10). It will be impossible to fool someone who knows

BECAUSE THE LORD IS YOUR SHEPHERD

and sees all things before they take place (Psalm 121). We can be provided with mercy in Jesus' name, but we must experience consequences, whether great or small, to learn from our mistakes, which will remind us never to repeat the actions again.

The majority of earthly parents will follow the instructions provided by the Spiritual Living God when training up a child (Proverbs 16:20-22; 19:18; 20; 22:6, 14-35, 23:13-16; Ephesians 6:1-4). Otherwise, we can look forward to the children becoming a menace to society, causing the parents much heartache and pain. The Spiritual Living God usually steps in and provides the discipline we fail to minister in their disobedience, which is much greater than we could have provided. Nevertheless, we were given a promise for the children before we were born with the consequences being listed (Exodus 20:12; Matthew 15:3-9; Galatians 3; Ephesians 6:1-4; 2 Timothy 3:14-17). In Moses' generation, the Spiritual Living God's relationship with the people came by Moses' interceding on their behalf (Exodus 20:18-21). Nevertheless, they still managed to displease the Spiritual Living God, until He promised everyone over the age of nineteen, except for Joshua and Caleb, would not enter the Promised Land (Numbers 14). They actually went in the same circle for forty years never locating the exit provided by the Spiritual Living God for being disobedient, until, "Ye have dwelt long enough in this mount" (Deuteronomy 1:1-8).

This is like entering a loop (freeway) that circles the city and missing the exit; every time, you come close and cannot get over. You must continue to circle the city because this is the only exit for your destination, without getting totally

WE NEED A RELATIONSHIP, NOT RELIGION

lost. As children of the Spiritual Living God, we also have a destination (Malachi 4; 1 John 5). For those who choose to have a spiritual personal relationship, not a **religion,** with the Spiritual Living God, He has established a way for those who desire to know Him personally (Jeremiah 31:31-35; Joel 2:28-32; Hebrews 1; 8), to have this spiritual relationship through His Son, Jesus Christ (John 1:1-18; 3). Never forget, the Spiritual Living God is a Spirit and only deals with Spirit and the Truth (John 4:23-24). He had to provide the breath of life (Genesis 2:7) for us to breathe, so we are not Spirits, but humans created in His image. Jesus has arrived to allow us to experience life in the Spirit (John 1:1-18; 3:16-21; 14-16; Romans 8; Hebrews 1; 8). This relationship allows us to participate in the promises the Spiritual Living God made to His children here on Earth. Lord, have mercy on those with a hardened heart (Hebrews 3:7-11), which allows them to become confused and disillusioned in this generation (Psalm 14; 53; Romans 1:21-32; 1 Corinthians 1:18-31; 2 Thessalonians 2:11-12).

Financial Freedom Comes from the Spiritual Living God

It really is amazing how people had problems with handling money before Jesus' arrival as the Son of the Spiritual Living God, and it is still occurring in this generation of the twenty-first century. We have technology where we just step up to an ATM (automatic teller machine) and access any funds that are available for us to operate in this world. We never think twice about the electricity coming to a standstill, ceasing all electronic transactions in this world. (ASK someone about HOUSTON, TEXAS' experience with Hurricane IKE in September 2008!). If this situation should ever take place in this generation, those who have a spiritual personal relationship with the Spiritual Living God know all they need to do is go back to the original ATM (ask the Master) to supply all your needs according to His riches in glory (Philippians 4:19). The day we remember to focus on the Spiritual Living God regarding anything our hearts desire (OOPS! THIS ACTUALLY TOOK PLACE IN HOUSTON, TEXAS), we will be provided with the guidance of the Holy Spirit before we make any financial decision (Proverbs 3:5-6; Matthew 6:25-33).

When we finally begin to grow spiritually, we will finally get things right financially. You will never experience the "more month than money," as His children while living here on Earth. We have been reminded by Malachi (3:6-15) in

BECAUSE THE LORD IS YOUR SHEPHERD

his generation, the Spiritual Living God's expectations for those who have been blessed is to bless the less fortunate in their generation. Malachi is asking the question we need to continually ask in each generation: Are we robbing the Spiritual Living God? If your answer is no, then why are you constantly having a loss in the profit margin, when it could have been a gain? Think, are you robbing Peter to pay Paul? You knew the promotion was yours, you felt it in your Spirit, but someone else received it. Every time you fix something, something else always breaks. You have experienced a total loss of every material thing you own. Every time you look up, something is attacking your body. This has nothing to do with Murphy's Law; stop listening to the different excuses man has spoken. Read Malachi 3:8-9; according to the Scriptures, curses can be experienced for choosing to ignore the Spiritual Living God. He has commanded this generation just like past generations to provide for His kingdom building (Malachi 3:10-12).

He also reminded us He will not change (Malachi 3:6), so we need to be obedient in this generation, also (Matthew 5:17-20).

We must always remember the Spiritual Living God has asked this generation like previous generations not to overlook the need He has for His kingdom building (Nehemiah 13:10-14), just like Nehemiah's generation.

Starting with Adam and Eve, the children were taught to remember the blessings from the Spiritual Living God and to always give thanks (Genesis 4:1-9). Geez, they did not have money, but the spirit of jealousy still was able to show up among the brothers. This is why Cain killed his brother Abel--Abel was offering the Spiritual Living God his very best, and

FINANCIAL FREEDOM COMES FROM THE SPIRITUAL LIVING GOD

this pleased the Lord more than Cain's offerings.

Those in Abraham's generation also knew it was necessary to honor the Spiritual Living God (Genesis 14:17-20). Jesus taught us in His generation that a decision needed to be made regarding our loyalty (Matthew 6:24). It is impossible for those created in the Spiritual Living God's image to have two masters. Surely, we can relate to this in the twenty-first century, trying to have a spiritual personal relationship with the Heavenly Father, who resides in heaven.

If we are going to trust the promises provided by the inspired words from the Spiritual Living God in Matthew's generation (6:19-23), there is no reason for us to be overly concerned about taking care of things according to the teaching of Jesus Christ. Whenever we are following His teachings, we are choosing to trust Him, according to the inspired words found in the Holy Bible. Therefore, we should not have anxiety over anything taking place in this world (Matthew 6:25-34). Spiritual maturity allows you to say, "Heavenly Father, according to your inspired words and based on my obedience to You as Your child (Romans 8; Ephesians 4:14-32), I am turning this situation over to You and going to sleep. Since You never slumber or sleep, there is no reason for two of us to be awake to handle my problems (Psalm 121). Surely, You can do a better job than I can in the name of Jesus."

Jesus Christ, His only begotten Son, provides the Helper (John 14-16; Acts 2), the guidance of the Holy Spirit, for those who have accepted the Gospel (Psalm 22; Isaiah 53; John 3:16; 12:28-50; Romans 1:16-20; Ephesians 1:13-14; Hebrews 1; 1 John 1-2). Otherwise, we become totally confused trying to communicate spiritually without the guidance of the Holy

BECAUSE THE LORD IS YOUR SHEPHERD

Spirit about spiritual things (1 Corinthians 2).We must put our relationship with the Spiritual Living God before our finances (Proverbs 3:5-10). Otherwise, we will never be allowed to experience His financial blessings in this generation. This is why we are reminded to make a decision. If we would like to be acknowledged as the Spiritual Living God's child (Romans 8; Ephesians 4:14-32), we cannot love money more than the Spiritual Living God (1 Timothy 6:10); otherwise, the love of money will cause us to make the wrong decisions spiritually.

Many can testify how the Spiritual Living God had to totally remove or put a dent in their financial situation to find out where their loyalty lay (Matthew 6:24). Anytime we come to the realization, only through Jesus Christ can we have a spiritual personal relationship with the Spiritual Living God, this spiritual knowledge informs us it is necessary to be enlightened by the Holy Spirit before we can understand His inspired words. Remember, all the past and present generations' resources and source of strength are provided by the Spiritual Living God (Deuteronomy 8:11-20; Matthew 6:25-34).

Do not become concerned about the people in this generation with old money (passed down through the generations) and new money (recently acquired) becoming confused and disillusioned about their ability to maintain their wealth without giving the Spiritual Living God His glory (Matthew 19:16-30). Remember, the Scripture states charity covers a multitude of sins (1 Corinthians 13; 1 Peter 4:8); there are some that freely give in order to bless the less fortunate. They make it a standing engagement to always have or attend functions to provide for the less fortunate.

FINANCIAL FREEDOM COMES FROM THE SPIRITUAL LIVING GOD

We need to remember, money might extend your health with man's many devices while living here on Earth. Nevertheless, when the Spiritual Living God decides your time is up for existing among the living, man cannot interfere with His decision (Proverbs 10). Sometimes we look at those with an abundance of financial wealth and say, "They cheated death," but we are reminded of the experience of a man and his wife in Peter's generation (Acts 5:1-11, 29-32).

We should be very careful about the promises and vows we make to the Spiritual Living God. If we are not spiritually mature, it is very easy to renege on the promises we made before we receive the blessing. Remember, the Spiritual Living God reminded those in Moses' generation, when they made a vow (Leviticus 27:32-34), "your tithes cannot be changed." We can start small with providing a tenth to the Spiritual Living God for His purposes and plans. As we grow spiritually, acknowledging all blessings are from the Spiritual Living God, we will be inspired by the guidance of the Holy Spirit to give more than the originally requested tenth (Luke 6:38).

We really need to understand the Spiritual Living God trusts us to make the right decision about tithes and offerings for His plans and purposes. The government (Uncle Sam) does not trust anybody. Uncle Sam takes his money before you gain access to your own money. He takes his taxes based on the gross (before taxes) amount of your income, but you want to give to the Spiritual Living God based on your net (after taxes) income. I am not going to tell you which income you should use to make your tithes and offerings to the Spiritual Living God's kingdom building. When your heart is ready to receive the truth based on the Scriptures, you will make

BECAUSE THE LORD IS YOUR SHEPHERD

the right decision (Luke 12:22-40). The Spiritual Living God provides your health and strength, including the provision of being in your right mind to make daily living decisions. We show our appreciation by struggling with providing Him a tenth of our gross, not net, of our income. If we have a problem with providing the tenth on this level of income, exactly why would the Spiritual Living God bless you with additional income (Luke 12:48)? Geez, it would get worse before it gets better, because now you are expected to give even more of your income for His plans and purposes. This has nothing to do with the leadership of the Spiritual Living God's church. He is very capable of providing for the needs of those whom He has called into obedience according to His plans and purpose for their lives. We are given a chance to provide for His kingdom building, taking care of those He called to be leaders of His church. Just like generations did before we were born (Genesis 28:22; Leviticus 27:32; Malachi 3; Hebrews 7:1-10), they bless those who were less fortunate also. Anytime we have been blessed with our health, strength, and the intelligence to go forth and make a living to sustain us in this life, we really should be grateful, with provisions being made available to us. Otherwise, how would you like to change places with a person who made a bad decision, and now he is disabled--just for a week, not even a month? I bet they would be willing to do whatever it takes to please the Spiritual Living God if they only had one more chance to choose a life of obedience.

Always remember to never allow the right hand to know what the left hand is doing when it comes to giving to the Spiritual Living God (Matthew 6:1-4). Otherwise, you have

FINANCIAL FREEDOM COMES FROM THE SPIRITUAL LIVING GOD

your reward for obedience; why should He bless you when others will praise and bless you?

Choosing to be mindful and bless others when you are blessed is very pleasing to the Spiritual Living God.

This allows the Spiritual Living God to bless you for your obedience to His inspired words, found in the Holy Bible.

Just think, the Spiritual Living God could have said He needs the ninety, and you take the tenth. Thank You, Lord, for not being like mankind; we can relate to greed in this generation. We give You the tenth, and then we have strings attached to Your tenth for Your kingdom building. We never realize the ninety is getting away from us, without the ability to account for the ninety.

We really need to understand, the Spiritual Living God holds everyone with access to His tenth accountable to Him. We can relax; we have done our part. Now pray the ones handling His tenth really fear Him as the Spiritual Living God (Malachi 2). Otherwise, they are going to suffer greatly for handling His tenth without the guidance of the Holy Spirit. Nevertheless, we need to let go of the tenth so we can observe the Spirit of the Spiritual Living God dealing with those who choose to misuse and abuse His children's trust (Genesis 28:20-22; Psalms 146-147). The day we realize the Spiritual Living God can handle all situations in life better than we can is the day we will learn to work smart and not hard.

The Presence of the Lord Is Here

How do you know when you feel the presence of the Spiritual Living God (Galatians 5:16-26)? Those called into obedience with the guidance of the Holy Spirit know within their Spirit, when they experience the Holy Spirit (Jeremiah 31:31-34; Joel 2:28-32; Romans 11:4-10; 1 Corinthians 2; 3:16-23; 2 Corinthians 6:17; 1 Peter 2:9-10).

Past generations provided inspired words from the Spiritual Living God starting with Moses (Deuteronomy 1:23-33). Jacob wrestled with an angel, saying, "I will not let you go till you bless me" (Genesis 32:24-30). Joseph had a dream of things to come, which others could not relate to, but the Spiritual Living God brought it to pass just like he dreamed it would take place (Genesis 37:1-11; 42:6; 45:1-8, 26-28; 46:29-30). Moses prayed for the presence of the Spiritual Living God in his generation to lead the people. He also asked for a visual, but was told "no man can look on the Spiritual Living God and live" (Exodus 33:12-23). Moses actually received a confirmation: "I will do this thing also that thou has spoken: for thou has found grace in My sight, and I know thee by name" (33:17). He had already experienced the Spiritual Living God by observing the burning bush and the voice that spoke to him originally (Exodus 3). Moses had a pillar of fire by night and a pillar of clouds in the day to recognize the presence of the Spiritual Living God was

BECAUSE THE LORD IS YOUR SHEPHERD

there (Exodus 13:21-22). This activity also let them know a meeting was needed in the tabernacle (Exodus 40:34-38). The Spiritual Living God also communicated by the sound of thunder and lightning in past generations, especially in Moses' generation (Exodus 19:16; 20:18-21). Samuel also received communication from the Spiritual Living God in his generation (1 Samuel 2:9-10; 7:9-10; 12:14-18). Job, David, and others spoke about lightning and thunder being used in their generation (Job 26:13-14; 37:3-5; 40:8-10; 2 Samuel 22:12-16; Psalm 18:12-14; 29:2-4; 77:16-20; 104:6-8; 144:5-8; Isaiah 29:5-7; Jeremiah 10:12-14; 51:15-17; Luke 10:17-19; 17:24; John 12:28-30; Revelation 4:4-6; 6:1-3; 14:2-3; 19:5-7). The generations before the twenty-first century had enough intelligence to acknowledge the Spiritual Living God was busy, and they should sit and be still (Psalms 46-50) during thunder and lightning. Some cultures also covered anything that looked like a mirror. You might call it superstitious, but those who have been struck by lightning and lived to tell someone would probably beg to differ with you; they probably have high respect for the Spiritual Living God during this activity of lightning and thunder after their experience. Ask someone to share his or her testimony; maybe you can become a believer without having your own testimony.

I personally know someone who was hooked on the soaps. The person insisted on watching the programs when it was lightning and thundering, knowing their training was to turn off anything making unnecessary noise during this activity. To make a long story short, lightning entered the home, hit the mirror, and turned off the television they insisted on watching. This action was enough to teach a lesson that was supposed to be passed down to each

THE PRESENCE OF THE LORD IS HERE

generation, but sometimes those in the younger generation have to experience things for themselves.

There is probably a swimmer who has a testimony about lightning and swimming. We make all kinds of excuses in this generation about water and lightning, but I totally believe the movement of the water draws lightning in that direction. Otherwise, any standing body of water without movement would constantly be hit. If you disagree, try to agree to disagree; you just might live a little longer here on Earth by not trying to prove your theory.

My point is, when we observe the lightning and hear the thunder in this generation, we need to try to honor and respect the Spiritual Living God is still working in this generation, like Moses' generation. The Spiritual Living God demands and will receive His respect when He gets tired of our disrespecting Him. We will experience Him at work in this generation also; a man really has no control over this activity (Isaiah 6:9-10; Romans 11:8).

Sometimes we just need another confirmation when the actions of other people make you question your faith and belief in the Spiritual Living God (Hebrews 11; James 5:7-20). When we surrender our lives to follow the Spiritual Living God's plans and purposes (Proverbs 3:5-6; Matthew 6:25-33), we can really feel His presence. Just like the song states, "When the Spiritual Living God is in the building, the sin sick are really healed. You can feel His presence all over this place." Job's (4:12-17) experience is for those who have experienced a funny feeling with your skin, you are not alone. Sometimes there is a feeling of warmth around you when it is cold, or you are in a comfortable temperature.

The Spiritual Living God has decided not to communicate

BECAUSE THE LORD IS YOUR SHEPHERD

with anyone who chooses to retain any sin, totally refusing to give it up (Hebrews 10; 1 John 1-2). He looks at our hearts and knows our minds, so it is impossible to communicate something that is not true (1 Samuel 16:7; Psalm 7:9; 139; Jeremiah 17:9-10; Mark 2:8; Romans 2:5-9; Revelation 2:22-24).

He has already told us, He has His way of delivering His children from temptation (2 Peter 2:9; 1 John 1-2). When we repent and ask for forgiveness of all sins, in the name of Jesus (Acts 2:37-40), this is the first step to acknowledging we have sinned against the Spiritual Living God. He already knows if the situation is being provided as a thorn in your side (2 Corinthians 12:7-10). Just like Paul experienced in his generation, with a reminder the Spiritual Living God's grace is sufficient.

Those located in Houston, Texas, (September 2008) can actually testify, we actually experienced a pillar of clouds by day (the temperature was very nice) and a pillar of fire by night (the moon was full and very bright). Those who can be identified as His children (Romans 8) actually experienced the presence of the Spiritual Living God during Hurricane IKE. We actually had more than 2 million people living in the dark without electricity for more than two days. We must tell the current and future generation the Spiritual Living God (those who call Him Mother Nature) is still very much in control of His World (Psalms 46-50). The problem with calling the Spiritual Living God "Mother Nature" has very little significance of His spiritual power and control. Nevertheless, His children know without a doubt, He is responsible for all things that take place here on Earth. Other spirits must seek His permission before any destruction can take place in this world, which belongs to Him.

Disobedience Has Consequences

Yes, Jesus has come for those who choose to accept Him as the Spiritual Living God's only begotten Son (John 1:1-1; 3:16-21; Hebrews 1; 1 John 1-5). We are forgiven for our sins anytime we choose to repent and ask for forgiveness in Jesus' name. We forget sometimes consequences must follow sins; otherwise, we would never learn from our mistakes in this life.

If the Spiritual Living God took the time to forgive David, who was very special to Him and had spiritual guidance (Acts 13:22b), He knew him by name. Remember, the Spiritual Living God sent Samuel to anoint David's head with oil (1 Samuel 16). David received the anointing of the Holy Spirit during his time as a leader of the Spiritual Living God's people. David still made mistakes and had to go before the Spiritual Living God in prayer, repent, and ask for forgiveness for his sins. The Spiritual Living God forgave David each time, but the consequences of his sins were experienced by him personally, as well as those under his leadership, which were the Spiritual Living God's people (2 Samuel 12; 24).

The reminders were to help remind David of the Spiritual Living God's holiness. The mistakes (sins) of David were also a reminder for future generations. When we accept the Gospel (Psalm 22; Isaiah 53; Romans 1:16-20; Ephesians 1:13;

BECAUSE THE LORD IS YOUR SHEPHERD

1 Thessalonians 1:5-6; Hebrews 1) of Jesus Christ (John 3:16-21, 14-16; Acts 2), we can establish our own spiritual relationship (Romans 8; Ephesians 4:14-32) with the Spiritual Living God, in the name of Jesus. As children of the Spiritual Living God, we should never disrespect the holiness of the Spiritual Living God. Otherwise, we will also experience consequences for our mistakes (sins). After we accept this understanding (1 Corinthians 2), we will grow spiritually, never wishing to travel this road again because our Heavenly Father, who resides in heaven, is the Righteous, Holy, and Spiritual Living God. The Holy Spirit can provide the guidance needed to serve the Righteous, Holy, and Spiritual Living God (Romans 8). We just need to remember to seek our help, provided by the Holy Spirit in Jesus' name (John 14-16; Acts 2; Hebrews 1).

Moses received insight of things to come from the Spiritual Living God before he died. He told the Israelites they would use their hands to sin against the Spiritual Living God, and He would also become angry with the future generations (Deuteronomy 31:16-29). These sins would cause them many heartaches and troubles (2 Corinthians 4). Moses provided a song to help them remember all things the Spiritual Living God had provided during the wilderness. In this song, he also spoke of things the future generation would experience due to their disobedience (Deuteronomy 32:1-45). Surely, these same things are not taking place in this day and time, which is the twenty-first century. Anyone with the guidance of the Holy Spirit can observe things said then really are actually taking place in this generation.

Do you think this is why past generations' songs, the hymns and songs of Zion, were provided for us to tell their stories to future generations?

DISOBEDIENCE HAS CONSEQUENCES

The Spiritual Living God has provided eyes and ears for us to see spiritual things spoken in Moses' generation (1 Corinthians 2). These experiences in past generations took place before Moses' and after Moses' generation.

The Spiritual Living God opened the Red Sea and the Jordon River (Exodus 14:21-31; Joshua 3:14-17), allowing the people to cross the waters on dry land. Who among us has the ability to part waters and allow men to cross in this generation? We must reflect and remember, there is nothing too hard for the Spiritual Living God to accomplish in this generation. Joshua reminded them in his generation to never forget (Joshua 4:24) the awesome power of our Spiritual Living God. He resides in heaven as our Heavenly Father in this generation. These actions should always cause man to fear, honor, and respect our Holy, Righteous, and Spiritual Living God, and always give thanks for His darling Son, Jesus Christ. He provided the guidance of the Holy Spirit for those who desire a spiritual personal relationship with the Holy, Righteous, and Spiritual Living God.

When the Spiritual Living God chose those whom He wanted to lead His people, He always provided spiritual guidance. He spoke in detail of things He wanted to take place and the consequences for choosing to disobey Him.

The Spiritual Living God told Joshua to inform the Israelites regarding the city of Jericho and everything in it being accursed. Only Rahab and those in her household would not be cursed. They could bring out the silver, gold, vessel of brass, and iron consecrating them to Him, the Spiritual Living God for His treasury (Joshua 6). One person during the battle chose to ignore the warnings of the Spiritual

BECAUSE THE LORD IS YOUR SHEPHERD

Living God, which were provided in detail, and removed items from Jericho. This person forgot the Spiritual Living God knows all things and there is not anything you can hide from Him.

It appears someone forgot to tell the story of Adam and Eve to Joshua's generation; maybe the person would have made a better decision about removing those items in Joshua's generation. In the beginning, the Spiritual Living God knew what Adam had done in the Garden of Eden, after being warned of the consequences. When He said, "Adam, where are you?" He gave Adam a chance to tell the truth without any help. Just like this generation, Adam thought he could cover his sin without the Spiritual Living God knowing exactly what had taken place in the Garden of Eden (Genesis 3:1-13).

During the next battle after Jericho, the people were encouraged by their success to take on the next battle at AI. When they were defeated and thirty-six men lost their lives, the leaders humbled themselves and went before the Spiritual Living God with questions (Joshua 7). The Spiritual Living God supplied in detail to Joshua, how to find the problem that caused them pain. When they found the culprit in the tribe of Judah, the people of Israel stoned the whole family for the pain they caused within the camp. They cleaned house without asking questions (7:19-26).

In this generation of the twenty-first century, we would probably try and justify the person's actions and become emotionally attached. Nevertheless, anytime we choose to ignore the warnings from the Spiritual Living God, in the name of Jesus, thinking it is okay to sin against the Spiritual Living God, He sent His Son, Jesus, to die for our sins (Hebrews

DISOBEDIENCE HAS CONSEQUENCES

10), He will forgive us; "that could be your relatives who sinned--would you want us to kill them?" This is why everyone related to Achan had to be removed from the face of the Earth. The Spiritual Living God needs us to always put His desire before ours (Proverbs 3:5-6; Matthew 6:25-33), with the understanding He has the power to deliver His children from temptation (2 Peter 2:9). The question remains in this generation, Are you ready to give up things that interfere with your spiritual personal relationship (Romans 8; Ephesians 4:14-32) with Him, as your Heavenly Father? He also has the power to deliver you from any sin you are ready to release (Hebrews 10; 1 John 3:5-10).

Jesus' death on the cross was not carte blanche to sin without facing consequences in this generation. His life was provided for those who desire to have a spiritual personal relationship with His Heavenly Father, the Spiritual Living God, who resides in heaven. Only then will we receive the guidance of the Holy Spirit to live a life of obedience, which will be pleasing to the Heavenly Father, Son, and Holy Spirit.

The consequences of sinning will always be experienced by us. Otherwise, we would never learn to respect the holiness, righteousness, and love the Spiritual Living God provides for His children in this generation, those who desire to be accepted as His children (John 12:28-50; Romans 8; Ephesians 4:14-32) by believing the report of the Gospel (Psalm 22; Isaiah 53; Romans 1:16-20; Ephesians 1:13; 1 Thessalonians 1:5-6), in the name of Jesus (John 1:1-18; 3:15-21; 14-16; Hebrews 1). The Spirit relates to the Spirit, and the flesh relates to the flesh. We need to make a decision to live in the Spirit (Galatians 5:16-26) in order to

BECAUSE THE LORD IS YOUR SHEPHERD

honor, fear, and respect our Heavenly Father, who resides in heaven, in the name of Jesus. Otherwise, we could live in the flesh, observing and choosing to follow the ways of the world (Romans 1:21-32; 1 Corinthians 1:18-31). The choice is ours, along with the consequences for choosing to be disobedient in this generation.

When we become prideful because of the Spiritual Living God's blessing, we need to reference the book of Job 38-41. It was never Job's desire to experience this disobedience while trying to be obedient, but it happened until he was reminded by the Spiritual Living God. The majority of people will tell you that you have become a "monster" when pride leads your decision making.

The book of Job reminds us of the monster (Leviathan), the great monster created by the Spiritual Living God (Job 41:1-34; Psalm 104:26). Sometimes we observe others around us choosing to live a life of sinful behavior (Ephesians 6:10-20). They appear to be successful in all things, according to the world's standards of living. David observed the same thing and wondered, *How was this possible?* Knowing he personally experienced consequences for his disobedience (Psalm 37), he provided insight regarding the Spiritual Living God never slumbering or sleeping (Psalm 121).

When the Spiritual Living God blessed David and allowed peace in the land, this took place because David actually grew spiritually with the need to fear, honor, and respect the Holy, Spiritual Living God. David inquired of the Spiritual Living God and waited for a response before going into battle (1 Chronicles 14:8-17). David's obedience caused others to look upon the man David with fear. They realized the success David had was bigger than David. He never

DISOBEDIENCE HAS CONSEQUENCES

failed to praise and thank the Spiritual Living God for his success during his battles. He even wrote his first Psalm of thanksgiving in 1 Chronicles 16:7-36. David humbled himself in 1 Chronicles 17:16- 27 with additional prayer and thanksgiving to the Holy, Righteous, Spiritual, and Living God, who resides in heaven.

Nevertheless, after the Spiritual Living God's provisions and David had given thanks to Him for His mercy and grace, Satan still found a way to provoke David to sin against the Holy, Righteous, and Spiritual Living God (1 Chronicles 21:1-6). The Spiritual Living God granted David mercy by providing a choice for his consequences of this sin (1 Chronicles 21:7-17). David realized the punishment from the Spiritual Living God was better than the punishment of man. He knew the Spiritual Living God would have mercy on him, whereas man would not show this kindness.

David's fear, honor, and respect for the Holy, Righteous, Spiritual, and Living God after experiencing his consequences caused him to build an altar with great cost. He realized his Holy, Righteous, and Spiritual Living God is really worthy to be praised and needed to be highly honored for His mercies and grace (1 Chronicles 21:18-30). David's actions caused the Holy, Righteous, and Spiritual Living God to command the angel of the Lord to put up the sword of destruction. When we look at the life of David and the mistakes he made, we realize the consequences he experienced for his disobedience to the Holy, Righteous, and Spiritual Living God, who resides in heaven, were just a reminder of their relationship in David's generation. We must not forget the Spiritual Living God had a very special relationship with David (2 Samuel 7:4-29; Acts 13:22b). We have decided in this generation because of the Spiritual Living God's love and compassion provided through His Son, Jesus Christ (Romans 9-10; 1 Corinthians 3), we can sin, choosing to be more disobedient and rebellious than David and others before Jesus Christ's arrival as the only begotten Son (Hebrews 1; 1 John 1-2), knowing we have been forgiven for our sins, when we repent and ask for forgiveness (Luke 13:1-5; Acts 2:38) in the name of Jesus. Nevertheless, we refuse to accept the help provided by Jesus with the guidance of the Holy Spirit (John 14-16; Acts 2; 1 John 1-2), acknowledging this is the only way we can overcome any sin (Romans 5-6; Hebrews 10; 2 Peter 2:9). Until we sincerely believe in our hearts and become tired and brokenhearted (Psalm 51), we will continue to sin and experience consequences for our sins against the Holy, Righteous Heavenly Father, who resides in heaven (Psalm 19:7-14). The Spiritual Living God provided consequences for David when he chose to be disobedient. Do you think we are more desirable to the Spiritual Living God than David? Surely, the Holy Spirit has revealed the truth about David's relationship with the Spiritual Living God (Psalm 89; Acts 13:22b).

Never forget, we are the clay, and He is the potter (Isaiah 29:15-16; Romans 9:18-24). Choosing to do the same thing the same way and expecting different results provides you with a picture of a dog chasing his tail and never catching it, but he becomes tired and eventually gives up hope (Romans 8; Ephesians 4:14-32). The Spiritual Living God provided His Son, Jesus Christ, so we could have an abundant life (John 10) of success while residing here on Earth according to His plans and purpose. Choosing to sin

DISOBEDIENCE HAS CONSEQUENCES

and never accepting help from the Holy Spirit (John 14-16; Acts 2; 1 John 1-2) to overcome our sins sends the wrong message to those observing our lives as children (Romans 8; Ephesians 4:14-32) of the Spiritual Living God (Hebrews 10; 2 Peter 2:9). Sometimes your life is the only truth others have to observe and learn from our experiences as they question if their lives are worth living. A life worth living says to others, "I have been crucified with Christ; it is no longer I who live, but the Holy Spirit provided by Jesus Christ lives through me" (Galatians 2:20-3:29). If they observe you as never being successful in overcoming sins, which displeases the Holy, Righteous, and Spiritual Living God, in the name of Jesus (Romans 6; Hebrews 10), they feel it is impossible for them to experience a spiritual personal relationship with the Heavenly Father, Son, and Holy Spirit. Surely, someone called into obedience can succeed in following the guidance of the Holy Spirit (1 Corinthians 9:11-14; 15:20-58; 2 Corinthians 3). We should take the time and start depending on the Holy Spirit (Proverbs 3:5-6; Matthew 6:25-33). Then we can have wisdom, knowledge, and understanding in all things (1 Corinthians 2).

When we quote Philippians 4:13 and Romans 16:25-27, we really will be able to do all things through Christ, who strengthens us. We will have a sincere desire to do the will of the Holy, Righteous, and Spiritual Living God, acknowledging it was because of the Spiritual Living God's love and compassion, He sent His Son to die and rise for our sins (John 1:1-18; 3:16-21); only by the blood of Jesus are we cleansed from our sins (Romans 3:23-26; 4-7; Hebrews 1; 1 John 1-2). Our relationship with Jesus and the guidance of the Holy Spirit allow us to come before the Holy, Righteous,

BECAUSE THE LORD IS YOUR SHEPHERD

and Spiritual Living God as His children (Romans 8; Ephesians 4:14-32). We have a Mediator, the Spiritual Living God's Son, Jesus Christ, interceding on our behalf to the Heavenly Father, who resides in heaven (Romans 8:34; 1 Timothy 2:4-6; Hebrews 1).

Jesus resides at the right hand of our Heavenly Father, the Spiritual Living God (Hebrews 1), interceding constantly for the Spiritual Living God to have mercy on His children (Romans 8; Ephesians 4:14-32) living here on Earth (John 14-16; Acts 2). This is the reason the Spiritual Living God's children do not experience His wrath without mercy and grace, in this generation. Moses' generation's experiences (Exodus 15:26; Psalm 103) are a reminder for future generations to be thankful.

He realized we are weak and without Him, we would never become strong (Romans 15:1-6). David reminds his son Solomon to serve the Spiritual Living God with a perfect heart (1 Chronicles 28:9). The Lord searches all hearts and understands all the imaginations of thoughts when we seek the Lord GOD (Psalm 7:9; 139:23-24; Jeremiah 17:9-10; Romans 3:9-20; Hebrews 11:6). He will be found by those who diligently seek Him (1 Peter 1-2). Anytime we turn our back on the Spiritual Living God, we will experience the consequences that come from being disobedient in this generation (Romans 6), which can also affect our children (2 Peter 2:14). We really need to receive the inspired words of wisdom (1 Corinthians 2) so we might experience a long life with our Heavenly Father, who resides in heaven. We can look forward to experiencing eternal life with Him as His children in the name of Jesus (John 5:17-47; 10; Romans 4:13-5:21; 1 John 5).

You Must Believe Me to Trust Me

Jesus Christ used a child as an object lesson during His generation. He said, "We must have a child's simple trust to enter the kingdom of heaven." The Truth can be easy to understand but difficult for some to practice. We have been told by past generations, according to the inspired words of the Spiritual Living God, His children (Romans 8; Ephesians 4:14-32) must accept Jesus Christ, as the only begotten Son of the Spiritual Living God (John 1:1-18; 3:16-21; Hebrews 1). Jesus' **birth** (Matthew 1:24-25; Luke 2:1-7), **life** (four Gospels), **death** (Matthew 27:51-56; Mark 15:38-41; Luke 23:44-49; John 19:16-42), **resurrection** (Matthew 28; Luke 24:1-48; John 20; 1 Corinthians 15), and His **ascension** (Mark 16:19-20; Luke 24:49-53) into heaven are provided in the four Gospels (Matthew, Mark, Luke, and John). They provided details according to their observation of the life of Jesus Christ while He lived here on Earth the same way four humans can observe a car accident today in this generation. Most of the information would be the same, but each would speak about what they thought was the most important facts to them.

When babies are born in this generation, many are perceptive to the sound of their parents' voices (Luke 1:39-45), just like John the Baptist acknowledged the sound of Mary's voice when she greeted her Aunt Elizabeth. The sheep

BECAUSE THE LORD IS YOUR SHEPHERD

always knows the voice of the shepherd (John 10). Many cultures have found music and reading have an impact on a baby being carried in the mother's womb. What are we doing in this generation for pleasure that can have an effect on the child in the womb without positive results? Therefore, when they enter this world, they relate more quickly to the sounds provided for them. When a mother speaks, they turn toward the familiar sound they are hearing (John 10:4-18). Jesus Christ used children many times (Matthew 18:1-5; 19:13-15; Mark 10:13-16; Luke 18:15-18) when He was trying to help past and present generations understand the level of trust needed and protection He provides. We must be able to trust the Heavenly Father, Son, and the guidance of the Holy Spirit regarding the promises that were made available to the children of the Spiritual Living God (Romans 11:13-36; Ephesians 5:1-21). Whenever a baby moves to a level of being a child with understanding, everything the parent said or did will be carried out by the child, mostly before the age of two. The child's training should begin to take place early in his life. It is highly urgent for parents to start before the child reaches the stage of a rebellious two-year-old.

The parents have a responsibility to mold and make this little person into someone who will not cause them hurt, harm, shame, or danger later in life (Proverbs 13:24; 19:18; 22:6, 15; 23:11-16; 30:11-17; Ephesians 6:1-4). When we choose to allow children the freedom to mold and make themselves, they are later called a menace to society. Eventually, they will be locked away like animals and told when they can get up, eat, exercise, or sleep. Why would any human being intelligent enough to observe the life of someone incarcerated (prison) set his or her own child up for defeat in this day and time?

The Holy Bible provides all the details needed for a successful life here on Earth. It is obvious based on generations before our birth, humans had a very hard time choosing a life of obedience according to the Spiritual Living God's plans and purpose for their lives here on Earth (Proverbs 3:5-6; Matthew 6:25-33; John 3:14-21). The Spiritual Living God realized He needed to provide an example and someone who could remove sins so He could have a spiritual personal relationship with those He created in His image (Genesis 1:26-28; John 3:22-36). He provided His Son, Jesus Christ (John 1:1-18; 3:16-21; 5:17-47; 10; Hebrews 1), and His Son provided a Helper, the Holy Spirit (John 14-16; Acts 2) when He returned to the Father as our intercessor (Romans 8:34). John 4:23-24 reminds us the Spirit provided by the Spiritual Living God (Jeremiah 31:31-35; Joel 2:28-32; John 6:44-71) must be drawn by the Heavenly Father before you can receive the Son. The problem with receiving the Holy Spirit is the flesh's desire to live according to its own plans and purpose (Romans 8; Galatians 5:16-26; Ephesians 4:14-32; 6:10-20). The flesh and Spirit are in a constant battle for our attention; Jesus Christ is the Light, and the flesh is darkness (John 1:1-18; 3; 8:12-30; Romans 7:7-25; 8). We have been provided with insight to help future generations; we must stay focused (Proverbs 3:5-6; Matthew 6:25-33) with the guidance of the Holy Spirit to comprehend spiritual things (1 Corinthians 2).

Jesus' teachings were hard for His disciples to comprehend before they received the guidance of the Holy Spirit (John 6:59-65; 12:16). Exactly how in the world did we become intelligent

BECAUSE THE LORD IS YOUR SHEPHERD

enough to understand spiritual things in this generation without the guidance of the Holy Spirit (Psalm 53; Romans 1:21-32; 1 Corinthians 1:18-31)? You can only have spiritual guidance by having a relationship with Jesus Christ, who provided the Holy Spirit as a Helper for the children (Romans 8; Ephesians 4:14-32) of the Spiritual Living God (John 14-16; Acts 2). The Spiritual Living God knew from past experiences in generations before the twenty-first century (Psalm 14; 53; Isaiah 6:9; Acts 28:26-28; Romans 1:21-32; 3:10-18; 10:3-31; 1 Corinthians 1:18-31), we would be deceived by humans and other spirits that exist in the world today (1 John 4:1-6; Acts 19:11-19).

How can anyone without the guidance of the Holy Spirit (1 Corinthians 2) challenge words inspired by the Holy, Righteous, and Spiritual Living God? We are reminded in the Scripture (Deuteronomy 29:29) to be still and know He is the Spiritual Living God (Psalms 46-50). We do not have an excuse in this generation because He promised each generation (Jeremiah 31:31-35; Joel 2:28-32; John 14-16; Acts 2; Ephesians 1:13; Galatians 4:4-7; Hebrews 1; 8; 1 John 1-5) as long as we desire to be obedient (Romans 8; Galatians 5:16-26; Hebrews 10), His children have access to His promises. We need to remember, our Heavenly Father (Luke 11:11-13) will always provide above and beyond anything His children ask or expect in this generation (key words: "His children"). Nevertheless, when the Jews found themselves in Egypt, Jeremiah had a word from the Spiritual Living God about their disobedience (Jeremiah 44). Anytime we become comfortable in the middle of unrighteousness, we need to remember all the evil the Spiritual Living God allowed to take place in Judah and Jerusalem. They provoked the Spiritual Living God to become angry, and they experienced great consequences (44:1-9). The people were warned of the evil experiences coming their way (44:10-11). When they arrived in Egypt, they forgot about the Spiritual Living God and turned a deaf ear regarding the words spoken by Jeremiah (44:16-19). Whenever he tried to help the people understand the consequences of their sins (44:21-26), they refused to listen and had to experience the consequences for themselves. When all was said and done, they had to learn the hard way (44:28-29). Whenever we decide not to humble ourselves with fear, honor, and respect regarding the Spiritual Living God, we can also reference Malachi; the priests (servants of the Spiritual Living God) were rebuked for not showing respect (Malachi 1:6).

Anyone in this generation who refuses to receive spiritual knowledge (1 Corinthians 2) that is being provided by the guidance of the Holy Spirit (John 14-16; Acts 2), our decisions allow us to become defeated regarding living an abundant life here on Earth (John 10). We will never be able to accept the promises provided for the Spiritual Living God's children, as they experience life in the Spirit (Romans 8; 11:13-36; Hebrews 1). There were many before our generation that learned the hard way; we can also learn the hard way. The Spiritual Living God's words will stand forever (Isaiah 40:6-8; 1 Peter 1:13-25).

Those who have been called into obedience regarding the inspired words of the Spiritual Living God (Isaiah 51), Isaiah reminds us to remember the Spiritual Living God's relationship with those in past generations, how He came through for them, and they passed their test in order to be strengthened in their faith (Hebrews 11). Their experiences were written for our benefit, to help this current generation

BECAUSE THE LORD IS YOUR SHEPHERD

(Job 1-3; Romans 15:1-6; John 1:5-10; 1 Peter 4:12-19). Just think, if we did not have these experiences and our own experiences, the distractions in this generation would cause those who are not grounded in their faith (2 Peter 1:12-21) and belief of the Heavenly Father, Son, and the guidance of the Holy Spirit to doubt and question exactly whose report we believe (Psalm 22; Isaiah 53; John 1:1-18; 3:16-21; 12:38-50; Romans 10:9-21). This is why it is necessary to search the Scriptures with the guidance of the Holy Spirit (John 5:39-47). We will need to take a stand in this generation or fall for everything, thus said man (John 16:13; Philippians 4:6-19). Whenever Israel finally turned back to seek the Spiritual Living God and His righteousness (Isaiah 54), she was reminded of the mistakes made in her youth. The Spiritual Living God told her He would have mercy and gather her (54:7-8), for He is the Lord, her Redeemer.

We have also been redeemed in the United States of America, just like the Spiritual Living God's everlasting love was provided for Israel in Isaiah's generation (Isaiah 43). All those who desire to know the Spiritual Living God can receive the promises found in Isaiah (chapters 55-56), as long as we have the guidance of the Holy Spirit (Romans 8:8-17; 11:13-36; 1 John 4:12-15). We will not be confused about spiritual things (Isaiah 44:24-25; Romans 1:18-32; 1 Corinthians 1:18-31). The promises found in Isaiah (54:17) will always hold true for those who are a part of the Spiritual Living God's heritage (Romans 8:4, 14-17; 11:13-36; Ephesians 1:5; 4:14-32). We really do not fight our own battles; they belong to the Spiritual Living God (1 Samuel 17:47; Romans 7:13-25; Galatians 5:16-26; Ephesians 6:10-20). Jeremiah tried to help Judah, but she refused to receive words from

YOU MUST BELIEVE ME TO TRUST ME

the Spiritual Living God's messenger (Jeremiah 15:1-14) regarding His anger with Judah. They experienced a lot of pain and heartache for their constant need to sin against the Spiritual Living God (Jeremiah 16).

Surely, the United States of America can learn from these mistakes and consequences experienced by other nations before the Spiritual Living God established her as a nation with Christian principles and standards (Romans 11:13-36). The people suffered greatly because of their disobedience regarding the Spiritual Living God's plans and purpose for their nation.

Do you think He established America with plans and a purpose to glorify Him as the Spiritual Living God, who resides in heaven and observes all things (Psalm 121)? We should never cease from thanking the Spiritual Living God for His Son, Jesus Christ, who sits at His right hand, interceding on our behalf, asking the Heavenly Father to have mercy on the United States of America (Mark 16:19; Acts 7:55b; Luke 24:51; Colossians 3:1; Romans 8:34; Hebrews 1; 7:25).

Malachi was sent to warn the people about things displeasing to the Spiritual Living God in his generation (Malachi 1-4). He spoke about how the Spiritual Living God's favored nation disrespected Him (1:1-14). Those He put in position to lead and teach, according to His plans and purpose, failed and received consequences (2:1-17). The Spiritual Living God told Israel He requires certain things to take place, but they had become confused about His righteousness and holiness. We must remember, in this generation, He is a Spirit (John 4:23-24), and we can only worship Him in Spirit and Truth. The Spiritual Living God defined righteousness and wickedness for the people to

BECAUSE THE LORD IS YOUR SHEPHERD

understand there is a difference (Malachi 4:1-6), reminding them, He shall return one day. All who desire to know Him personally will not have an excuse (Isaiah 56:3-8; 66:18-20, 23; Jeremiah 31:31-35; Joel 2:28-32; John 1:1-18; 3:15-21; 4:23-24; 5:17-47; 14-16; Acts 2; 1 Corinthians 2; Ephesians 1:13; Hebrews 1; 1 John 1-5) before His Son reappears here on Earth to judge the people (Matthew 24:29-44).

Surely, we can learn from this experience and make better decisions in this generation regarding the Spiritual Living God and His plans and purposes. Remember, He originally established the United States of America as a Christian nation. He has called some into obedience in this generation (2 Chronicles 7:14) also. Those who are called really need to answer the call in this generation, because we sincerely need the Spiritual Living God to bless His people in this generation. The help has been provided before our birth to keep you focused according to His plans and purpose (John 14-16; Acts 2; Romans 8; 1 Corinthians 2; Galatians 5:16-26; Ephesians 4:14-32; 6:10-20). These Scriptures provide the details needed to perform the duties of the Christian faith in order to please the Spiritual Living God (Proverbs 3:5-6; Matthew 6:25-33).

The people in this generation who refuse to acknowledge the difference in the Spirit and the flesh (natural) (Romans 7:13-24; 1 Corinthians 3; 5; Galatians 5:16-26; 6:1-10; Ephesians 6:10-20) must understand they are not wrestling with flesh and blood; this is a spiritual battle (1 Samuel 17:47).

The Spirit and flesh are in a constant battle for your obedience (Acts 19:11-19; 1 John 4:1-6). Hosea had a message for the people in his generation; he tried to help Israel understand, the Spiritual Living God was not pleased

YOU MUST BELIEVE ME TO TRUST ME

with them (Hosea 4:1-6). They chose to listen to so many things spoken during this time without those speaking being guided by the Spirit, until they had become confused about the Truth (John 4:23-24). The Spiritual Living God allowed them to experience Hosea (4:3). Our fish are also disappearing in this generation. Do you think the Spiritual Living God is capable of multiplying the fish to feed the people in this generation? If Jesus took two fish on dry land, prayed, and blessed them to feed more than five thousand people, exactly why are the fish not multiplying in this generation (John 6:1-14)? Could it be possible, America is being confused in this generation just like Hosea's generation was confused? Always remember the inspired words found in Hosea (4:6-19). The people were destroyed for lack of knowledge, but we have access to the Holy Spirit through Jesus Christ. Why are we experiencing what they experienced in their generation? Surely, we are not causing the Spiritual Living God to reject us in this generation. He has provided His Son with the guidance of the Holy Spirit so we might have wisdom, knowledge, and understanding about spiritual things (John 5:19-47; 1 Corinthians 2). We need to remember the provision of His Two Commandments (Matthew 22:34-40; John 13:1-35; 14-16), which covers the Ten Commandments given to Moses in his generation (Exodus 20:1-21). Otherwise, we can also look forward to experiencing heartache and pain in this generation, for choosing a life of disobedience.

The Spiritual Living God is always willing to show us where we are spiritually as long as we have a spiritual personal relationship with Him, as our Heavenly Father (Job 1:5-12; 4:17-21; 36-42; Galatians 4:4-7; 1 John 1-2). He will never

BECAUSE THE LORD IS YOUR SHEPHERD

leave or forsake you during these tests (Job 1:8-12; Hebrews 13:5-6). We need to take the time and remember, Satan had to request permission from the Spiritual Living God to test Job (Job 1:6-12), which the Spiritual Living God granted with a condition (1:12). Why would those who believe in the Gospel regarding the Heavenly Father, Son, and the guidance of the Holy Spirit (1 Corinthians 2; Galatians 5:16-26; Ephesians 1:13; 6:10-20; 1 John 1-5) bypass any spiritual testing (remember, it is a fixed fight)? We would never know if we spiritually and personally know Him as the Spiritual Living God in this generation.

We really need the test in this generation; we need to know if we would speak like Job during a test or like his wife (1:21-22; 2:9-10).

Surely, those with the guidance of the Holy Spirit would have the strength to endure all things (John 16:13; Philippians 4:13). It would be okay to reference Psalms 30-35 during this time, while we wait patiently for Jesus to intercede on our behalf (Romans 8:34) because we chose to live according to Romans (8; Ephesians 4:14-32), trusting the Helper provided in John (chapters 14-16); nevertheless, Job (5:17-27) reminds us of the blessings provided by the Spiritual Living God. We have also received blessings from the Spiritual Living God as His children in this generation. We should try not to be like Thomas; he has already made the mistake of saying, "Unless I see the print from the nails, I will not believe" (John 20:24-31). Nevertheless, Thomas was told, just like the other disciples, of things Jesus must accomplish before His departure and return (John 14:1-14).

Remember, Jesus sent a Comforter (John 14-16) and prays for those who belong to the Spiritual Living God as His

YOU MUST BELIEVE ME TO TRUST ME

children (John 17; Romans 8; Ephesians 4:14-32). We do not have to stress ourselves about spiritual things; just remember (1 Corinthians 2), it is easier to believe and receive your help in this generation. We have been warned about being with unbelievers (1 Corinthians 6:11-18). They have found fault with the inspired words provided by the Spiritual Living God (2 Timothy 3:14-17; Psalm 14; 53; Romans 1:21-32; 1 Corinthians 1:18-31), planting seeds of doubt about the Spiritual Living God (John 4:23-24) in the minds of those not grounded in their faith and belief (Matthew 13:13-30; Hebrews 11; 2 Peter 1:12-21). Nevertheless, we have been given choices in this generation and examples from past generations. Find a mustard seed (Matthew 13:31-32), observe the size; you only need this much faith to receive eternal life (Hebrews 11; 1 John 1-5), which will eventually take place with or without your making the right decisions regarding your life here on Earth (John 1:1-18; 3-5; Romans 14:11). Only by the guidance of the Holy Spirit will our decisions be according to the Spiritual Living God's plans and purposes for our lives. Job reminds us, regardless of what the world believes, the Spiritual Living God is still very much in control in this generation of the twenty-first century (Job 9:1-13). Jesus reminded those in His generation, the hatred of the world is expected. Remember, they hated Him also (John 15:18-27). We should keep our eyes on Him, because nothing is impossible with the Spiritual Living God (Proverbs 3:5-6; Matthew 6:25-33; Mark 10:27; 2 Thessalonians 1:2-10; 2:4-13; 5:2-11).

He also reminded us, with the guidance of the Holy Spirit, we could overcome the world just like He had (John 16:25-33).

BECAUSE THE LORD IS YOUR SHEPHERD

Our peace will always come from within, provided by Him, with the guidance of the Holy Spirit (John 14:15-31). Anytime a seed is planted without water, it cannot live; Jesus is the Living Water for this generation. The Spiritual Living God created each human being in His image (Genesis 1:27-28; 5:2; Matthew 19:4-5). He provided a Son (John 1:1-18; 3:16-21; 17:1-3; Hebrews 1) to plant the seed of faith for those who believed the Gospels (Romans 1:16-20; Matthew; Mark; Luke; John). Those who think the Gospel is weakness (Romans 1:21-32; 1 Corinthians 1:18-31), this Scripture has been provided for you. Now you know the reason you do not believe the inspired words of the Spiritual Living God. Paul provided a warning regarding the spirit of deception being powerful enough to confuse those in Thessalonica in his generation (2 Thessalonians 2:5-12). Jesus, the Spiritual Living God's, Son, came so those who desire to know the Spiritual Living God would have access to Him (John 1:1-18; 3; 4:23-24; 5:17-47; 10; 14-16; Hebrews 1). We are allowed to communicate with the Spiritual Living God, who is a Spirit (John 6:44-65), anytime we receive the Helper provided by His Son, Jesus Christ (John 14:15-31; Galatians 5:16-26; Ephesians 1:13; 6:10-20). We must acknowledge Jesus as the Living Water needed for the seed of faith (Matthew 17:20; 21:21-22; Mark 9:23-24; Romans 1:16-20; Hebrews 11). We can look forward to inner growth (Ephesians 3:14-21), then, we will experience Acts 2. The promises that were made before our birth still hold true in the twenty-first century (Isaiah 44:3-4; Ezekiel 11:19-20; Joel 2:28-32; Zechariah 13:6-9; John 7:38; 15:1-16; 1 Corinthians 15:58).

The wisdom, knowledge, and understanding provided by the Holy Spirit (Acts 2:43-44; Ephesians 1:3-5, 13; 2:11-

YOU MUST BELIEVE ME TO TRUST ME

22; 4; Colossians 3:1-11) remind us, those who belong to the Spiritual Living God have all things in common. Do not waste your time defending inspired words found in the Holy Bible provided by the Spiritual Living God (Psalm 14; 53; Romans 1:21-32; 1 Corinthians 1:18-31). We should be willing to plant the seed and allow the guidance of the Holy Spirit to provide the increase (1 Corinthians 3:5-10). Sometimes those with spiritual guidance do not have spiritual insight (Deuteronomy 29:29), according to this Scripture. Whatever the Spiritual Living God decides to reveal, it will be His choice, and this Scripture should provide insight about His decision, just like He provided spiritual guidance for you revealing His inspired words were true (John 6:44-65). He could have provided this same guidance for anyone He chose to call into obedience (Romans 9).

If Pharaoh's heart was hardened in Moses' generation in order for the Spiritual Living God to reveal Himself to His people in that generation, what makes this generation, which is diffidently the adulterous generation (Proverbs 30; Matthew 12:38-41; 13:13-17; Mark 8:35-38; John 4:48; James 4:1-10), think the Spiritual Living God needs a human to reveal something spiritual to those whose hearts are hardened (Hebrews 3:7-11)? The Spiritual Living God provided His Spirit (Jeremiah 31:31-35; Joel 2:28-32; 1 Corinthians 2; Hebrews 8) and His Son as an example of obedience (John 1:18-31; 3:16; 4:23-24; 5:17-47; 14-16; Romans 8; Ephesians 1:13; Hebrews 1). Why should He entertain those who choose not to believe His inspired words in this generation (Hebrews 10)? *Remember, it is harder to pull someone up and easier to pull someone down. (Stand on a chair and try it for yourself.)* We have been given a chance to receive and believe

BECAUSE THE LORD IS YOUR SHEPHERD

the Gospel (Romans 1:16-20; 10:9-21; Ephesians 1:13-14). Otherwise, we have been warned by Isaiah (44:24-25), the Spiritual Living God is still in control. The Spiritual Living God also reminded Moses' generation and future generations, "He would have compassion on those whom He wanted to have compassion on" (Romans 9:15-33; 1 Corinthians 9:10-27). Man cannot change anything the Spiritual Living God does not allow to be changed. Otherwise, we suffer the consequences for being disobedient, creating heartache and sorrow for those who follow our leadership without the guidance of the Holy Spirit (Matthew 15:10-14).

We are reminded (Romans 8:28-39), we are more than conquerors through Jesus Christ, who strengthens us. Joshua had to remind the people in his generation, they should be strong and encouraged, for the Spiritual Living God will always be with them (Joshua 1:9). We can look around in this generation of the twenty-first century, observing the many cultures that choose not to be strong and encouraged according to the inspired words of the Spiritual Living God (Luke 21:5-38). David found himself in a situation where he had to encourage himself (1 Samuel 30:6). As children of the Spiritual Living God, we need to remember to encourage ourselves as we call on the name of Jesus, in this generation. Sometimes things spoken before our birth can be seen taking place in this generation. We need to be still and acknowledge the Spiritual Living God is still the Lord GOD (Psalms 46-50). Anytime we choose not to have a spiritual relationship with the Spiritual Living God, who is a Spirit and must be worshiped in Spirit and Truth (John 4:23-24; 6:44-65), we will observe different cultures experiencing life's woes, without the guidance of the Holy

Spirit. One culture is so strong, they choose to live under the bridge before they humble themselves and pray, refusing to ask for forgiveness for their errors in life, which cause these circumstances they are experiencing (Psalm 19:7-14; James 5:19-20).

The Spiritual Living God provides for His children (Romans 8; Ephesians 4:14-32); the righteous are not forsaken, and His seed does not have to beg for bread (Psalm 37; Luke 15:11-32; John 6:31-51; 10). There is a culture of people who choose to leave the land of the living anytime their lives here on Earth become overwhelming without the guidance of the Holy Spirit. Just because you experienced Matthew's words while Jesus was teaching (19:16-30), only by the guidance of the Holy Spirit (John 14-16; Acts 2; 1 Corinthians 2) will life in this world not become overwhelming. There are cultures where family means everything to them; the only problems are they must have a spiritual relationship with the Spiritual Living God. They cannot serve other gods and receive the promises found in the Holy Bible (Proverbs 3:5-6; Matthew 6:25-33; 22:37-40; 23). Surely, we cannot be identified as Scribes (experts in legal matter, questioning Jesus' authority, sometimes they believed, Matthew 8:19) and Pharisees (blind regarding spiritual things, John 3:1-10, they refuse to accept Jesus Christ, Matthew 12:24-34) in this generation. The parents must also teach their children to respect both parents, not just one (Exodus 20:5-6; Matthew 15:3-9; Ephesians 6:1-4). Only by the guidance of the Holy Spirit will the child have the strength to accomplish this very hard commandment. When their peers have more influence than their parents, encouraging them to be disobedient because everybody else is disrespecting their

BECAUSE THE LORD IS YOUR SHEPHERD

parents in this generation, could this be why the children are dying by record numbers in this generation (Matthew 15:4-9)? Check the statistics of past generations; parents were respected, and children lived longer for choosing to live a life of obedience. This was the first commandment with a promise (Galatians 6:1-3). Whenever parents decide they are not going to train up their children according to the Spiritual Living God's expectation, they are going to experience some very painful and brokenhearted days, as long as these children live here on Earth (Proverbs 19:18; 20:11; 22:6, 15; 23:13-14).

The people were warned in Moses' generation not to take their eyes off the Spiritual Living God (Deuteronomy 8:11-20); otherwise, they would perish for their disobedience. Surely, this generation can relate to their experiences and consequences in this day and time (2 Chronicles 19:6-9; Proverbs 3:5-6; Matthew 6:25-33; Romans 2:11; 9:18-33; Acts 10:34-48; Ephesians 6:9; Colossians 3:25; James 2:1, 9). The Spiritual Living God is not a respecter of persons (Romans 2:10-16).

We were reminded (John 14-16; Acts 2; 1 Corinthians 2), the Holy Spirit will always provide enlightenment, wisdom, knowledge, and understanding for the children (Romans 8; Ephesians 4:14-32) of the Spiritual Living God. We must remember this promise as long as we accept His only begotten Son, Jesus Christ (Hebrews 1). We will have insight regarding living life in the Spirit (Galatians 5:16-26; Ephesians 6:10-20), you really will be able to accomplish all things (John 16:13; Philippians 4:13). Otherwise, we must remember what Jesus said to the disciples in the Garden of Gethsemane (Matthew 26:41; Luke 22:40, 46; Romans 8:1-4;

YOU MUST BELIEVE ME TO TRUST ME

15:1-6): "Watch and pray that ye enter not into temptation: the Spirit indeed is willing, but the flesh is weak." Jesus Christ has already died for those weak in their Spirit so they might be strengthened (John 14-16; Acts 2; 1 Corinthians 8:11-13). We need to remember what Joel told the people in his generation (Joel 3:10b). James reminded us there is a difference in true and false wisdom in his generation (James 3:13-18). Worldliness and pride were also problems (James 4). Those who are wealthy in material things in this generation need to try and be mindful of the warning to the rich in his generation (James 5). The Spiritual Living God is not a respecter of persons (2 Chronicles 19:7; Acts 10:34-48; Romans 2:10-16; Ephesians 6:6-9; Colossians 3:23-25; James 2:1-9). He reminds us, He will love and have compassion on whom He desires in this world (Exodus 33:17-23; Psalm 103; 119:73-176; Jeremiah 15:1-14; Romans 9:18-33). Surely, we can do what (2 Chronicles 7:14) was spoken before our generation. Joshua reminded the people in his generation to be strong and encouraged, for the Spiritual Living God will fight their enemies (Joshua 10:25). Do you think with the guidance of the Holy Spirit in the name of Jesus, we can reference this Scripture in this generation? We must believe the Spiritual Living God still provides for His children (Romans 8; Ephesians 4:14-32; 1 John 1-3) in this generation also. Always remember (1 John 4:1-6), many have been deceived following the wrong spirits (Acts 19:11-19).

Until You Can Fear, Honor, and Respect the Holy, Spiritual Living God, Stop the Questions

Did your parents allow you to disrespect them as a child (Matthew 15:3-9)? Here lies the problem with you not being able to respect the Holy, Spiritual Living God. They have done a disservice to you, and you are probably passing the ignorance (Galatians 6:1-9). We must remember the Spiritual Living God is not your "Buddy, Pal, Bro, Big Guy Upstairs," or "The Big Boy." When was the last time you called a judge of the law here on Earth one of these names or the president of the United States of America a name of this nature? We do not use these words in their presence; otherwise, we would be looked upon as being ignorant and totally disrespectful.

Guess what? They are not able to save you from your sins (Romans 5-6; Acts 2:21; 1 John 1-5). They are not capable of providing a healing hand during your sickness, an abundant life (John 10), a long life, or a chance to experience eternal life. Nevertheless, you honor and respect a human just like you, more than the Spiritual Living God. When Abraham wanted to intercede on behalf of Sodom and Gomorrah, he was speaking to angels who represented the Spiritual Living God (Genesis 18:22-33). Pay attention to how he humbly (18:27, 30-31) spoke with them, as he acknowledged their holiness.

After Moses made the mistake of hitting the rock instead of speaking to the rock (Numbers 20:8-13) while leading

BECAUSE THE LORD IS YOUR SHEPHERD

the Spiritual Living God's people, He forgave Moses, but the consequences remained for his disobedience. In Deuteronomy (3:24-25), Moses speaks of the greatness of the Spiritual Living God, he was missing on this journey. He wanted to experience life in the Promised Land, but the Spiritual Living God said, "No," and, "Let us not have this conversation again" (twenty-first century comprehension) (Deuteronomy 3:26-29). Moses was instructed to prepare Joshua to become the leader of the Spiritual Living God's people. Moses explained to the current generation the need to choose a life of obedience to the Holy, Righteous, Spiritual, and Living God (Deuteronomy 4:1-8). Moses wanted the people to understand the Spiritual Living God was to be feared, honored, and respected always (Deuteronomy 4:9-14; 7:1-26). He also reminded them of the consequences for choosing disobedience (Deuteronomy 4:15-40; 8:11-20). The Israelites had the responsibility to teach future generations (Genesis 18:19-20; Deuteronomy 4:10; 11:19-21), just like we must teach the future generations in this day and time (Hebrews 1-2; 8; 10-11). Otherwise, it is very possible the words spoken during Moses' generation will come to pass in this generation. Their level of intelligence will never comprehend, they do not have a spiritual relationship with the Spiritual Living God (Exodus 20:5-6; 32:31-35; Psalm 53; Romans 1:21-32; 1 Corinthians 1:18-31; 2 Peter 2:14).

It appears Moses gained some spiritual growth when he began to see the splendor and glory of the Holy, Spiritual Living God, whom he had been communicating with while traveling to the Promised Land.

If the wisest man in the world knew how to humble himself before the Spiritual Living God (1 Kings 3:7), for "I am but a

UNTIL YOU CAN FEAR, HONOR, AND RESPECT...

little child; I know not how to go out or come in," we should accept the words spoken in 1 Kings (3:6-15) regarding those desiring to know the Spiritual Living God personally. We must first have the mind-set of a little child (Matthew 18:1-5; 19:13-15). Children who are obedient will always follow the leadership of their parents (Ephesians 6:1-4), providing the parents live a life of obedience regarding the Spiritual Living God's inspired words; otherwise, look forward to their rebellion that's coming your way.

This generation has decided their level of intelligence does not allow childlike obedience to the Spiritual Living God. We have too many of man's technologies (Ecclesiastes 7:29), which encourages us to exalt ourselves (Jude 3-16). We just need to remember, whatever goes up must come down. The Spiritual Living God provides us with the knowledge we have to glorify Him (Proverbs 1:7-33). When we choose to be glorified, we will experience consequences for being disobedient, pride before the fall (Job 34:31-37). We need to remember, without Jesus Christ, we are like a ship without a sail; it is impossible to be anchored in spiritual knowledge in the flesh (1 Corinthians 2; Galatians 5:16-26).

Solomon was given wisdom to make a decision in 1 Kings (3:16-28) that only the Spirit of the Spiritual Living God could provide. He had no prior knowledge before rendering an honest verdict. The Spiritual Living God really can do all things (Isaiah 45:7; John 15:13; Philippians 4:13). We should watch the questions; without the guidance of the Holy Spirit provided by Jesus Christ in this generation, we are heading for disaster (Isaiah 45:18-25; Ezekiel 20:1-44; 1 Timothy 4:1). Eventually, every knee will bow and tongue, confess about our Heavenly Father, who resides in heaven, and His relationship with His only begotten

BECAUSE THE LORD IS YOUR SHEPHERD

Son, Jesus Christ (Isaiah 45:22-23; Romans 14:10-12; Ephesians 3:13-15; Philippians 2:9-11). We need to reflect back on Psalm 111:10-115 and be encouraged.

This is like getting an oil change to keep the car running in order to avoid future problems, or drinking fluids in order not to become dehydrated and experience sickness in this generation. We have been provided with reminders of who the Spiritual Living God really is, in this generation (Psalm 112). Psalm 118 should help those with a **religion** and not a spiritual personal relationship with the Spiritual Living God understand, trusting the Lord GOD (Psalm 118:4-9) will pay off very soon.

We need to reflect on Moses and others' mistakes in past generations in order not to duplicate their mistakes in this generation, hopefully, learning and accepting the messages provided about fear, honor, respect, and the need to serve the Holy, Spiritual Living God. Their experiences with being disobedient in past generations actually encourage His children (Romans 8; Ephesians 4:14-32) in this generation to be still (Psalms 46-50). Granted, we have the guidance of the Holy Spirit available to us, constantly reminding us to make a better decision, in the name of Jesus, if we are His children.

This generation's worldly knowledge is causing many to forget all that the Spiritual Living God asked of His children (Jeremiah 10). When parents spoil a child, refusing to teach him fear, honor, and respect for them as the parents (Matthew 15:4), they set their child up for a life of constant disobedience, if they do not have respect for adults. How can they fear, honor, and respect the Spiritual Living God, whom they cannot see, when they disrespect those in authority, whom they can see? The consequences can be very grave. The children constantly ask for things of the parent, realizing the answer should be no. Nevertheless, the parent, because of his or her weakness, says yes, instead, which allows the child to experience consequences for not being trained according to the Spiritual Living God's standards (Proverbs 13:24; 19:13-29; 20:7-22; 22:4-8, 14-16; 23:12-18, 22-28; 30:11-17; Ephesians 6:1-4; 2 Timothy 3:14-17). Their disobedience can be overwhelming without spiritual strength to understand the need for the training. The children really have the power to wear you down without strength supplied by the guidance of the Holy Spirit.

The Spiritual Living God told Moses no about entering the Promised Land, but the Spiritual Living God did allow Moses to look upon the Promised Land before entering his resting place (Deuteronomy 3:27-28). As parents, we have a responsibility to teach our children to honor, fear, and respect our Heavenly Father, who resides in heaven, in the name of Jesus. He has provided the Helper, the guidance of the Holy Spirit (John 14-16; Acts 2; 1 Corinthians 2), for His children (Romans 8; Ephesians 4:14-32).

We need to understand, everybody does not desire to have a spiritual relationship with the Spiritual Living God, in this generation. This knowledge should be made available to your child as part of his or her life training (Psalm 53; Romans 1:21-32; 1 Corinthians 1:18-31). They are being put at a disadvantage being here on Earth without this knowledge and past generations' experiences for choosing a life of disobedience (Deuteronomy 4:29-40; 6).

The Spiritual Living God promises things will be well with those who choose a life of obedience, according to His

BECAUSE THE LORD IS YOUR SHEPHERD

will (Deuteronomy 5:29-33). Psalm 103 reminds us to thank the Spiritual Living God and to not forget the benefits for choosing to honor, respect, and acknowledge the righteousness of the Spiritual Living God.

If you do not feel the inspired words of the Spiritual Living God were written for your benefit of a better life while living here on Earth in this generation (Psalm 14; 53; Romans 1:21-32; 1 Corinthians 1:18-31), praise the Spiritual Living God, He allowed you to make a choice about choosing to know Him spiritually and personally in this world. There were many before you were born who experienced the same ignorance (Ephesians 4:18-20). Peter tried to help those before your generation; he was put in prison (Acts 12). Be encouraged; he reminds those during his generation, "We should obey the Spiritual Living God and not man" (Acts 5:17-42). No man has the power to stop the Spiritual Living God's plans and purpose for those called into obedience, when they answer the call. Never allow anyone to tell you ignorance is not expensive (Psalm 14; 53; Romans 1:21-32; 1 Corinthians 1:18-31). We can either learn the hard way or the easy way, from others or our own mistakes in this life. Look at the expense associated with teaching and training a child while he is in his formative years. Now consider the heartache and pain you experience when he is disobedient and locked up like an animal in a cage, or dies for being a menace to society. Anytime we choose to be disobedient according to the inspired words found in the Holy Bible, these are some of the consequences; nevertheless, the choice is ours to bear. The Spiritual Living God has already provided His Son to bear the sins of those who have a spiritual personal relationship with Him (1 Timothy 4:8-12; 1 John 1-5).

UNTIL YOU CAN FEAR, HONOR, AND RESPECT...

We have a Spiritual Living God who refuses to force us into obedience. We will always come to Him with a willing heart (John 6:44-65), realizing life outside the plans and purpose of the Heavenly Father, Son, and the guidance of the Holy Spirit is not worth living. We need a spiritual personal relationship (Romans 8; Ephesians 4:14-32) with the Heavenly Father, Son, and Holy Spirit. According to John (4:23-24), the Spiritual Living God is a Spirit. That which is born of the Spirit is Spirit; that which is born of the flesh is flesh (John 1:1-18; 3:5-6, 16-21; Romans 8:8-17; Galatians 5:16-26).

As human beings, we are born of flesh with a Spirit (Jeremiah 31:31-34; Joel 2:28-32; 1 John 4:12-14; Romans 1:16; 8-10; 1 Corinthians 2). We cannot access the Spirit until we accept the spiritual connection. Jesus Christ is the Spiritual Living God's only begotten Son (Hebrews 1). This connection is provided by the Son of the Spiritual Living God, Jesus Christ (John 1:1-18; 3; 5:17-47; 14-16; Ephesians 5; Acts 2). He provided the guidance of the Holy Spirit when He ascended back to the Heavenly Father, who resides in heaven (Romans 8:34; Colossians 3:1).

For those who do not believe in the Heavenly Father, Son, and the guidance of the Holy Spirit, it is okay! According to John 10, we need to be sheep to follow the Shepherd (John 10:22-42). When you are ready to call on the name of Jesus, He will open your understanding (Luke 24:44-48). Until then, continue walking around here on earth quenching the Spirit (Ephesians 4:29-31; 1 Thessalonians 5:19).

You are walking around in darkness without the Light (John 1:1-18). Be careful of those other spirits the Holy Bible speaks of; they will reside within you, without a personal invitation (Acts 19:11-19; 1 Timothy 4:1; 1 John 4:1-6). They can be aggressive and do not give you a choice; they just take control of your life. If you do not think so, reference Matthew 12:43-45; and Acts 8:7 and 19:11-20. Ask someone on drugs, or with a sexual addiction, or with a gambling or alcohol problem, or engaging in any other sinful behavior if he or she has tried to stop the madness. Just look around at the person you always thought was quiet and sweet; when someone crosses this person in this generation without the guidance of the Holy Spirit, it is scary, right?

We have been warned (2 Thessalonians 2), let no man deceive you. The mind will be confused beyond your control regarding spiritual things to come (Psalm 14; 53; Romans 1:21-32; 1 Corinthians 1:18-31; 1 Timothy 4). Those who desire other gods and become deceived, Isaiah 47:10-15 and Jeremiah 10 inform us of the heartache and pain you will experience for following unbelievers here on Earth.

Moses provided words of wisdom for the Israelites regarding the Spiritual Living God's expectations for those who desire a relationship with Him (Deuteronomy 12). Those who desire to eat flesh may eat all the flesh they kill, with His blessings. He only requested that we refuse to eat any blood (Leviticus 17:10-16; 15:19-33). Oh! "That was then; this is now"--just remember those words when you experience the consequences for being disobedient.

The Spiritual Living God's request should not be that difficult to follow, when we think about the blood and power provided by His Son, Jesus Christ (OOPS! No rare meats with blood oozing). There have been stories told about women desiring to be evil using blood released monthly (Leviticus 18:19; 20:18; Ecclesiastes 7:26; Ezekiel 18:6c). Only the Spiritual Living God knows how much devastation she can cause another human being who is not covered by the blood of Jesus. Why do you think He said we can also have these same promises because of our spiritual relationship with Jesus Christ? We are now sons and daughters of the Holy, Righteous, Spiritual Living God, who resides in heaven as our Heavenly Father (Romans 8:14-17; Galatians 4:1-7; Ephesians 1:5; 4:14-32). Let us thank the Spiritual Living God for His mercy (Psalm 103). When the Spiritual Living God promises to send a prophet (Deuteronomy 18:15-22) and put His words in His mouth, He is stating things to come for the benefit of future generations (Romans 15:1-6; Hebrews 1). We need to plant seeds in future generations regarding the promises of the Spiritual Living God, also informing them of His ability to make everything come true according to His inspired words found in the Holy Bible, for future generations (Deuteronomy 1:10-12; 1 Kings 8:55-57; Psalm 77:7-14; Luke 24:49; Acts 1:3-5; Romans 4:13-25; Galatians 3:11-29; Ephesians 3:4-7; 6:2; 1 Timothy 4:6-16; Hebrews 1-2; 4:1-6; 9:15-28; 11).

When we choose to put our hope in the promises of the Spiritual Living God and His plans for our lives, we can stand on a sure foundation (Proverbs 3:5-6; Matthew 6:25-33; 2 Timothy 2:19). We must come to the realization, there is nothing in this world to stop the plans and promises of the Holy, Spiritual Living God, providing you desire to know Him personally through His darling Son, Jesus Christ. Remember, the Lord hears the righteous, according to Psalm 34 and John 9:31. If you are experiencing Luke 10:17-24, you observe things taking place, knowing it had to be the guidance of the Holy Spirit, in order for it to be accomplished. Be sure and give thanks to the Spiritual Living God; let Him know

BECAUSE THE LORD IS YOUR SHEPHERD

you are grateful for this experience because you are able to grow spiritually with this personal experience (Ephesians 3:14-21), knowing He hears your prayers in the name of Jesus, His Son, the Mediator (Romans 8:34; 1 Timothy 2:4-6).

As we perceive the life of Jesus Christ, the Holy Spirit has to open our ears and allow us to focus our eyes on the holiness of our Lord and Savior, Jesus Christ (John 14-16; Acts 2; 1 Corinthians 2). If we are not allowed to hear and see the holiness of the Spiritual Living God, who resides in heaven, we become like the Israelites during Moses' generations. We are wandering in the wilderness of the world, without the guidance of the Holy Spirit. We are moving, but we are not really arriving at any set destination.

This experience is like being on a loop inside the city and missing the exit. You continue to drive, thinking, *I thought I passed by here last time.*

In other words, you are doing the same things, the same way, getting the same results, and do not have the wisdom to know you are not making any progress in life.

The Spiritual Living God promised the Israelites things could be different, but they had to make the right decision regarding obedience or disobedience to Him, the Holy, Spiritual Living God. All thanks are to the Spiritual Living God for providing details in these chapters: Deuteronomy 27-28. The blessing for choosing obedience and the curses for choosing disobedience to the Holy, Spiritual Living God are listed for future generations.

Choosing a life of disobedience without the guidance of the Holy Spirit allows us to experience the Spiritual Living God's anger and His wrath. The leaders in past generations were usually provided with details about conditions needed,

UNTIL YOU CAN FEAR, HONOR, AND RESPECT...

and which things would stop His anger and wrath (Isaiah 41-43).

When the dust settled, many had lost their lives because of their rebellion against the Holy, Righteous, Spiritual Living God during Moses' generation (Numbers 16); we are supposed to learn from their mistakes in future generations.

Now, we have some insight as to why we experience things in this generation, without the guidance of the Holy Spirit, exactly why things are taking place according to the inspired words of the Holy, Spiritual Living God. The Israelites had to observe past and present experiences of the leaders the Spiritual Living God called into obedience in order to make the right choices about serving Him as the Spiritual Living God who resides in heaven.

Remember, the Spiritual Living God provided the guidance of His Spirit for those called into obedience (Exodus 31). By keeping their focus on the holiness of the Spiritual Living God, they were capable of leading the people He needed them to lead (Exodus 32).

When the people rebelled against the Spiritual Living God, He never asked the leaders about the rebellious people. He told them, "Hear what the people are saying."

Then, the Spiritual Living God answered the people in anger and wrath. The Spiritual Living God realized as a Spirit (John 4:23-24), He needed to live among the people on Earth, providing them with an example of love and compassion (1 John 4:7-14). This caused Him to provide love and compassion of Himself with spiritual guidance, into the womb of a young girl named Mary (Luke 1:26-56). When Mary brought forth the male child and called His name Jesus (Luke 2), she was only being obedient to the promises

BECAUSE THE LORD IS YOUR SHEPHERD

made by the Spiritual Living God in past generations of things to come forth in future generations (Psalm 22; Isaiah 53; Luke 1-2). Jesus' experiences here on Earth were for the benefit of all humans (John 1:1-18; 3:16-21; 5:17-47; 6:31-63; 8:12-30; 10; 12:25-50; Hebrews 1; 8; 11; 12; 1 Timothy 4:10; 1 John 1-5). He provided in detail the life needed to have a spiritual personal relationship with the Holy, Righteous, Spiritual, and Living God (Isaiah 56:3-8; 66:18-20, 23). Jesus made a promise to provide a Helper to make all things possible for our success (John 16:13; Philippians 4:12-14). If we only believe what He said on His departure from Earth (John 14-16; Acts 2; Romans 8; Hebrews 1), He taught many things for our benefit, showing us what steps would be needed to have a spiritual relationship with the Holy, Righteous, Spiritual, and Living God.

He provided the knowledge of the Spiritual Living God being a Spirit. Anytime we desire to have a relationship with Him, it must be a spiritual interaction. We must recognize Him as a Spirit (John 4:23-24), and we must access Him in the Spirit, through Jesus Christ, His Son (John 3:16-21; 1 Corinthians 2; 1 John 1-5). It must be a spiritual relationship (Romans 8; 1 Thessalonians 4:7-8); we need to accept the process found in Romans 5-7. We must acknowledge, there is a difference in the Spirit and the flesh (Romans 8; Galatians 5:16-26). We could only have this relationship when Jesus opens our hearts and minds, revealing the holiness of the Spiritual Living God by the guidance of the Holy Spirit (Matthew 13:13-17; Luke 24:44-47; Colossians 1:14-29; 1 John 3). We must accept the promises provided by the Spiritual Living God about the arrival of His only begotten Son, Jesus. If we accept the Gospel (John 3:16-21; 5:17-47;

UNTIL YOU CAN FEAR, HONOR, AND RESPECT...

Acts 10:42-43; 1 Timothy 1:8-11), the report Isaiah (Psalm 22; Isaiah 53; Romans 1:16-20; Ephesians 1:13; 1 Thessalonians 1:5-6; Romans 10:6-21) spoke about the birth, life, death, resurrection, and ascension of Jesus Christ, the Spiritual Living God's only begotten Son (John 1:1-34; 3; Galatians 1; Hebrews 1; 2:5-18), we could have the guidance of the Holy Spirit (John 14-16; Acts 2; Romans 8; 1 Corinthians 2). The Holy Spirit would provide wisdom, knowledge, and understanding regarding anything and everything we need to make the right decisions while living here on Earth (1 John 4-5).

Whenever the Spiritual Living God had to remind the Israelites of their journey in the wilderness, He provided in detail things that took place because He was there with them on this journey. He spoke about how He used Moses to lead them and without his leadership, they were not able to perceive things with their hearts. They would not hear or see things provided by Him, the Spiritual Living God, if they chose to forget Him (Deuteronomy 29). He met all their needs during this time, trying to reveal Himself to the Israelites through Moses with signs and miracles.

The Spiritual Living God also reminded them of their need to keep His inspired words in the covenant. If they chose obedience according to His will, they would prosper in all things. They could trust His promises He made to the generations before them. If they chose to be His people, He would always be their Spiritual Living God. We need to take the time and reflect on Deuteronomy 29:1-15. He reminds the people these promises are for them and those who choose a spiritual relationship with Him in future generations. We need to also reflect on verse 29:29; this

BECAUSE THE LORD IS YOUR SHEPHERD

Scripture teaches us to hold our peace regarding all things, especially spiritual things. The Spiritual Living God reveals only what He desires us to know, with the guidance of the Holy Spirit. Those who accept Jesus Christ as His only begotten Son, with the guidance provided by the Holy Spirit, actually have spiritual insight (Romans 8; 9:16-33; 1 Corinthians 2). Surely, we are intelligent enough to accept things revealed spiritually will not be comprehended by those living in the flesh (Psalm 14; 53; Romans 1:21-32; 1 Corinthians 1:18-31). He is the Spiritual Living God with total control of His world; we should be still and trust His promises made to His children (Psalms 46-50; Romans 8; Ephesians 4:14-32).

We are invited into the family of our Heavenly Father, the Spiritual Living God, who resides in heaven (Isaiah 56:3-8; 66:18-20, 23). We are the future generations because of our Lord and Savior, Jesus Christ (Romans 8:8-17; 2 Corinthians 3:2-6, 14-18). We have the ability to hear and see spiritual things (Romans 8:28-39); when Jesus ascended into heaven to reside at the right of our Heavenly Father (Hebrews 1), He provided the guidance of the Holy Spirit for the children of the Holy, Righteous, Spiritual, and Living God (Romans 10). We can choose to become the Spiritual Living God's children, in Jesus' name. Otherwise, we can live like the Israelites and never experience the guidance of the Holy Spirit provided by Jesus Christ (John 14-16; Acts 2; 1 Corinthians 2).

The guidance of the Holy Spirit is the only way we will be able to perceive with our hearts, hear with our ears, and see with our eyes spiritual things, accept the Gospel (Psalm 22; Isaiah 53; Romans 1:16-20; Ephesians 1:13; 1 Thessalonians 1:5-6; Hebrews 1), which is His Son's purpose for being here

UNTIL YOU CAN FEAR, HONOR, AND RESPECT...

on Earth, in detail, provided by inspiration from the Spiritual Living God about His only begotten Son, Jesus Christ (Romans 8:34; Hebrews 1). As children of the Spiritual Living God, we have a responsibility to take care of what belongs to Him. Our bodies are considered temples of the Spiritual Living God (1 Corinthians 3:16-23). With spiritual guidance, this is very attainable. The guidance of the Holy Spirit gives us the strength (John 16:13; Philippians 4:13) to accomplish all things according to the Spiritual Living God's plans and purposes for our lives, while living here on Earth.

Before we can receive wisdom from the Spiritual Living God in the name of Jesus, we must appear foolish to the world. Only through spiritual guidance can we receive wisdom from the Spiritual Living God and become wise (1 Corinthians 2). Remember, the Spiritual Living God knows the thoughts of the wise in the world; they are vain (1 Corinthians 3:16-20). We should always remember (Psalm 100; John 8:12-30; 10), these Scriptures will remind us of the awesome Spiritual Living God we serve here on Earth. We must be able to acknowledge that He actually made us in His image (Genesis 1:27-28; 5:2; Matthew 19:4-5). Whenever we choose to create humans in our likeness with advance technology, we are providing help for the Spiritual Living God, who has the ability to do all things according to His plans. David reminds us (Psalm 100:3), know ye that the Lord, He is the Spiritual Living God; it is He that made us and not we ourselves.

How Do We Know God Hears Us When We Pray?

According to the Scriptures, certain things were required of those who sincerely sought the Spiritual Living God of heaven. The Spiritual Living God required those inquiring of Him to be from the tribe of Levites, before the arrival of Jesus as His only begotten Son. They had to follow given procedures before coming into His holy presence. The details only reminded others of the holiness of the Spiritual Living God, who resides in heaven. Anyone choosing to overlook this procedure would suffer death. Aaron was from the tribe of the Levites. He had four sons; only two lived to remind the people of the Spiritual Living God's holiness (Numbers 3:1-13).

David, in his generation, was reminded of the Spiritual Living God's holiness also. He was bringing the Ark of God back to his city, when it rocked and almost tipped over. A young man, who was not from the family of the Levites, was trying to keep the Holy Ark of God from falling. I guess no one shared the requirements stated by the Spiritual Living God regarding only a certain tribe of people (Levites) interacted with Him because of His holiness. Uzzah touched the Holy Ark of God (carried things representing the Spiritual Living God) and lost his life on the spot (2 Samuel 6:1-11). David taught his son Solomon about the holiness of the

BECAUSE THE LORD IS YOUR SHEPHERD

Spiritual Living God. Solomon was crowned king after his father, David, but he knew how to come before the Holy, Righteous, and Spiritual Living God, who resides in heaven (2 Chronicles 6:12-42). The Spiritual Living God answered Solomon's prayer (2 Chronicles 7:1-3) by accepting the offering placed before Him. After reading these Scriptures, you will understand why we need Jesus as a Mediator (Romans 8; Hebrews 1) in this generation. Otherwise, we might not live to tell others about the Holy, Righteous, and Spiritual Living God we inquire about during prayer. David provided inspired words for future generations, reminding us about the Spiritual Living God and our prayer life.

- The Lord hears the righteous (Psalm 34).
- We can be rescued from our enemies (Psalm 35).
- The prayer of a penitent heart (Psalm 38).
- A prayer for self-understanding (Psalm 39).
- We need to always remember to praise the Spiritual Living God for answered prayer (Psalm 40).

Sometimes the children of the Spiritual Living God become discouraged, when they take their eyes off Jesus, in this generation. It appears those who choose to be disobedient are being blessed, without living according to His plans and purpose, here on Earth. David also provided inspired words about this situation. He really loves His children (Psalm 36); we need to consider the true state of the wicked (Psalm 37).

John 4:23-24 and 9:31 remind us in this generation that the Spiritual Living God is a Spirit. We need to read Psalm 51; Romans 8; and Ephesians 4:14-32 before we can

HOW DO WE KNOW GOD HEARS US WHEN WE PRAY?

communicate with our Heavenly Father, who resides in heaven, through His Son, Jesus Christ. The Lord's covenant with Solomon was written for future generations, also. We need to accept the holiness of the Spiritual Living God so we might hear from Him in the name of Jesus (John 9:31; 1 John 1-2). The inspired words provided by David in the Psalm help the children of the Spiritual Living God keep things in perspective, when we acknowledge Him. We need to be thankful for what He has already accomplished in our daily lives before petitioning Him for additional things (Psalms 141-143).

We have been asked to accomplish certain things so our prayer life would not be hindered in this generation (Galatians 5:16-26; James 5:12-20). If we refuse to follow these instructions, our prayers will not be heard. The Spiritual Living God has informed past and present generations, He refuses to interact with sinful people (those who intentionally sin without spiritual guidance) (Psalm 19:7-14; John 9:31; Hebrews 10; 1 John 1-2).

Past generations died on the spot, no questions asked, because of their disobedience. We have been provided with the Spiritual Living God's (John 4:24) Spirit (Jeremiah 31:31-35; Joel 2:28-32; 2 Corinthians 3; Hebrews 1; 8:10-12; 10:16-17). The generations after Jesus Christ's generation have been provided with a Light to access the spiritual connection (John 1:1-18; 8:12-59; 10; 14-16; 1 Peter 2). In order for us not to die on the spot like Aaron's sons, who chose to dishonor the Spiritual Living God, and still come before His presence, we need to accept the Gospel (Psalm 22; Isaiah 53; Romans 1:16-20; Ephesians 1:13; 1 Thessalonians 1:5-6; Hebrews 1) regarding His only begotten Son (John 3:16; 14-

BECAUSE THE LORD IS YOUR SHEPHERD

16; Acts 2; 1 John 1-5). We need to believe the Scriptures were provided by those inspired by the Spiritual Living God (John 5:39-47; 2 Timothy 3:15-17; 2 Peter 1:12-21).

We must also receive life in the Spirit in order to be acknowledged as the Spiritual Living God's children (Romans 8; Galatians 5:16-26; Ephesians 4:14-32; 1 Peter 2:9-10). This spiritual relationship allows those who are His children to receive the promises. He provided for His children (Romans 8; Ephesians 4:14-32; 5-6) according to their spiritual relationship (Ephesians 3:4-6; Hebrews 4), which can only be accomplished through His Son, who provided the Helper, the guidance of the Holy Spirit (John 14-16; Acts 2). Otherwise, the Spirit provided for each person created in the image of the Spiritual Living God (Jeremiah 31:31-35; Joel 2:28-32; 1 Corinthians 2; Ephesians 1:11-13; Hebrews 8; 1 John 4:12-14) remains dormant, as we live our lives in darkness, here on Earth. Jesus Christ is the Light (John 1:1-18; 8:12-30; 10; 2 Corinthians 6:14-18; 1 John 2:24-29) provided by the Spiritual Living God; without Him, we are totally without spiritual knowledge (1 Corinthians 2).

If the Spiritual Living God has decided He will not communicate with sinful people (John 9:31; Hebrews 10; John 1-2), we must give up sin in order to go into prayer with the Spiritual Living God. If we are the adulterous generation (Proverbs 30; Matthew 12:39-41; 2 Peter 2:14), look around, we can claim that generation. Our prayers will never get past the ceiling covering our head in this generation (1 Timothy 2:1-8; 1 Peter 3:7). The Spiritual Living God will always deliver His children from temptation (2 Peter 2:9) to keep their prayers from being hindered. As children of the Spiritual Living God (Romans 8), we can always look forward to our

HOW DO WE KNOW GOD HEARS US WHEN WE PRAY?

help, the guidance of the Holy Spirit, and our Mediator, Jesus Christ (Romans 8:34; Hebrews 1). The Holy Spirit speaks on our behalf when our hearts are too heavy to pray to our Heavenly Father, who resides in heaven (Romans 8:26-27; 1 John 5:13-15). As long as we choose a life of obedience with the guidance of the Holy Spirit, and can identify with Romans 8, there is no reason for your Heavenly Father not to hear you when you pray.

Those who are called by the Spiritual Living God need to answer the call. Many are experiencing things that could be avoided if someone could hear from heaven, so the Spiritual Living God can bless the land in this generation (2 Chronicles 7:14). We are instructed regarding the benefits of choosing a life of obedience, when the Spiritual Living God calls us into obedience. Those who desire to follow the commandments (Matthew 22:35-40; John 3:16-21; 1 John 1-5) provided according to the inspired words of the Spiritual Living God will have the guidance of the Holy Spirit (John 14-16; Acts 2; Ecclesiastes 8:5-13). We actually need spiritual guidance if we are going to take a stand for what is right according to the Spiritual Living God (Luke 12:1-12; John 14:26; 16:13; Philippians 4:4-9, 13, 19) in this generation. The spirit of deception is very aggressive in this generation. Without totally surrendering your life to the will and purpose of the Spiritual Living God, it will be easy for those identifying themselves as His children to begin to question what the Holy Spirit has revealed to strengthen our faith and belief in this generation (Proverbs 3:5-6; Matthew 6:25-33).

There is also Scripture reminding us of the consequences when we choose to be disobedient and the possible effects it can have on others and future generations (Proverbs 30; 2

BECAUSE THE LORD IS YOUR SHEPHERD

Peter 2:14). Anytime we decide to turn away from the Spiritual Living God and choose disobedience, the consequences (2 Chronicles 7:19-22) are reminders for future generations. We must have a mediator in this generation before we can interact with the Spiritual Living God. Jesus Christ is our intercessor, who provides the spiritual connection (John 14-16; Acts 2; Hebrews 1) in this generation. We cannot have a spiritual life (Romans 8) without accepting the Gospel (Psalm 22; Isaiah 53; Romans 1:16-20; Ephesians 1:13; 1 Thessalonians 1:5-6; Hebrews 1). The Gospel allows us to benefit from the promises made by the Spiritual Living God for His children. Nevertheless, when we choose life without the spiritual connection provided by His Son, we are not His children, and the things said about curses and devastation are experienced for being disobedient in this generation, also. The things experienced by others hopefully will steer the current generation in a different direction. Surely, we can learn from the mistakes of others, so we will not be living in vain. Whenever we choose to be obedient to the plans and purposes the Spiritual Living God has for our lives here on Earth, we are allowed to experience eternal gain up the road, as long as we follow His Son, Jesus Christ (1 John 5).

When our prayers are not being answered, we need to make sure there are no sins interfering, things you needed to ask forgiveness for in the past, which you refuse to release (Psalm 19:7-14; John 20:23). This is causing your prayer life to be hindered. We really need to bring everything to Jesus and leave it on the altar, to be free from any obstacles interfering with our prayer life.

Take the time and reflect on any and all situations the Holy Spirit brings to remembrance. Read Psalm 51 and cry

HOW DO WE KNOW GOD HEARS US WHEN WE PRAY?

in brokenness, asking for forgiveness for any disobedience, with a sincere heart in the name of Jesus.

Just think, what if Jesus would have been like the people in this generation? Remember, He was born with flesh and blood just like us, those who have the breath of life. He came into this world created in the image of the Spiritual Living God, just like us (Colossians 1:14-29; Hebrews 1).

He could have taken on the attitude of the humans like you and me, who choose to be disobedient more than being obedient to the Spiritual Living God. Otherwise, He could have decided to be like the angels who were kicked out of heaven. We really need to understand, it was pride that caused Satan, who was an angel, to be removed from heaven (2 Peter 2:4). Jesus has the power and authority to accomplish all things here on Earth (John 5:17-47). Nevertheless, He never forgot the purpose and plans for His life here on Earth. Satan even tried to recruit Him with promises of things to come (Matthew 4:1-17). Jesus Christ took a stand for righteousness regarding the plans and purposes of His Heavenly Father, who wanted to show the humans created in His image living here on Earth His love and compassion (Luke 24:44-47). Jesus experienced many things while living here on Earth. Anytime the humans wanted to take His life before time, His Heavenly Father hid Him from their natural eyesight. He actually chose not to become discouraged with all He observed taking place, even if He reacted sometimes raising the eyebrows of others. The Spirit His Heavenly Father provided gave Him the strength to endure all things--including things taking place in this generation; this is still His Heavenly Father's world. We create many things during this generation to turn the hearts

BECAUSE THE LORD IS YOUR SHEPHERD

of men away from His Heavenly Father. Nevertheless, we receive reminders in this generation about His displeasure, but He is still totally in control of His world (Psalms 46-50).

When the time came for Jesus to lay down His life, many did not fully understand all the things He said leading up to this fulfillment. The Spiritual Living God, who is His Heavenly Father, still provided a choice regarding His life, and He knew this for a fact. When He prayed in the Garden of Gethsemane (Matthew 26:36-46; Mark 14:32-42; Luke 22:39-46), "not My will but Thy will be done," Jesus was still living a life of obedience and performing miracles at His point of death. When Peter pulled his sword and cut the soldier's ear off, Jesus touched the ear, and it became whole again.

How many of us with the guidance of the Holy Spirit at the point of death can follow the footsteps of Jesus Christ, in this generation? The examples He set in His lifetime were for the benefit of the children (Romans 8; Ephesians 4:14-32) of the Spiritual Living God.

There is really no excuse for this generation to choose not to serve the Spiritual Living God, in the name of Jesus. Anytime we pray with a sincere heart, asking in faith, without wavering in doubt, but standing (Proverbs 3:5-6; Matthew 5:25-33) according to the Spiritual Living God's promises to His children, we will also be able to exemplify the life of Jesus Christ to others who observe our lives here on Earth in this generation.

It is possible you can have your spiritual breakthrough you have been waiting and praying for in the name of Jesus. Always remember, there are conditions for praying and receiving your answers from the Spiritual Living God (Matthew 7:7-11; 21:21-22; Mark 11:23-26; James 1:4-7; 1

HOW DO WE KNOW GOD HEARS US WHEN WE PRAY?

John 3:22). The Holy Spirit will provide the deliverance you have been waiting for. There will never be a reason for you to return to a battle, which belongs to the Lord (1 Samuel 17:47). Feel free to sing, "I am free. Praise the Lord, I am free. There are no more chains holding me."

You Inquire of the Spiritual Living God's Will, but You Do Not Like His Answer

There was a generation before this generation with a prophet named Jeremiah. The people asked him to inquire of God about His decision for their lives (Jeremiah 42-44). The Spiritual Living God told Jeremiah to tell the people not to go into Egypt. He already knew the troubles they would face. They had no idea what destruction awaited them, and they would sin against Him, the Spiritual Living God, with hardened hearts. They were afraid someone bigger than they, would cause them harm. They thought they would be protected in Egypt, but failed to realize the Spiritual Living God knew what they were going to face and was trying to redirect their fears. They found themselves worshiping idols and burning incense, serving other gods. They were totally connected to Egypt's form of worship (44:2-5).

The Spiritual Living God became angry and supplied them with consequences for their disobedience through Jeremiah (44:7-29). They ignored Jeremiah, telling him, "We will not listen" to your words from the Spiritual Living God (44:16). The Spiritual Living God told them to let the games begin (twenty-first century jargon) in these verses: 44:28-30. He allowed the people to observe His power, glory, and honor. Then, the people wanted to use "Woe is me, Lord," standing in the need of prayer (Jeremiah 45:3). Our current

BECAUSE THE LORD IS YOUR SHEPHERD

generation's (Psalms 120-121) life's woes are listed for this generation:

- Woe, I cannot put You before all things here on Earth.
- Woe, I cannot treat people the way I would like to be treated.
- Woe, I cannot accept Jesus Christ as Your only begotten Son.
- Woe, I cannot be enlightened by the guidance of the Holy Spirit.
- Woe, I cannot see the Light, because I am in darkness.
- Woe, I cannot stop lying when I know the truth.
- Woe, I cannot stop cursing like a sailor.
- Woe, I cannot stop desiring the same sexual gender for affection.
- Woe, I cannot stop entering the marriage bed without marriage.
- Woe, I cannot control my alcohol or drug intake.
- Woe, I cannot stop the desire to enter others' marriage beds.
- Woe, I cannot stop removing things that do not belong to me.
- Woe, I cannot stop eating, and I know I am full.
- Woe, I cannot keep money when I make above and beyond my need.
- Woe, I cannot retain this job when I know I was blessed to receive it.
- Woe, I cannot control those children of mine, who should be a blessing.

YOU INQUIRE OF THE SPIRITUAL LIVING GO'DS WILL...

Surely, we can learn from past generations' mistakes, if the Spiritual Living God has stated in His inspired words found in the Holy Bible, we should follow His instructions regarding all things pertaining to living an abundant life (Exodus 34:6-10; Isaiah 56; John 10; 1 Timothy 1:12-17; 1 Peter 1:3-25) with the guidance of the Holy Spirit. We must remember, the instructions are for His children (Romans 8; 1 Corinthians 2; 2 Corinthians 3:2-6, 14-18; Ephesians 1:13; 4:14-32). If you refuse to accept the Gospel of His only begotten Son (Psalm 22; Isaiah 53; John 1:1-34; 3:16-21; 4:23-24; 5:17-47; 6:44-65; 8:12-30; 10; 12:28-50; 14-16; Hebrews 1; 1 John 1-5), it will be impossible for you to claim the promises for His children. He reminded us before our birth, He would not change to satisfy each generation (Malachi 3:6; Colossians 1:14-19; Hebrews 13:8). Why do we need to suffer with hurt and pain, if someone has already experienced these situations in past or present generations (Genesis 18-19; Numbers 23-24; Isaiah 5-6; Ezekiel 24-28; 2 Timothy 2-3; Titus 1-3)? Why do we allow this world, with the guidance of the media, to influence our decisions to sin against the Holy, Righteous, and Spiritual Living God (Isaiah 26:3-4; Romans 1:21-32; 1 Corinthians 1:18-31)? They will not suffer your consequences for disobedience, but they can influence your decision making, which causes you much heartache and pain. ***Something is sincerely wrong with this picture. Do you see the division and corrupt morals provided by others without spiritual leadership, nevertheless?*** When it is, "Woe is me, Lord," standing in the need of prayer, they cannot help you during your personal struggles in life.

We should always look to the hills (Psalm 121) for our help, which comes from the Spiritual Living God, through His Son,

BECAUSE THE LORD IS YOUR SHEPHERD

Jesus Christ (Romans 8:34), who provides the guidance of the Holy Spirit (John 14-16; Acts 2), in this generation. This is the spiritual connection being made available in this generation so we can have a spiritual personal relationship with the Spiritual Living God, who resides in heaven. **As children of the Spiritual Living God, remember, you are never alone here on Earth.**

> **Psalm 121: "The Spiritual Living God's sustaining power."**
> **Psalm 141: "Prayer for help in trouble."**
> **Psalm 142: "Thou art my refuge."**
> **Psalm 143: "Teach me to do Thy will."**

When Your Wisdom Allows You to Look Foolish

Anytime we decide the Spiritual Living God, who is holy, righteous, and a Spirit, functions on the level of a mere human, we are in trouble (John 4:23-24; Romans 1:16-20; 8; 1 Corinthians 2; Ephesians 1:13-14; 4:14-32; 5-6; Hebrews 1; 8; 10). He will allow us enough rope to hang ourselves (Psalm 14; 53; Proverbs 30; Romans 1:21-32; 1 Corinthians 1:18-31). Your ignorance will cause you much heartache and pain (Romans 1:24-32); you will be lacking spiritual insight to problems regarding relationships with men and women. They are no longer pleased with the natural use of the opposite sexual gender, but they begin desiring the same sexual gender. No wonder we are experiencing the same problems with sin, they had in Sodom and Gomorrah during Abraham's generation (Romans 9; Jude 5-7). We are in the twenty-first century, and those bad seeds planted by past generations are coming up again, with this generation being so disobedient (Proverbs 30). How can one culture be so totally confused about the expectation of humans created in the Spiritual Living God's image (Genesis 1:26-28; 5:1-2)? Whenever we decide to ignore the only begotten Son of the Spiritual Living God (Romans 4-6), we are not allowed to have access to the guidance of the Holy Spirit (John 14-16). Therefore, we do not have the intelligence to acknowledge there is

BECAUSE THE LORD IS YOUR SHEPHERD

a difference in your natural and spiritual understanding (Romans 8; 1 Corinthians 1:17-3:23).

Those who thought the Spiritual Living God made a mistake when He created them need to understand, there is no failure in the Holy, Righteous, Spiritual, and Living God, who resides in heaven. Never underestimate His ability to allow us to fulfill our desires and lifestyles in this century, according to Romans 1:26-28. He knew before you were born the choices you would make and you would try to justify your actions. The problem with this ignorance is you are satisfied with your disobedience, according to the inspired words found in the Holy Bible. Misery loves company and usually can convince anyone not grounded in his or her faith to come on board (Colossians 1:3-29; 2 Peter 1:12-21). There is a need to protect our minds (Isaiah 26; Ephesians 6:10-20) in this generation; it is absolutely necessary (Isaiah 26:3-4). The media provide only a little acceptance of the Spiritual Living God's existence and total control in this generation (Psalms 46-50; Isaiah 45:22-23; 46:9). Once you observe and listen to something constantly, you become like a fish.

They draw you in hook, line, and sinker, until you are caught in their views without making your own decisions (Isaiah 47:10-15). The Spiritual Living God provided choices for those created in His image with possible consequences for making the wrong decisions. If the media are capable of overwhelming us with their views, totally confusing our original wisdom, knowledge, and understanding regarding spiritual things (Romans 8; Ephesians 4:14-32; 1 Corinthians 2; 1 Timothy 3:14-17), it will be obvious, we are not grounded in the Truth (John 4:24), according to the inspired words found

WHEN YOUR WISDOM ALLOWS YOU TO LOOK FOOLISH

in the Holy Bible (2 Peter 1:12-21). If you are enlightened by the Holy Spirit, provided by the only begotten Son, Jesus Christ, your observance of darkness will not impact the Truth as a child of the Spiritual Living God. Otherwise, anytime we observe, listen to, and read anything in this generation, the seeds of doubt will be planted in our minds regarding the Truth (Psalm 22; Isaiah 53; John 1:1-34; 3:16-21; 4:23-24; 14-16; Acts 2; Romans 8; 1 Corinthians 2; Ephesians 4:14-32; Philippians 4:6-9; Hebrews 1; 8). He warned us before our birth of the need to protect our minds and the consequences if you do not protect your mind (Romans 2:8-9).

The consequences will follow our decisions, but we are always given choices. The Spiritual Living God, who resides in heaven, is no respecter of persons (Romans 2:10-16). He requires each of us to live a life of obedience according to His inspired words found in the Holy Bible (Romans 1:16-20; 1 Corinthians 2). We are not capable of spiritual understanding without the guidance of the Holy Spirit (John 16:13; Romans 1:21-32; 1 Corinthians 1:18-31). Therefore, it is impossible to be (Philippians 4:6-9) right, fair, and honest when we prey on those who are weak (Romans 15:1-21; 1 Corinthians 3:1-3; 2 Corinthians 4; 15), there will be consequences. Just like we made the decision to choose a life of disobedience, they should be given a chance to make their own decisions (Romans 9-10). Anytime the Spiritual Living God decides to apply consequences to our lives for choosing to be disobedient, Jesus is the only One who can mediate on our behalf (Romans 8:34; Hebrews 1). No human can interfere with the Spiritual Living God's decision outside the covenant He has with His only begotten Son (Romans 8; Ephesians 4:14-32).

BECAUSE THE LORD IS YOUR SHEPHERD

Those who desire to know the covenant of the Spiritual Living God and His Son need to read these Scriptures: Psalm 22; Isaiah 53; Matthew 5:17-20; 6:25-33; John 1:1-34; 3:15-21; 4:23-24; 5:17-47; 6:31-65; 8:12-30; 10; 12:35-50; Hebrews 1; 1 John 1-5. Focus on the Gospel, which is the birth, life, death, resurrection, and ascension of the Spiritual Living God's Son, Jesus Christ (four Gospels: Matthew, Mark, Luke, and John). They each provide insight from the writer's perspective based on their inspiration. They try to help us visualize the relationships and their experiences with the Spiritual Living God's Son, Jesus Christ, the same way we would speak about someone we knew personally. We would provide insight based on our own experience with this person, then meditate on John 14:6-7 and Romans 1:16-20, pray in Jesus' name for the guidance of the Holy Spirit (John 14-16; Acts 2; Ephesians 1:13). Only by the guidance of the Holy Spirit will we receive wisdom, knowledge, and understanding in all things (1 Corinthians 2). Then and only then will Philippians 4:4-9, 13, and 19 become a true statement while living here on Earth (Proverbs 3:5-6; Matthew 6:25-33).

Why Should I Be Submerged for Baptism?

Anytime we desire to be like someone, we must follow in his or her footsteps. If someone lays a path for you to follow and provides guidance to keep down your stress level, without man-made medicinals, do you follow or lead in that situation? Depending on your answer, your level of spiritual maturity will be revealed. It really does take time to arrive at a certain level of spiritual maturity. Only by the guidance of the Holy Spirit are we allowed to have wisdom, knowledge, and understanding about all things in this world, especially spiritual things (John 14:15-31; Acts 2:38-40; 1 Corinthians 2). The promises found in the Holy Bible, which are the inspired words provided by the Spiritual Living God (Galatians 3), were written for His children (Romans 8; Ephesians 4:14-32; 5-6). We are only allowed to receive spiritual guidance by accepting the Gospel (Psalm 22; Isaiah 53; Romans 1:16-20; 9; Ephesians 1:13) of His only begotten Son, Jesus Christ (John 1:1-34; 3:16-21; 4:23-24; 5:17-47; 8:12-30; 10; Hebrews 1). He provides the Helper, the guidance of the Holy Spirit, so we can receive spiritual enlightenment about spiritual things (John 14-16; Acts 2; 1 Corinthians 2).

Otherwise, it is impossible to be just like Jesus Christ, following the steps He took here on Earth. Only by the guidance of the Holy Spirit will we be able to claim the Spiritual Living God as our Heavenly Father (Romans 8).

BECAUSE THE LORD IS YOUR SHEPHERD

This spiritual relationship with the Spiritual Living God (John 4:23-24) encourages you as a believer to seriously follow in the footsteps of Jesus Christ (John 1:1-34; 3:16-21; 4:23-24; 10). The Spiritual Living God sent John the Baptist as a forerunner for His only begotten Son. John was obedient to the purpose and plans for his life here on Earth (Isaiah 40:3; Malachi 4:5-6; John 1:1-34; 3:22-36). When he baptized the only begotten Son of the Spiritual Living God, he received confirmation, "This is My beloved Son." The Spirit of a dove also landed on Jesus when He descended from the water of baptism (Matthew 3:13-17; Mark 1:9-11; John 1:24-34). Peter reminded the people (Acts 2:38) in his generation after the ascension of Jesus into heaven to reside at the right hand of the Heavenly Father (Mark 16:19-20; Luke 24:50-53; Romans 8:34; Hebrews 1; 1 Peter 3:18-22). They should repent so they could be baptized like Jesus, as well as the sufferings and rewards for their faith. Phillip took the time to baptize men and women in his generations (Acts 8:5-40) who believed (John 1:1-34; 3:16-21; 4:23-24; 8:12-30; 10; 12:28-50; 14-16; Hebrews 1; 8; 1 John 1-5).

Therefore, if Jesus Christ was submerged, we should be willing to take the steps He took and receive a spiritual confirmation, just like Jesus.

If you have an opportunity to experience being submerged in water to be baptized, take it; the experience actually rejuvenates you. It is very different from anything else you have participated in here on Earth. The renewed feeling is almost like being freed from burdens; they are lifted, and you have a new lease on life. Maybe this is our confirmation from the Spiritual Living God, we are one of His children (Romans 8; Ephesians 4:14-32). As our Heavenly

WHY SHOULD I BE SUBMERGED FOR BAPTISM?

Father, He is reminding us, as adopted sons and daughters of the Spiritual Living God, He will take care of things from now until eternity if we trust Him (Proverbs 3:5-8; Matthew 6:25-33).

We really need to follow the examples set by Jesus Christ, His only begotten Son. He has provided the steps needed to please the Spiritual Living God (John 8:12-30). There is a difference in your Spirit if it is possible to experience being submerged in water (Acts 1:5; 2:38). Nevertheless, always remember, this is only an outward confirmation of your desire to follow the same steps Jesus took while living here on Earth. **This is not a requirement to experience eternal life (1 John 5).** We need to accept the facts found in Acts 2; Romans 5-7; Hebrews 10; 1 Peter 3:21-22; and 1 John 1-2, remembering, as long as we repent and ask for forgiveness for our sins, acknowledging, "You know, it was the blood of Jesus. One day when you were lost, He died upon the cross; you know it was the blood He shed for you!" regardless of the different **religions** available today in order to deceive others (Romans 14), a spiritual relationship with the Spiritual Living God sets you above all those other gods that exist in this day and time (Isaiah 56:3-8; 66:18-20, 23; 2 Corinthians 2:14-17; 1 John 4:1-6). If they disagreed with Paul in his generation after his Damascus road experience (Acts 9), why should the people listen in this generation (Hebrews 4)? We have more gods than past generations; ours even talk to interfere with the guidance of the Holy Spirit (John 10).

We have already been warned, everyone will be given an opportunity to accept the Gospel (Psalm 22; Isaiah 53; Romans 1:16-20; Ephesians 1:13; 1 Thessalonians 1:5-6;

BECAUSE THE LORD IS YOUR SHEPHERD

Hebrews 1), but many will harden their hearts (Hebrews 3:7-19) regarding the Truth (John 1:1-18; 3:16-21; 4:23-24; Romans 1:16-20; Hebrews 1). Everybody that has breath in his or her body and became a living soul (Genesis 2:7) has been provided with the Spiritual Living God's Spirit in this day and time (Jeremiah 31:33-34; Joel 2:28-32; Acts 2:17-21; 10:43; Romans 16:25-27; 1 John 4:12-14). The Spirit from the Spiritual Living God is dormant until we accept His only begotten Son, Jesus Christ, in this generation (John 14-16; Acts 2). We receive enlightenment from the guidance of the Holy Spirit if we choose to believe the Gospel. Nevertheless, the choice is ours to receive or reject the Light provided to bring us out of darkness in this generation (John 1:1-34; 3:16-21; 4:23-24; 5:17-47; 6:44-65; 8:12-30; 20:31). We really need to stop claiming the promises found in the Holy Bible. They are only for those who believe the Gospel (Psalm 22; Isaiah 53; John 1:1-18; Romans 1:16-20; Ephesians 1:13-14) and can be identified as children (Romans 8; Ephesians 4:14-32) of the Spiritual Living God in this generation, which means, without the acceptance of Jesus Christ as the Spiritual Living God's only begotten Son (John 3:16-21; 5:17-47; 14-16; Hebrews 1), you are experiencing the things said in the generations before Jesus Christ's (Hebrews 3) arrival in the flesh as a human without a sinful nature. We must keep reminding ourselves, the promises are for the children of the Spiritual Living God only (Hebrews 2:14-18).

The Galatians (chapter 3) were warned in their generation by Paul about being foolish (3:1-3), just like Paul tried to explain to the Galatians before you were born. The Spiritual Living God hardened Pharaoh's heart to reveal Himself to His people in Moses' generation. He warned

WHY SHOULD I BE SUBMERGED FOR BAPTISM?

the people against being disobedient and informed them of the consequences for choosing a life of disobedience (Deuteronomy 6:10-25).

We are experiencing a lot of weather turbulence in this generation, including fires, floods, and drought. Nevertheless, man is providing excuses for those who will listen to the world's explanation for things said before their birth. The Spiritual Living God said certain things would take place when we choose to ignore His existence. Do you think He can use the hardened hearts (Hebrews 3:7-19) of the people in this generation so we can observe His power, majesty, and glory in this day and time? We have currently experienced 800-plus fires originally started by lightning in one state (Ezekiel 20:45-49). Who do you think allows this devastation to take place and is responsible for lightning and thunder? Please do not say what the meteorologists teach you; before they were born, the Spiritual Living God communicated with Moses and others through thunder and lightning (Exodus 19:16; 20:18-21; Job 40:9; Psalm 77:17-20; 144:6; Jeremiah 10:10-13; Luke 17:24; John 12:28-30). Why should His level of communication stop in this generation? Because we have taken the time and used our minuet minds to elaborate our level of intelligence about the power of the Spiritual Living God (Romans 1:21-32; 1 Corinthians 1:18-31).

Whenever you decide to really surrender your life to the Spiritual Living God, your life experiences with Him are breathtaking. It is obvious, He is really displeased with some things currently taking place in His world.

Whenever He allows disasters to take place in this generation, you do not make excuses; remember to just reflect on the Spiritual

BECAUSE THE LORD IS YOUR SHEPHERD

Living God's promises for His children (Romans 8; Ephesians 4:14-32).

The majority of children usually understand their parents' actions because of their personal relationship with them as parents. Whenever we acknowledge the Spiritual Living God as our Heavenly Father and accept His Deity as a Spirit, we will find He only accepts His Truth (John 4:23-24). He reminds His children spiritually He is totally in control of His world we live in (Psalms 46-50). He actually provides spiritual understanding about things taking place around you, and why they are taking place (1 Corinthians 2). There is currently a lot of flooding taking place in this generation; some cities in the state of Iowa have been devastated by water. Just about any state in the path of these waters is experiencing a flood, as the waters are destined for the Mississippi River. I am speaking from my spiritual personal experience regarding knowing the Spiritual Living God, through His darling Son, Jesus Christ, with the guidance of the Holy Spirit (Ephesians 1:13). I am very thankful for the spiritual personal relationship and not the **religions** others speak about in this day and time.

We need to always remember, the Spiritual Living God has the power to start and stop any devastation we are experiencing in this generation. Whatever He decides to use to gain our attention is His choice, not ours. He created us in His image; we did not create Him (Genesis 1:27-28; 5:2; Matthew 19:4-5)! Sometimes this is the only way we learn to be still and observe the power of the Spiritual Living God (Psalms 46-50). Anyone can have a spiritual personal relationship because everyone created in His image (Genesis 1:27-28; 5:2; Matthew 19:4-5) has been provided

WHY SHOULD I BE SUBMERGED FOR BAPTISM?

with His Spirit (Jeremiah 31:31-35; Joel 2:28-32; Hebrews 1; 8). We just need access to be enlightened, which can only be provided by His only begotten Son, Jesus Christ (John 1:1-34; 3:16-21; 4:23-24; 14-16; Acts 2; Romans 1:16-20; 8; Ephesians 1:13-14; Hebrews 1; 1 John 1-5), with the guidance of the Holy Spirit. If you have surrendered your life to the Spiritual Living God through Jesus Christ, asking for forgiveness for any and all sins, known and unknown, accepting the Gospel as His inspired words of Truth (Psalm 19:7-14; Romans 10:9), remember, you can claim the promises found in the Holy Bible for His children (Isaiah 56:3-8) in order to experience an abundant life while we currently live here on Earth (John 10).

Otherwise, we really need to stop claiming things promised to others. The disciples were commanded to go out and baptize all nations in the name of the Heavenly Father, Son, and the Holy Ghost (Spirit). They were told to teach everyone, they would always have Jesus with them through the guidance of the Holy Spirit, until the end of time (Matthew 28:16-20; John 10:28-30). Everyone has been given the Spirit of the Spiritual Living God; only through His Son can we have access to the guidance of the Holy Spirit (Jeremiah 31:31-35; Joel 2:28-32; John 1:1-34; 3:16-21; 4:23-24; 1 Corinthians 2; Hebrews 1; 8). We need to follow the instructions (Acts 2) before our birth (2:38-44) or reject those instructions and create our own. Just remember the consequences (1 John 1-5). Life really can beat the life out of you without the guidance of the Holy Spirit. Devastation comes from choosing to ignore the Truth, according to the inspired words found in the Holy Bible (John 16:13; Romans 1:16-20; Philippians 4:4-9; Galatians 5:16-26; Ephesians 6:10-20).

BECAUSE THE LORD IS YOUR SHEPHERD

When Jesus returns, it really will not be about baptism, an outward action, but the ability to confess about the blood (Revelation 5:8-12). We are reminded (Isaiah 66:18-20, 23; Matthew 25:31-45), all nations will receive His judgment, regardless of their speech, as long as the Scripture is fulfilled (Matthew 24:14; Mark 13:10). Everybody that has breath, created in the image of the Spiritual Living God, will be able to experience eternal life (1 John 5:19-20) because they claim the blood of Jesus (Isaiah 56:3-8).

Sin Can Be White as Snow

The Spiritual Living God spoke in Isaiah (1:13-20) regarding those who chose to sin and tried to serve Him at the same time. He told them to make a decision, if they wanted Him to acknowledge them. They should remove evil so their prayers could be heard. He told the people their sins were scarlet, but they could be as white as snow.

When they refused to be obedient according to His inspired words, a sword would devour them. The choice of obedience allowed them to receive the blessings provided by the land. We are provided with spiritual guidance in this generation (Psalm 51; John 9:31; Romans 6; Hebrews 10). We have the guidance of the Holy Spirit, who provides wisdom, knowledge, and understanding in all things (John 14-16; Acts 2; 1 Corinthians 2; Ephesians 1:13, 17-18), if we have accepted Jesus Christ as the Spiritual Living God's beloved and only begotten Son (Psalm 22; Isaiah 53; John 1:1-34; Hebrews 1). Otherwise, there is the adversary, the devil, waiting to seek whom he can devour (Hebrews 1-2; 1 Peter 5:6-8; 1 John 3:8-10). The only way to have true fellowship with the Spiritual Living God is to accept His inspired words found in His Holy Bible (Hebrews 2:14-18; 1 John 1:5-2:6).

Why do you think, "it would be easier for a camel to go through the eye of a needle (Luke 18:18-30) than a rich person to enter into the kingdom of the Spiritual Living God"?

BECAUSE THE LORD IS YOUR SHEPHERD

Anytime we think we are capable of providing all things, our hearts will be hardened (Hebrews 3:7-19) regarding spiritual things (Psalm 14; 53; Romans 1:21-32; 1 Corinthians 1:18-31). As long as we can rely on ourselves, there is never a need to rely on someone else (John 10; Hebrews 3:7-11). The Holy Bible provides spiritual insight regarding having a child's understanding to enter the Spiritual Living God's kingdom. Children always believe someone more powerful and bigger than themselves can accomplish much more than they can (Luke 18:15-17). Only through Jesus Christ can we have the guidance of the Holy Spirit to communicate with the Holy, Righteous, and Spiritual Living God (Luke 19:1-9), who is a Spirit (John 4:23-24).

He already knows what you are experiencing here on Earth. The question is, Do you need Him, or can you handle things without Him? There was a song written before this generation that stated, "I need thee every hour, Lord, I need thee." Do you think they had a reason for petitioning the Spiritual Living God of their need for Him?

If the Spiritual Living God allowed Judah and Jerusalem to experience Babylon, there was a need to reach His people. The people were so busy listening to false prophets and others without spiritual guidance (Jeremiah 27), they forgot about the Spiritual Living God.

Nevertheless, the Spiritual Living God had to bring them to a halt, allowing them to experience suffering to get their attention (Jeremiah 28-30). He told Jeremiah to encourage them regarding their return from bondage one day. The trials they would experience would cause their hearts to turn back to Him (Jeremiah 29:10-32). If they would sincerely seek Him and desire His plans for their lives here on Earth,

SIN CAN BE WHITE AS SNOW

He would provide the guidance needed for bringing them back unto Him from other nations (Jeremiah 31; Joel 2:28-32). We should observe Israel's errors in life, which caused their captivity and suffering. Realizing we need to change our ways in this generation so we do not experience unnecessary hardship, so we can see the One who died on Calvary's cross in order for us to be set free (John 8:32-47; Romans 6:14-23; 1 Corinthians 7:22; Galatians 5:1; 1 Peter 2:15-17), Jesus is the name we need to call on. He has risen and now resides at the right hand of the Heavenly Father (Romans 8; Hebrews 1). We actually have someone in this generation interceding for those who can be identified as the children of the Spiritual Living God. He promised them a Helper (John 14-16; Acts 2; 1 Corinthians 2), the guidance of the Holy Spirit, in time of need. Only by faith can we please the Spiritual Living God (2 Corinthians 4; Hebrews 8-11) in the name of Jesus. We must remember, Jesus has paid it all with His blood shed on Calvary's cross. A spiritual relationship with the Heavenly Father, Son, and the guidance of the Holy Spirit keeps us mindful of all sins being paid in full. Now, we are allowed to be identified as His children (Romans 8; Ephesians 4:14-32), to claim the blood used to wash our sins white as snow (Romans 3-5; Ephesians 1-2; Hebrews 9-10; 1 Peter 1:13-25; 1 John 1-5).

SABBATH

What if the Spiritual Living God took six days and gave us one day to accomplish the things we desire in life? Remember the "Sabbath" was made for man and not man for the Sabbath (Mark 2:23-28). You probably never thought about this situation, right? It is okay; we really do take a lot of things for granted regarding the Spiritual Living God. When it comes to really getting to know Him spiritually, we will be totally amazed at the number of things we actually do outside His will, and He continually spares our lives here on Earth. The Holy, Righteous, Spiritual, and Living God, who resides in heaven, decided before we were born to love us and have compassion on everyone created in His image (Genesis 1:26-28; 2:7; Luke 24:44-47).

He has already provided instructions for those of us (John 1:1-18; 3:16-21; 4:23-24; 5:17-47; 6:44-65; 10; 14-16) who desire to have a spiritual personal relationship with Him, as our Heavenly Father. He helps us identify the Truth, by accepting His only begotten Son, Jesus Christ (Hebrews 1), so we might have access to the guidance of the Holy Spirit (Romans 8; 1 Corinthians 2; Galatians 3-6; Ephesians 4:14-32; 5-6). Otherwise, we would not be able to comprehend spiritual things in the flesh (Psalm 53; Romans 1:21-32; 1 Corinthians 1:18-31). He is a Spirit and only deals with Spirit and Truth (John 4:23-24) as the Spiritual Living God.

BECAUSE THE LORD IS YOUR SHEPHERD

Isaiah (chapter 48) had to remind Israel they had become confused, and he rebuked them for their unfaithfulness. The Spiritual Living God reminds them of things that would take place before they participated in them regardless of their actions; He is still the Spiritual Living God. We should observe their mistakes and learn from their disobedience in this generation. The day we learn from past generations' mistakes regarding keeping the Sabbath holy, for the Holy, Righteous, and Spiritual Living God (Job 22:26-27; Isaiah 56:3-8; 58:13-14; Jeremiah 17:19-27), this will be the day we gain great spiritual insight about the blessings available to us for our obedience to the Spiritual Living God's holy inspired words found in the Holy Bible.

If the Spiritual Living God commanded past generations to remember the Sabbath and keep it holy, starting with Moses' generations (Exodus 16:26-31; 20:8-26; 23:12-13; 32:12-17; 35:1-3; Leviticus 19:2-4; 23:3), therefore, never providing inspired words instructing future generations the day of Sabbath was not needed (Isaiah 56:2-7), who told this generation, we were permitted to cease in having a day of total worship and praise of the Spiritual Living God? Oh! That was then; this is now, we have been reminded on many occasions of ignorance being bliss (Psalm 14; 53; Romans 1:21-32; 1 Corinthians 1:18-31). There is Scripture that allows works of mercy to be performed (Matthew 12:12; Luke 6; 13:11-17). The Scripture states pray Jesus' return is not on the Sabbath (Matthew 24:20). Why do you think this is not a good day for His return? The Spiritual Living God (Job 23:8-17; Psalm 121) never slumbers or sleeps. He already knows He will find many who are not acknowledging His day of praise and worship in this generation. We will not have a legitimate excuse for choosing to be disobedient on

SABBATH

this one day. We must remember this is a commandment required of His children (Romans 8; Ephesians 4:14-32), to always observe in all generations.

Growing up in Texas had its advantages before the 1970s regarding Sunday being the Sabbath. Some people like to call Texans slow, but slow is a good thing when we are allowed to think before we act. I am speaking of Sunday being the Sabbath, but any day you decide is the first day of the week for your culture is considered your Sabbath. The only problem with us picking our own Sabbath is the day might be different from Jesus' day of Sabbath (John 20:19-23). He recognizes the Sabbath as a possible day of His return (Matthew 24:20). If you are not disciplined, it helps to stop when the majority of people decide to stop, pray, and worship. We can sincerely stay focused on being obedient to the Spiritual Living God, without interference from things that can easily distract us spiritually (Proverbs 3:5-8; Matthew 6:25-33).

You did not have a lot of distractions on Sunday after returning home from Sunday worship before the twentieth century in Texas. Most families spent time together and had downtime. They actually found time to relax and do absolutely nothing but be still (Psalms 46-50). We did not have the distractions of malls and superstores to focus on during these times (Jeremiah 10-11; 17:21-22). We are currently breaking two Commandments when we love our children more than the Heavenly Father, Son, and the guidance of the Holy Spirit, and refuse to observe a day of worship in this generation of the twenty-first century (Leviticus 19:2-4; Matthew 22:34-40). If something was needed, we retrieved it before Sunday, or we waited until Monday.

269

BECAUSE THE LORD IS YOUR SHEPHERD

How did this generation manage to become so distracted with needs and wants, never having the patience to wait until after the Sabbath (Monday)? Probably, greed is the culprit, along with the desire to succeed in our desired professional careers.

We only slow down in America halfway on Sunday in some states, which is considered the Sabbath for most. Other states do not acknowledge a Sabbath day at all; each day is like the previous, and we wonder why this generation has more burdens than past generations. Never forget, disobedience always has consequences. Even if you do not believe in the Gospel (Psalm 22; Isaiah 53; John 1:1-34; 3:16-21; 4:23-24; 5:17-47; 10; 14-16; Romans 1:16-20), they will still be experienced by you (Hebrews 1; 8). Always remember, we are blessed in each generation because of our obedience to the Holy, Righteous, and Spiritual Living God. Jesus' life here on Earth provided a way for everything to be totally taken care of; we do not have a legitimate excuse for not serving the Spiritual Living God in this generation (Hebrews 2).

Hopefully, this generation will consider the Sabbath a day of rest from worldly adventures, focusing on spiritual things (Isaiah 56:3-8; Philippians 1:3; 2:1-18; 3; 4:6-9), according to Nehemiah 10:31; 13:15-22, he had to remind his generation the sale of wares would not take place on the Sabbath.

Just because the Spiritual Living God has compassion on those who can be identified as His children (Romans 8; Ephesians 4:14-32), loving us in the name of Jesus, it is not a good reason to take advantage of the situation. If Jesus could find time to acknowledge His Heavenly Father once a week without unnecessary interruptions, by worshiping

SABBATH

the Holy, Righteous, Spiritual, and Living God, His Heavenly Father (Mark 6:2), how did we become so obsessed with other things and steal this day? He commanded His children in past and present generations to remember the Sabbath and keep it Holy (Exodus 20:8-11).

Anytime a generation decides its heirs do not need to worship, honor, and respect the Spiritual Living God in this manner, we are setting them up to experience a life of frustrations and defeat. Anytime we refuse to teach the future generations to regard a day of Sabbath, for the Holy, Righteous, and Spiritual Living God (John 20:19), in this generation, we are providing the future generations with a disservice of things to come for their disobedience, including their future generations (Isaiah 30:8-14; 56:3-8). Remember, the Spiritual Living God only asked for one day to reflect on His holiness, righteousness, and the fact that He is a Spirit (John 4:23-24; 9-10), which means access to Him requires life in the Spirit (Romans 8), which can only be obtained by having a relationship with someone spiritually, provided by the Spiritual Living God, His only begotten Son, Jesus (John 1:1-34; 3:16-21; 5:17-47; 6:44-65; 14-16; Acts 3:20-26; Hebrews 1; 1 John 1-5). The Spirit communicates with the Spirit, and the flesh communicates with the flesh (Romans 8; 1 Corinthians 2; Galatians 5:16-26; Ephesians 1:13; 6:10-20).

Do not be deceived with evil spirits, thinking you are in (1 John 4:1-6; Acts 19:11-19) communication with the Holy Spirit. Jesus came so we might have access to the Holy, Righteous, Spiritual and Living God (John 14-16; Acts 2). If we do not have the guidance of the Holy Spirit provided by Jesus, we are denied access to the Holy, Righteous, Spiritual, and Living God, who resides in heaven (John 6:62-69).

BECAUSE THE LORD IS YOUR SHEPHERD

Remember, the choice is ours to receive or reject that which has been freely given for our benefit (2 Thessalonians 2:1-12). The Spiritual Living God inspired others before our birth to write about past and present situations, instructing future generations to learn from past generations' mistakes (Romans 1:16-20; 15:3-6; 1 Corinthians 10:1-13; 2 Timothy 3:15-17; 1 Peter 1:13-25; 2 Peter 1:12-21). If we are not teaching things taught to generations before our generation, our children are experiencing great heartache and pain in their generations for never receiving the enlightenment of their Spirit and the Truth, according to the Gospel (Psalm 22; Isaiah 53; John 1:1-18; 3:16-21; 4:23-24; 5:17-47; 6:44-65; 8:12-30; 10; 12:27-50; 14-16; Romans 1:16-20; 1 Corinthians 2; Galatians 3; Ephesians 1:13-14; Hebrews 1; 8; 1 John 1-5). This is why they choose to take their parents' lives in this day and time (Proverbs 30). Those other spirits take up residence in their minds and become successful (1 John 4:1-6), because the parents fail to teach them and live according to the inspired words of the Spiritual Living God, in this generation (Proverbs 13:24; 19:18; 22:15; 23:11-16; 30:11-17; Matthew 15:4-9; Ephesians 6:1-4). We must remember, wisdom, knowledge, and understanding about fearing, honoring, and respecting the Spiritual Living God comes from Him (Leviticus 19:2-4; Ecclesiastes 12:9-14; Acts 5:26-32; 1 Corinthians 2), not textbooks written by men in their generation (Isaiah 40:6-8; Hebrews 13:8; 1 Peter 1:13-25).

The Spiritual Living God Is Still in the Blessing Business

He made promises to the Israelites during their generations. We are the Spiritual Living God's children in this generation. Providing we have taken the time to accept His darling Son, Jesus Christ, as our Lord and Savior (John 1:1-18; 3:16-21; 4:22-25; 5:17-47; 6:44-65; Hebrews 1), we have access to the Holy, Spiritual Living God with the guidance of the Holy Spirit, provided in Jesus' name (John 14-16; Acts 2; Romans 8; 1 Corinthians 2).

The Spiritual Living God promised the Israelites, if they would choose to listen and follow the commandments He provided--the most important commandment was to love and serve Him, with all their heart and soul (Deuteronomy 11:12-25)--they could look forward to His blessings. He instructs each generation to teach the next generation (Genesis 18:19-21; Deuteronomy 4:10; 11:19-21). He also informs them of the disadvantage of choosing disobedience. The Spiritual Living God presents options for the people (11:26-32). Their blessing will flow for choosing to be obedient and follow His plans for their lives. We have been given promises (Jeremiah 31:31-35; Joel 2:28-32) in our generation of His expectation for those whom He calls His children (John 1:1-18; 3; 4:23-24; 10; 14-16; Romans 1:16-20; 8-10; 1 Corinthians 2; Ephesians 1:3-23; 4:14-32; 6:1-3; Philippians 4:6-9, 13, 19; Hebrews 1; 8; 1 John 1-5). Consequences are provided

BECAUSE THE LORD IS YOUR SHEPHERD

for choosing our own plans in this generation. The Spiritual Living God already had His plans and purpose for our lives, according to His inspired words, before our birth (Isaiah 49:1-6). He has a commandment for those who belong to Him (John 5:17-47; 6:31-65). We should reflect on Psalm 32, realizing David spoke of the blessedness of forgiveness.

Jesus has come for this generation to receive the promises spoken during Moses' generations (Acts 26:6-7; Romans 15:7-13; 1 Corinthians 6:9-7:1; Titus 1:2; 2:11-15). Jesus is the key for us to have a spiritual personal relationship with a Holy, Spiritual Living God and still live to tell others (Matthew 3:13-17) in this generation. Jesus' baptism was the confirmation from the Spiritual Living God regarding His Deity. Anytime we accept Jesus' birth, life, death, resurrection, ascension, and provision of the Holy Spirit (John 1:1-18; 3:16; 4:24; 14-16; Acts 2; 1 Corinthians 2; Hebrews 1), we can also keep the Spiritual Living God's commandments to love Him with all our heart and soul, and love our neighbors as we love ourselves (Matthew 22:37-40).

This is the only way we will be in a position to receive the blessings promised by the Holy, Spiritual Living God. The Holy Spirit provided by Jesus enlightens us to receive wisdom, knowledge, and understanding in all things (John 6:44-65; 14-16; Acts 2; Romans 1:16-20; 8; 1 Corinthians 2; 1 John 1-5). Those who choose life without the guidance of the Holy Spirit, depending upon their human knowledge, which is very limited, you do not realize your deficiency until you encounter a child (Romans 8; Ephesians 4:14-32) of the Spiritual Living God who exemplifies Jesus Christ in his or her daily walk (Galatians 5:16-26; Ephesians 1:13-14; 6:10-20), with the guidance of the Holy Spirit.

THE SPIRITUAL LIVING GOD IS STILL IN THE BLESSING BUSINESS

We read about how Jesus sat in the Temple among doctors and highly educated men (Luke 2:46-52). They were astonished at the questions and answers the young child presented to them. Those who are educated in this century who think higher of themselves than they ought to, Job (38; Romans 12:3-8) has provided a message from the Spiritual Living God! "Whenever the 'I' in pride or any sin leads, and you follow, there will be consequences for your disobedience." Just like those in Jesus' generation, when He was a youth, they thought their knowledge was the highest level of intelligence until they encountered the Spiritual Living God as a man (God the Son) with flesh and blood (Isaiah 40:5; John 1:1-18; Galatians 4:4; Philippians 2:5-10; Colossians 1:14-22; 1 Timothy 2:5; Hebrews 1). The Holy Spirit will always be more intelligent than human understanding (John 14-16; 1 Corinthians 2). We are not in a position to know this without the guidance of the Holy Spirit (Psalm 14; 53; Romans 1:21-32; 1 Corinthians 1:18-31). Peter tried to help Simon (Acts 8:9-24) understand these words. He observed the Holy Spirit's working through Peter to glorify the Spiritual Living God, in the name of Jesus, realizing the difference in spiritual power and his power.

He wanted to pay for this power, provided by the guidance of the Holy Spirit; he observed things taking place through them (Acts 8:18-24). The warnings are for those who do not have the guidance of the Holy Spirit (Romans 8:4-17). A carnal mind hinders spiritual growth (1 Corinthians 3). "Jesus I know, Paul I know, who are you?" (Acts 19:11-19). Always remember to test the spirits by the Spirit (1 John 4:1-6). The Spiritual Living God warned the Israelites in their generation not to change His inspired words (Deuteronomy

BECAUSE THE LORD IS YOUR SHEPHERD

12:32). Shall we do the honors in this generation (Isaiah 40:6-8; Malachi 3:6; Hebrews 13:8; 1 Peter 1:13-25; 2 Peter 1:12-21) because we don't understand His holiness as the Heavenly Father, Son, and Holy Spirit? Heaven forbid, this should take place, and He becomes angry. Remember what He said about our intelligence in this generation (Psalm 53; Romans 1:21-32; 1 Corinthians 1:18-31). Some of us actually give man credit for natural disasters in this generation of the twenty-first century (Jeremiah 32:17-27). The only credit man shall take is receiving consequences for choosing to sin, over the guidance of the Holy Spirit (1 John 1-2). Wisdom is a gift (1 Corinthians 2) from the Spiritual Living God for those who can be identified as His children (Romans 8; Ephesians 4:14-32).

Sometimes we have a desire to be there for those who choose not to have a personal spiritual relationship with the Heavenly Father, Son, and the guidance of the Holy Spirit (2 Corinthians 6:14-18). The Israelites were warned in their generation of the consequences (Deuteronomy 13) for choosing to make decisions without the Spiritual Living God's leading. We are all given the same options (Jeremiah 31:31-35; Joel 2:28-32; John 3:16; 4:24; 6:44-65; 14-16; Acts 2; 1 Corinthians 2; Romans 1:16-20; Ephesians 1:13-14; Hebrews 1; 8; 1 John 1-5) when it comes to having a spiritual relationship with the Holy, Spiritual Living God. It is possible the Spiritual Living God has guided some, but we still have a choice to follow or ignore His call into obedience (Romans 8:28-39).

For those who feel they were never called into obedience, we should observe the life of those who choose to answer their call from the Spiritual Living God, if there is a

THE SPIRITUAL LIVING GOD IS STILL IN THE BLESSING BUSINESS

Light, where they appear different from others in this world (John 1:1-18; 3:16-21; 4:23-24; 5:17-47; 8:12-30; 10; Romans 8; 1 Corinthians 2; Hebrews 1; 1 John 1-5). We should focus and pray for the Spiritual Living God to grant us a spiritual relationship with Him, in the name of Jesus (John 6:44-65; 14-16).

We all have the option (Jeremiah 31:31-34; Joel 2:28-32; 1 Corinthians 2; Hebrews 1; 8) to make a decision, providing the Spiritual Living God has given us our right mind. Others who are here, not in their right mind, according to the Spiritual Living God, He takes care of those who belong to Him.

The Spiritual Living God needs His children who have a spiritual relationship with Him to be a Light in this dark World (John 1:1-18; 3:16-21; 5:17-47; 8:12-30; 12:28-50, 17; Romans 8; Ephesians 4:14-32; 5:1-21; Hebrews 1; 8).

Whenever we become confused about the Spiritual Living God's will, and the world's desires for our lives here on Earth (Proverbs 3:5-6; Matthew 6:25-33; Luke 12:48), we need to understand the only problem is those who choose to follow His inspired words in judgment; we must be judged accordingly, by the Spiritual Living God. In other words, those called into obedience must give up all things displeasing to the Spiritual Living God, here on Earth (1 Corinthians 9:10-27; 2 Corinthians 7:1; 1 Peter 1:13-25; 2:9-17). He will not accept our excuses for sin, when a way of escape has been provided for His children (1 Corinthians 10:5-22; 2 Peter 1:12-21; 2:9).

We will also be judged by the Spiritual Living God according to the judgment of others (Matthew 7:1-6). In Ezra's generation (7:11-26), the king commissioned him to follow the words given

BECAUSE THE LORD IS YOUR SHEPHERD

in Moses' generation according to the Spiritual Living God's Holy provision. The king also informed Ezra to move leaders into positions, to judge the people with knowledge regarding the Spiritual Living God's laws. Those who are without knowledge shall be taught the words of the Spiritual Living God, who resides in heaven. We are reminded in this generation, those who accept Jesus as the Spiritual Living God's Son will receive the guidance of the Holy Spirit (John 14-16; Acts 2; 1 Corinthians 2; Hebrews 1; 10:16). We will have the wisdom, knowledge, and understanding needed to judge others according to the Spiritual Living God's Holy inspired words.

This is why it is necessary to think twice before you sit in judgment of others here on Earth, in this generation. You must remember, the Spiritual Living God will judge you, after you judge others. He told them to judge justly to make sure they do not become a respecter of persons in Deuteronomy (16:18-22). Do not receive gifts because your eyes will become blinded of wisdom, and you pervert the words of righteousness. Anything received shall be from Him, the Spiritual Living God (Romans 2). We should remember not to become gods in the eyes of others (Colossians 2:6-9). He is still the one and only Holy, Spiritual Living God in this generation (Deuteronomy 6:1-9; 11:1-25; Philippians 2:2-11; Colossians 1:14-19, 26-28; Hebrews 1).

Ezra reminded the people (8:22), the hands of the Spiritual Living God are upon all who desire to do good, but His power and wrath are against all who choose to forsake Him. There is no need to debate inspired words found in the Holy Bible as children (Romans 8; Ephesians 4:14-32) of the Spiritual Living God (John 6:44-65; 1 Corinthians 2; 2 Timothy 2:14-26). He decides whom He will enlighten

THE SPIRITUAL LIVING GOD IS STILL IN THE BLESSING BUSINESS

regarding His inspired words, found in the Holy Bible. We have a choice to humble ourselves or harden our hearts (Hebrews 3:7-11) regarding spiritual things. We all have the Spirit of the Spiritual Living God within us (Jeremiah 31:31-35; Joel 2:28-32; 1 John 4:12-14; Hebrews 1; 8; Ephesians 1:13). We can be enlightened, or we can suppress the Spirit with darkness (Ephesians 1:15-2; 4:29-31; 6:10-20; 1 Thessalonians 5:19). Titus reminded those in his generation to avoid foolish questions (Titus 3:9-11); we like to quote in this generation, "No question is foolish." Just remember the Scriptures before communicating, we need to test the spirits by the Spirit (Romans 1:21-32; 1 Corinthians 1:18-31; 1 John 4:1-6). We have been given a choice by the Holy, Righteous, and Spiritual Living God, who desires to be our Heavenly Father by accepting His Son, Jesus Christ, with the guidance of the Holy Spirit (John 3:16; 4:24; 10; 14-16; Acts 2; 1 Corinthians 2; Romans 8; Hebrews 1; 8; 1 John 1-5).

The Scripture provides insight regarding the flesh and Spirit being as different as night and day (John 1:1-18; 3; 1 Corinthians 15:35-58; Galatians 5:16-26; 1 John 5). We are born of a woman, but before we can enter this world, there is usually a flow of water surrounding the baby that must burst forth first, with blood following thereafter. Those with common knowledge about the birth of a baby usually ask, "Has your water broken?" Whenever they observe a clear fluid from a mother looking forward to the birth of a child, I accept this water as the water spoken in John (3:3-5; 1 John 5:6). Humans are made in the image of the Spiritual Living God (Genesis 1:27; 5:2; Matthew 19:4-5; Hebrews 1; 1 John 5:6-12). Our bodies consist of a great amount of water for existence here on Earth. Anytime we observe a decaying human body, it is amazing how, without the fluids, you observe nothing but skin and bones. The generations before this generation did not have a lot of man-devised technology (Ecclesiastes 7:29). This made things more easily received and not questioned (Titus 3:9-11). The brain surgeon is not capable of working on any human being's brain unless Jesus provides healing hands (Acts 5:14-16; 19:11-12). Nevertheless, we will sing praises to man and sometimes overlook it was because of the Spiritual Living God's grace and mercy (John 12:43). You have made it through any brain surgery; statistics will always point to the truth. Those who lived without complications and those who never made it back among the land of the living are testimonies about miracles of the Spiritual Living God, in the name of Jesus.

As long as we pray and trust every inspired word in the Holy Bible is the Truth, provided by the Spiritual Living God (John 5:39-47), we will be taking our first steps to trust and acknowledge the Spiritual Living God is holy, righteous, and a Spirit (John 4:23-24).

We are humans and exist within flesh and blood (1 Corinthians 15:45-50; James 2:26); the Spiritual Living God provided a part of Himself for all humans (Jeremiah 31:31-35; Joel 2:28-32; 1 Corinthians 2; Hebrews 1; 8). Providing He created them according to Genesis (1:27; 2:7), He breathed the breath of life, and man became a living soul.

We are comprised of Spirit, soul, and body (1 Thessalonians 5:22-24). Our body, which is used to house our Spirit and soul, returns to dust at the point of death (Job 19:25-27; Ecclesiastes 3:20-21; 1 Corinthians 12:12-31). The Spirit and soul (Genesis 35:18; 1 Samuel 30:12b; Ecclesiastes 12:7; Ezekiel 18:4) go

THE SPIRITUAL LIVING GOD IS STILL IN THE BLESSING BUSINESS

back to the Spiritual Living God at the point of death. The Spirit (Jeremiah 31:31-35; Joel 2:28-32; 1 John 4:12-14) lies dormant until Jesus Christ, the Son of the Spiritual Living God, revives your Spirit within you. Some of us never receive the guidance of the Holy Spirit (John 14-16; Romans 8; 1 Corinthians 2). Anytime we choose not to believe there is a difference in Spirit and flesh (John 1:1-18; 3:6-21; 4:23-24; Romans 8; 1 Corinthians 15:35-58; Galatians 5:16-26; Ephesians 4:14-32; Hebrews 1; James 2:26), we are living in darkness without experiencing the Light.

There should never be any confusion about those not being capable of understanding spiritual things (Psalm 53; Romans 1:21-32; 1 Corinthians 1:18-31). This Scripture should provide enough insight for those guided according to the Holy Spirit (1 Corinthians 2). They understand, you do not debate spiritual things with people living in the flesh (Galatians 5:15-26; Ephesians 6:10-20; Titus 3:9-11). The Holy Spirit is powerful enough to enlighten anyone who accepts the Heavenly Father and Son (John 1:1-18; 3:16-21; 6:44-65; 14-16; Hebrews 1; 8:10-13), in this generation. Some of us are so educated with our PHDs (people have dementia), we are forgetful (Deuteronomy 8:11-20). These Scriptures were inspired and written before our birth for the benefit of future generations (2 Peter 1:12-21). It will be obvious we are spiritually ignorant (Psalm 53; Romans 1:21-32; 1 Corinthians 1:18-31) anytime we challenge the inspired words of the Spiritual Living God. We become totally confused about the Holy Spirit's providing wisdom, knowledge, and understanding in all things (John 14-16; Acts 2; 1 Corinthians 2). This was taking place before we were born, you think? The differences between each generation are, the more we can use our limited intelligence to figure out things, the more we harden our hearts regarding

BECAUSE THE LORD IS YOUR SHEPHERD

spiritual things (Hebrews 3:7-11), becoming totally delusional, choosing to refuse things we cannot comprehend (Psalm 14; 53; Romans 1:21-32; 1 Corinthians 1:18-31).

Be encouraged, there is not a battle in this world that is too big for the Spiritual Living God. Nevertheless, He requires your obedience before He provides the victory. When Solomon's son Rehoboam chose to follow the wisdom of his generation, overlooking the experience and wisdom of past generations (2 Chronicles 10), he experienced the loss of ten of the twelve tribes of Israel. The Spiritual Living God remembered His relationship with David, Rehoboam's grandfather. He decided to allow Rehoboam to lead Judah and Benjamin. The other tribes eventually rebelled against the house of David. Due to the wisdom provided by Rehoboam in his generation, Rehoboam wanted to fight the other tribes for their rebellion, but was warned by the Spiritual Living God not to go against Jeroboam (2 Chronicles 11:1-17).

Rehoboam eventually realized his mistake when he listened to the current generation and turned his heart back to the Spiritual Living God. Then, he was strengthened like his father, Solomon, and grandfather, David.

Jeroboam decided to reject the worship of the Lord, the Spiritual Living God. He decided to build idols for the people of Israel to worship. Just like our generation, Rehoboam became relaxed with the Spiritual Living God's blessings, choosing to mislead the people according to the Spiritual Living God's inspired words.

The Spiritual Living God sent a friendly reminder, allowing Judah to be invaded (2 Chronicles 12:2-12). This caused Rehobaom to humble himself and turn his heart back to

THE SPIRITUAL LIVING GOD IS STILL IN THE BLESSING BUSINESS

the Spiritual Living God. The Spiritual Living God eventually allowed the two tribes to battle (2 Chronicles 13:10-20). The Spiritual Living God gave the victories to the two over the ten because of their obedience to do His will. We should observe past generations' mistakes and always seek the Spiritual Living God before entering a battle, if they desired to have the victory (2 Chronicles 14:2-6, 9-15; 15:1-7).

If we are not being obedient, according to the will of the Spiritual Living God, our loss will be great just like past generations (Judges 2; 3:1-7). We really need to hear from heaven before the Spiritual Living God will bless our land (Judges 3:9-10; 2 Chronicles 7:14; Psalm 78). Anytime we make a decision not to lead the Spiritual Living God's people according to His inspired words, found in the Holy Bible, we allow our enemies to defeat us during any battle, including a personal battle, without the guidance of the Holy Spirit (Ephesians 6:10-20).

We really have too many things going on in the world today that the Spiritual Living God does not approve of. The world gives its approval, but the Holy, Righteous, and Spiritual Living God is very displeased, according to His inspired words found in the Holy Bible (1 Corinthians 10:14-33; 15:35-58; 2 Corinthians 4:7-18; 6:14-18; 10:3-5; Galatians 5:16-26; 6:6-10; Ephesians 1:15-2:10; 6:10-20; Hebrews 8). This is our blueprint and plans for living a life of obedience in this generation. We should learn from the experiences of past generations, learning what steps were needed for success and what step they took during defeat. We can only have the victory in battles when we choose to humble ourselves and turn from all sins, which are displeasing to the Holy, Righteous, Spiritual, and Living God. Only then will we

BECAUSE THE LORD IS YOUR SHEPHERD

hear from heaven and will the Spiritual Living God bless our land, in the name of Jesus Christ, our Lord and Savior (2 Chronicles 7:14; Isaiah 33; 34:16-17).

Ezra (chapters 9-10) spoke of those called into obedience, but chose to mingle and marry outside the will of the Spiritual Living God. Those who have been called in this generation by the Spiritual Living God into obedience, according to His Son, Jesus Christ, with guidance from the Holy Spirit, we also have a responsibility to lead the people of the Spiritual Living God, according to Scripture (1 Peter 1:9-17; 2 Peter 1:12-21). The Scriptures state, His will by inspired words found in the Holy Bible (John 5:39-47; 2 Timothy 3:16; Romans 15:4). As children of the Spiritual Living God, we have been empowered (Ephesians 6:10-20; Hebrews 8; Ephesians 4:14-32) to choose a life of obedience in this generation.

We have received our Helper in the guidance of the Holy Spirit (John 14-16; Acts 2; 1 Corinthians 2), which allows us to be successful in all things, according to Philippians (4:6-9, 13, 19). We need to remember, there is no failure in the Spiritual Living God (Isaiah 42-43). When we turn away from Him, we experience the consequences for choosing to be disobedient (2 Chronicles 24:17-22).

The Spiritual Living God is Holy, Righteous, and a Spirit. We must seek His guidance in Spirit and Truth (John 4:23-24). Only through Jesus can we have a spiritual (John 1:1-18; 3:16-21; 14-16; Acts 2; Romans 8; 1 Corinthians 2; Ephesians 1:13; Hebrews 1; 8; 1 John 1-5) relationship with the Spiritual Living God, who resides in heaven, as our Heavenly Father.

Do We Really Need to Battle with Other Countries?

Does the Holy Bible, which is the inspired words of the Spiritual Living God, really say things that have come true in this generation of the twenty-first century? Did the Holy Bible state the Spiritual Living God is a Spirit (John 4:22-25)? Did the Holy Bible state the Spirit communicates with the Spirit and flesh (John 3:5-6; Romans 7:13-17; 8:6-17; Galatians 5:16-26; Ephesians 6:10-20)? Do I have the Spirit of the Spiritual Living God within me (Jeremiah 31:31-34; Joel 2:28-32; 1 John 4:12-14) so I can communicate with Him (John 1:1-18; 3:16-21; 4:23-24; 14-16; Hebrews 1)?

Do we need the Holy Bible to find our purpose for being here on earth (Ecclesiastes 3; 8:5-7; Acts 11:23; Romans 8:28; Ephesians 1:11; 3:11; 2 Timothy 1:19; 3:10; John 3:15)? Do people live in this world and choose to be evil, according to the inspired words of the Spiritual Living God, who provides righteousness for all humans (John 3:16-21)? According to the books found in the Holy Bible, the inspired words of the Spiritual Living God (Exodus; Deuteronomy; Joshua), there are reminders for future generations regarding how the Spiritual Living God communicated in detail with His leaders. He actually told them when, where, and how His leaders Moses and Joshua were to go into battle (Numbers 31). David also sought the Lord before going to battle. As we focus on the personal battles David had before Goliath,

BECAUSE THE LORD IS YOUR SHEPHERD

he reflected on past experiences in his life with the Spiritual Living God, situations that caused him to encourage himself. This is why the confidence he shares with future generations is a reminder for the Spiritual Living God's children to recall our past experience in any battle (1 Samuel 17:32-51). The Spiritual Living God provides wisdom, which is better than war, but one sinner can destroy a nation without spiritual guidance from the Holy, Spiritual Living God (Ecclesiastes 9:16-18).

Those in past generations were required to have their hearts right with the Spiritual Living God before any battle. They could not be out of the will of the Spiritual Living God and go into battle. According to Psalm 33, we are reminded of those who choose to fear, honor, and respect the Holy, Righteous, and Spiritual Living God, who resides in heaven. He will bless the nation and the people who have His inheritance; they belong to Him (Isaiah 56:3-8)! If they chose to be disobedient according to the inspired words of the Spiritual Living God, they were defeated in battle.

The Spirit of the Spiritual Living God did not protect them when they led without the details. The Spiritual Living God provided instructions according to His inspired words found in the Holy Bible. Moses' through Joshua's generations chose to be obedient and experienced victories if the people followed His instructions. Otherwise, they were defeated and sought the Spiritual Living God, for a reason, for the defeat (Deuteronomy 1; Joshua 6-8; 12). The Spiritual Living God reveals outcomes based on obedience and disobedience to the people in their generation.

Do we have anything in our generation that can cause us to be defeated during any battle? The leaders from

DO WE REALLY NEED TO BATTLE WITH OTHER COUNTRIES?

past generations provided their experiences for future generations, exactly how they always sought the Spiritual Living God before going into battle, if they wanted to be successful. Who told this generation we could go into battle and become successful without seeking the Spiritual Living God first? Anytime the United States of America decides she needs to go into a battle with other nations, those called into obedience must humble themselves and pray, seek the Spiritual Living God, turning from their wicked ways, and (Galatians 5:16-26; James 1:12-18; 4:1-12; 2 Peter 2:9) repent for sins. Then, the Spiritual Living God will allow us to hear from heaven, so He can bless our land in this generation (2 Chronicles 7:14).

We must remember, the Spiritual Living God is a Spirit (John 4:23-24); He only communicates with Spirits. Humans are created in His image, are flesh (Genesis 1:27; 2:7; 5:2; Matthew 19:4-5). All humans put in a position as leaders must have access to their spiritual connection (Jeremiah 31:31-35; Joel 2:28-32); otherwise, they are without spiritual guidance. Jesus Christ is this generation's spiritual connection (John 1:1-18; 3:1-21; 10; 14-16; Acts 2; Romans 1:16-20; 8; 1 Corinthians 2; Ephesians 1:13; 4:14-32; Hebrews 1; 8). Remember, the Spirit communicates with the Spirit, and flesh communicates with the flesh (1 John 4:1-6; Acts 19:11-19).

Jesus is the only key to success in all wars in this generation. Anytime we decide as humans we do not need Him, we will have the opportunity to deal with man and become defeated (James 1:19-27). They were reminded in Deuteronomy (1:41-46) not to go into battle without permission from the Spiritual Living God, when Israel ignored His warning, and they were defeated by Hormah

BECAUSE THE LORD IS YOUR SHEPHERD

(Amorites). The message from the Spiritual Living God was loud and clear in their generation; surely, history can repeat itself in this generation. We must learn to follow the Spiritual Living God's spiritual guidance in this generation of the twenty-first century, also.

These questions were provided to make you think and seek the Spiritual Living God, in the name of Jesus, for some intelligent answers. Remember, the Spiritual Living God gave us the ability to think things through, only by the guidance of the Holy Spirit (1 Corinthians 2). We are allowed access to spiritual things provided in Jesus' name (John 14-16; Acts 2).

Jesus provided the Helper in the guidance of the Holy Spirit, who provides wisdom, knowledge, and understanding in all things (John 16:13; Philippians 4:6-9, 13) as long as we have accepted Him as the only begotten Son. Always remember, the holiness of the Spiritual Living God keeps us seeking the Mediator to intercede on our behalf (1 Timothy 2:1-8; Hebrews 1). The Spiritual Living God's Son, Jesus Christ, is the Mediator and the Holy Spirit enlightens us regarding spiritual things with knowledge that surpasses human intelligence (Romans 8:34; 1 Corinthians 2). Psalm 46 reminds us the Spiritual Living God is still in control of His world. He is our strength and refuge at all times, according to David's experiences in life. As we read the Holy Bible, with the guidance of the Holy Spirit (Proverbs 3:5-6; Matthew 6:25-33), this generation needs to fully understand, there is really nothing too hard for the Spiritual Living God to resolve for His children.

We are reminded of the Spiritual Living God's holiness and righteousness according to His plans and purpose for our lives here on Earth. He is really capable of bringing any

DO WE REALLY NEED TO BATTLE WITH OTHER COUNTRIES?

war to an end, in this generation. Nevertheless, we must decide to turn our hearts and mind toward seeking His will for this generation. We will not be able to stand still and observe the power and glory provided in the name of Jesus. The Spiritual Living God expects His children in this generation to turn from things that are very displeasing to Him (2 Chronicles 7:14). The book of Joshua provides detail of the battles the Israelites had to fight according to the inspired words of the Spiritual Living God (Joshua 10-11). All victories were due to their obedience and the promises the Spiritual Living God made to Moses. Joshua followed the inspired words provided according to the Spiritual Living God's will for His people. Joshua made sure he waited for the Spiritual Living God's directions before going into battle. These directions allowed him to receive his help from the Spiritual Living God (Joshua 10:11-14), which allowed him to receive the victory (Joshua 10:40; 21:42-45).

The land finally rested from war Joshua experienced (11:23) with others. The Spiritual Living God promised the Israelites, if they did not remove the Canaanites (Joshua 22-25), they would be a thorn in their sides (Joshua 23:13-16; 24). After Joshua's death, an angel of the Lord reminded them about entertaining the Canaanites in Judges 2. The Canaanites caused them many problems (pay attention, America). When the Spiritual Living God delivered the Israelites, they always went back to observe the Canaanites. This caused the Spiritual Living God to become angry with them. They would turn their backs on the Spiritual Living God and do evil, serving other gods.

The Spiritual Living God, who resides in heaven, would allow their enemies to overtake them. They would cry unto

BECAUSE THE LORD IS YOUR SHEPHERD

the Spiritual Living God and ask for forgiveness for sinning against Him. He would provide a spiritual leader and deliverer to bring them out from their enemies' control. They (Israelites) would choose to be obedient, and then serve other gods again. The Spiritual Living God of heaven would be angry and allow the enemy to suppress them again. The routine went on constantly in the book of Judges (10:16-18) through Malachi, for an example. The Spiritual Living God provided prophets, angels, seers, judges, kings, and priests to reach the people regarding His expectation for their lives here on Earth. There were successes and failures until the Spiritual Living God decided to have compassion on those created in His image (Romans 9).

The Spiritual Living God decided to arrive here on Earth in the flesh (John 1:1-18; 3:16-21; 10; Hebrews 1; 8; 1 Timothy 3:16; 1 John 5:1-12). He provided an example of His expectation of those who have a desire to know and follow Him personally (Hebrews 1-2). The Spiritual Living God's arrival as Jesus (God the Son, 1 John 5:6-12) in the flesh was a sure sign of His love and compassion. Whenever we read about past generations' experiences found in the Old Testament of the Holy Bible, we find the Spiritual Living God had patience, but He wanted the people to obey and acknowledge His holiness.

Whenever they fail, we observe their consequences for choosing disobedience. The Spiritual Living God is a Spirit and must be worshiped in Spirit and Truth (John 3:16-21; 4:22-25; 14-16; Acts 2; 1 Corinthians 2; Romans 8; Hebrews 1; 8; 1 John 1-5). Whenever we choose ignorance over the guidance of the Holy Spirit (God the Spirit, 1 John 5:6-12), we should rejoice and be glad (Psalm 53; Romans 1:21-32;

DO WE REALLY NEED TO BATTLE WITH OTHER COUNTRIES?

1 Corinthians 1:18-31; Hebrews 3:7-11). No one forced us to make these decisions; we were given a choice, and the consequences are ours to bear.

The Spiritual Living God was pleased with the humbling and instruction Jehoshaphat provided after his mistake with Ahab. Others sought to battle against Judah, creating a multitude (2 Chronicles 20) of challenges. The Spiritual Living God informed them not to be afraid or dismayed, for the battle belonged to Him. He told them to stand still and observe the salvation of the Lord (20:15-19). Jehoshaphat, along with all of Judah and Jerusalem, bowed and fell before the Lord in worship and praise for His mercy and grace.

What a blessing for those in this generation who need to be encouraged in times of trouble (2 Corinthians 4; Ephesians 6:10-20). We need to observe those in past generations after fighting in a battle; they never took the Spiritual Living God's glory. They realized their success was because He provided all things for them to have the victory. What are we doing in this generation after a battle, that is causing those who come back from the battlefield not to live a normal life? The Spiritual Living God does not send anyone into a battle in this generation to depend on man-made medicinals at the end of the battle (1 Samuel 17:47). Nevertheless, if we are going to be prideful and refuse to be right, fair, and honest in all things during a battle (John 16:13; Philippians 4:6-9, 13), this generation can look forward to suffering unnecessarily. We will always have consequences for choosing to sin against the Spiritual Living God (Psalm 51; 1 John 1-5). Isaiah had to remind Israel in his generation, there is no weapon that can form against them and prosper

BECAUSE THE LORD IS YOUR SHEPHERD

(Isaiah 54). As children (Romans 8; Ephesians 4:14-32) of the Spiritual Living God, the promise is still true in this generation: "There is no weapon that can form against us and prosper; it just will not work."

The Spiritual Living God revealed Himself to Asa and Jehoshaphat, his son, in 2 Chronicles 15-19. The Spiritual Living God blessed them, and they had peace as long as He was the focus in their life. Asa became too comfortable with the Spiritual Living God and suffered the consequences for his disobedience toward the Holy, Righteous, and Spiritual Living God, just like Hezekiah and his son, Manasseh (2 Chronicles 29-33). After being blessed by the Spiritual Living God, Hezekiah became prideful and Manasseh, his son, decided to become evil, which caused problems for the king and the people under their leadership. The Spiritual Living God sent a seer in 2 Chronicles (16:7-9) to remind Asa of his mistake. After all the blessings he had received from the Spiritual Living God, He allowed Asa to die of diseased feet. During his suffering, Asa actually sought physicians instead of the Spiritual Living God, who previously delivered him in times of trouble (16:12-13). Asa's son Jehoshaphat was greatly blessed due to his obedience to the Holy, Righteous, and Spiritual Living God, who resides in heaven (2 Chronicles 17:1). He made the mistake of having Ahab for a friend in his generation (1 Kings 16:30-33; 2 Chronicles 18:1-7; 19:1-2).

We have been warned (1 Corinthians 5:13; 2 Corinthians 6:14-18) of the disadvantage of associating with unbelievers in this generation. We need to remember the story about Jezebel, Ahab's wife (1 Kings 21-22:50; 2 Kings 9:30-37); she was successful in turning his heart away from the Spiritual

DO WE REALLY NEED TO BATTLE WITH OTHER COUNTRIES?

Living God. Therefore, they despised the Lord GOD; Ahab was no longer capable of making the right decisions as the king of Israel. Jehoshaphat decided to go into battle with Ahab; after all, Ahab actually provided a feast for a king upon his arrival (2 Chronicles 18:1-3).

Jehoshaphat probably felt obligated to go into battle with him (Deuteronomy 1:17; 16:18-20). Lying spirits were made available to help convince Jehoshaphat it was okay to participate in the Ra-moth-gil-e-ad battle with Ahab. Only one prophet spoke the truth of things to come and was rewarded with a jail sentence (2 Chronicles 18:12-34).

We really need to be careful whom we entertain, when they despise the Holy, Righteous, and Spiritual Living God, who resides in heaven. Jehoshaphat was warned, after he returned from the battle, of his mistake (2 Chronicles 19:2-7). The Spiritual Living God had mercy on him because he had a heart for the Spiritual Living God in past decisions. He reestablished his desire to please the Spiritual Living God by informing those under his leadership, they must follow the inspired words spoken before their arrival on Earth regarding leading others, and being fair, honest, and obedient to the Spiritual Living God. He told them to judge others for the Lord, the Spiritual Living God, not a man. Do not accept gifts and become respecters of persons, when it comes to the Spiritual Living God (2 Chronicles 19:5-10). We should pay attention to the same message being provided in Moses' generation for the Spiritual Living God's people. Do you think we can learn from two different people being provided with the same message, in this generation?

When beauty and royalty challenge you as a child (Romans 8; Ephesians 4:14-32) of the Spiritual Living God,

BECAUSE THE LORD IS YOUR SHEPHERD

will you fail or succeed? Someone before your generation succeeded in one area and fell in the next, when it came to women (2 Chronicles 9:1-12). The queen of Sheba admitted she had heard of all the Spiritual Living God had done for Solomon (9:22-23; Nehemiah 13:26-27). She also knew she was a woman with certain capabilities. The questions and challenges she presented to Solomon allowed the Spirit of the Spiritual Living God to speak through Solomon, providing answers, which caused her spirit to become weakened (2 Chronicles 9:4-6). The Holy Bible states how powerful women are in the Scripture (Ecclesiastes 7:25-27). Sometimes this power can be used to destroy any male who decides to challenge her outside the will of the Spiritual Living God (Genesis 34:1-4; Ecclesiastes 7:26). Anytime a male chooses to participate in adultery or fornicate (1 Corinthians 7:1-7), he needs to remember, he is tying lead weight around his body, which can hold him back when he is trying to go forward, because he bound his flesh (Genesis 2:24; 1 Corinthians 6:15-20) with an evil woman. According to the Scriptures, a male has power from the Spiritual Living God to withstand all things (Psalm 1; 3-8), but without the guidance of the Holy Spirit, men are like a deer caught in the headlights of a moving vehicle. They have been warned by the inspired words of the Spiritual Living God, they need spiritual protection (Proverbs 5; 6:20-35; 7; 9). The male gender is not capable of overcoming anything women set before them to destroy them (Proverbs 9:13-18; Ecclesiastes 7:26).

In this generation of the twenty-first century, males are killing females in record numbers because they thought they did not need the guidance of the Holy Spirit. Why

DO WE REALLY NEED TO BATTLE WITH OTHER COUNTRIES?

seek a relationship with a female before having the guidance of the Holy Spirit (John 14-16; Acts 2; Romans 8)? He enlightens you regarding all things, especially spiritual things (1 Corinthians 2). Being warned beforehand of her ability to destroy you without the protection of the Spiritual Living God, in Jesus' name (Proverbs 12:4-5), sets you up for defeat early in a relationship. Praise the Spiritual Living God for women who live according to Proverbs 31:10-31.

If any male is serious about serving the Spiritual Living God, he will need a wife (Proverbs 18:22) who can identify with the woman found in Proverbs 31:10-31. Only by the guidance of the Holy Spirit, a female will choose to be obedient, providing her husband is being obedient to the teachings of Jesus Christ (1 Corinthians 7:1-2; 11:3; Ephesians 5:22-33). The guidance of the Holy Spirit will always make sure the Spiritual Living God's children are on one accord. Then and only then, the husband will be capable of leading another human being according to the inspired words found in the Holy Bible. Anytime a male is called into obedience, he must follow (2 Corinthians 10; Galatians 5:16-26; Ephesians 5:22-33; 6:10-20; 1 John 1-5) Jesus Christ, who follows the Spiritual Living God; He has detailed plans for his life here on Earth. He will always realize the battle and vengeance belong (1 Samuel 17:47; Romans 12; 1 Corinthians 10:5-33) to the Spiritual Living God; it is not man's. Because of his obedience, he will have the victory.

America Was Established for the Spiritual Living God

We need to remember, the United States of America was established as a Christian (things Jesus Christ taught while living here on Earth) nation. Others were inspired with additional guidelines (Ephesians 5:1-21; Philippians 4:6-9; Colossians 3:1-17) for a nation with Christian principles. Anyone who desires to be a part of this nation must accept the standards of Christian living (Isaiah 56:3-8; Philippians 2:1-18; 4:1-20). Some of us have observed the lives of those claiming Christianity and become discouraged with the faith, which is not a **religion** (2 Corinthians 4; Hebrews 11; James 2:14-26). What you and they fail to understand about the Christian faith is you must live your life in the Spirit (Jeremiah 31:31-35; Joel 2:28-32; Job 32:8; 1 Corinthians 2; Hebrews 1) to become successful here on Earth.

Only by the guidance of the Holy Spirit do humans that have breath (Genesis 2:7) and are created in the image of the Spiritual Living God (Genesis 1:26-28) realize they must serve Him in Spirit and Truth (Isaiah 56:3-8; John 1:1-18; 3; 4:23-24; 5:17-47; 6:44-65; 10; 14-16; Acts 2; Romans 8; Ephesians 1:13, 15-23; 2-4; Hebrews 8; 11; 1 John 1-5). Otherwise, we are set up for failure and defeat (Genesis 5:1-3; Psalm 14; 53; Romans 1:21-32; 7:13-25; 8:1-17; 1 Corinthians 1:18-31). Others observing your life, without the guidance of the Holy Spirit, will become totally discouraged with the Christian

BECAUSE THE LORD IS YOUR SHEPHERD

faith (2 Corinthians 4; Galatians 5:16-26; Ephesians 6:10-20; Hebrews 11; James 2:14-26) because you fail to keep your eyes on the only Person who could empower you to do all things (Proverbs 3:5-8; Matthew 6:25-33; Philippians 4:4-9, 11-13, 19-20). In order to lead spiritually, you must be called into obedience (2 Chronicles 7:14; 1 Peter 1:3-25; 2:1-17), then, you must be equipped with the guidance of the Holy Spirit (John 14-16; Acts 2; 2 Timothy 2-3). You must be grounded in the Truth (2 Peter 1:12-21); you must believe the Gospel (Psalm 22; Isaiah 53; John 1:1-18; Romans 9; Ephesians 1:13; Hebrews 1; 8), **Jesus' birth** (Matthew 1:24-25; Luke 2:1-7), **life** (four Gospels), **death** (Matthew 27:51-56; Mark 15:38-41; Luke 23:44-49; John 19:16-42), **resurrection** (Matthew 28; Luke 24:1-48; John 20; 1 Corinthians 15), and **His ascension** (Mark 16:19-20; Luke 24:49-53) into heaven. These Scriptures are provided in the four Gospels (Matthew, Mark, Luke, and John), providing details of the only begotten Son, Jesus Christ's (Hebrews 1; 1 John 1-5) life experiences while living here on Earth and plans of salvation for the Spiritual Living God's children, who can look forward to experiencing eternal life.

The book of Romans provides details on experiencing life with and without the guidance of the Holy Spirit. Remember, the Spiritual Living God is a Spirit, and we must worship Him in Spirit and Truth (John 4:23-24; 6:44-65; 14-16; Romans 8; 1 Corinthians 2; 2 Corinthians 3:17; Ephesians 4:14-32). There is one Spiritual Living God with one Son, Jesus Christ, and one Spirit, provided by the Spiritual Living God (1 John 5:6-12). God the Father, God the Son, and God the Holy Spirit are three separate identities, which operate with one spiritual connection. The Spiritual Living God allows those

AMERICA WAS ESTABLISHED FOR THE SPIRITUAL LIVING GOD

who sincerely desire to know Him spiritually and personally access through His Son, Jesus Christ, with the guidance of the Holy Spirit (Luke 10:19-20; John 1:1-18; 3:15-21; 4:23-24; 5:17-47; 6:44-65; 10; 16-17; Acts 3:12-26; 1 Thessalonians 4:7-8; Hebrews 1; 8; 11).

Exactly how could your level of intelligence after being warned of the consequences (Romans 1:21-32; 1 Corinthians 1:18-31) begin to communicate with the Holy, Righteous, and Spiritual Living God? Many have tried before you were born, without the guidance from the Holy, Spiritual Living God (Numbers 14; 16; Acts 12:20-24; 19:11-19; 1 John 4:1-6). Do you think you can learn from their mistakes, trying to reference the Holy, Spiritual Living God without spiritual access through Jesus Christ (2 Thessalonians 2-3:5)? Keep on trying to ignore His holiness, many living in this century need to see for themselves just how holy the Spiritual Living God (1 Peter 4), really is. Your life can be used as a testament for future generations; now they can learn from your mistakes.

The United States of America was established before you were born; the standards were set in stone (Deuteronomy 6-8; 27-28; 1 Corinthians 5:4-13; Titus 3; Hebrews 1-2; 1 Peter 1-2). The guidance of the Holy Spirit enlightens us regarding all things, especially spiritual things (1 Corinthians 2), as children (Romans 8; Ephesians 4:14-32) of the Spiritual Living God (John 5:39-47; 2 Timothy 3:14-17). Nevertheless, any changes we make in this generation to discredit the inspired words spoken by the Spirit of God before our birth will always provoke the Spiritual Living God to become angry (2 Peter 1:12-21). Do you think the United States of America can handle the anger of the Spiritual Living God

BECAUSE THE LORD IS YOUR SHEPHERD

(Exodus 19:16; 20:18-21; Leviticus 26:14-46; Deuteronomy 28:15-68) in this generation? Focus on Isaiah's generation for a minute; surely, these things are not currently taking place in America, right, "say it is not so." Isaiah (29:1-16) spoke about this city and her disobedience; surely, we cannot identify with Ariel.

There is no way the United States of America is participating in things that cause the Spiritual Living God to become angry in this generation of the twenty-first century (cyclones, El Nino, global warming, hurricanes, tornadoes, levies breaking, cities burned by fires, tsunamis, floods), right. There were generations before this generation that never experienced things currently taking place in the United States of America. If you believe the Spiritual Living God is bigger than the problems we are facing today, we really need to stop giving credit to our small gods for causing the problems that exist in this generation; only the Spiritual Living God grants permission for things to take place in His world. Anytime a generation can be identified as the adulterous generation (Proverbs 30) before and after Jesus' teachings in His generation (Matthew 12:39-45; Mark 8:31-38; Luke 9:23-27; James 4:1-10) along with James' reminding them in his generation, we will not escape the consequences of the sins taking place in this generation. We have too many people committing fornication (having sexual contact without marriage vows) and married people disrespecting their marriage vow by committing adultery (sexual activity with someone who is married), not just adults, but children, also.

There are many inspired words found in the Holy Bible to help future generations understand, this is an area in life

AMERICA WAS ESTABLISHED FOR THE SPIRITUAL LIVING GOD

with grave consequences (Leviticus 20:9-27). All sins are committed outside the body except for fornication and adultery (1 Corinthians 6:9-20). The Spiritual Living God has already informed past generations, He has a problem with this activity we are commanded about adultery (Exodus 20:14; Deuteronomy 5:18; Leviticus 20:9-11; Proverbs 6:31-32; Matthew 5:31-33; 15:18-20; 19:8-10; Mark 2:20-22; Acts 15:19-21; Romans 1:28-30; 1 Corinthians 5:1-3; 6:12-14; 7:1-3; 10:7-9; Galatians 5:18-20; Ephesians 5:2-4; Colossians 3:4-6; 1 Thessalonians 4:2-4; 2 Peter 2:14; Jude 5-7). Jeremiah tried to help the people in his generation understand adultery is not acceptable to the Spiritual Living God (Jeremiah 3:7-10; 5:6-8; 7:8-10; 23:13-15); the Lord rebuked the leaders who were lying about adultery (Jeremiah 29:20-23). This activity provoked Him to become angry in Ezekiel's generation (Ezekiel 16:25-27). The people were provided with details about the consequences of their sins fornication and adultery being a generational activity without the Spiritual Living God (Ezekiel 16:27-58).

Do you think it is possible for the current generation to participate in fornication and adultery, in this day and time, as His children and please the Spiritual Living God? Remember, Jesus told us His purpose for being here on Earth was not to change anything the Spiritual Living God spoke before His arrival as the only begotten Son (Matthew 5:17-20). We have been given a chance to repent and ask for forgiveness for committing these sins, in this generation, because of the blood Jesus shed on Calvary's cross (Hebrews 10; 1 John 1-5). Nevertheless, the Spiritual Living God remembers His promises with past generations and established an everlasting covenant with His people (Ezekiel

BECAUSE THE LORD IS YOUR SHEPHERD

16:59-63; Galatians 3-4; Ephesians 2-3; 5; Colossians 1:3-29; 3).

Whenever we refuse to acknowledge the Spiritual Living God's Son, Jesus Christ, we do not have anyone who can intercede on our behalf to the Spiritual Living God to have mercy in this generation. We can look forward to Deuteronomy (28:15-20, 36-44); surely, we need the Son of the Spiritual Living God. Otherwise, how can we become the head, without becoming the tail in this generation (28:44)? Remember, we can only be blessed for choosing to be obedient (Deuteronomy 28:1-14; 2 Corinthians 6-7:1); the promises are still true in this generation.

The Spiritual Living God is powerful enough to start and stop any disaster we are experiencing in this century (Psalms 46-47). He is still in control. Only by the guidance of the Holy Spirit are we allowed to understand spiritual things (1 Corinthians 2; Galatians 5:16-26; Ephesians 1). Otherwise, we experience Psalms 14 and 53; Romans 1:21-32; and 1 Corinthians 1:18-31; it is foolishness to the natural mind. We need to remember His promises (Exodus 29:45-46; Deuteronomy 1:11; John 14-16; Acts 1:3-5; Galatians 3:3-6, 26-29; Hebrews 9:15-17, 32-34). Just like Joshua reminded the people in his generation, they must make a decision (Joshua 22:5; 23:6-16) about the Spiritual Living God, Paul spoke to those in his generation also (Galatians 3:19-4:7; 5:16-26; Ephesians 1-2). Joshua reminds them of the strength the other nations had, but the Spiritual Living God gave the Israelites the strength to drive them out of their own country (Genesis 13:15; 15:18-21; 26:3-5; 28:4-14; Deuteronomy 7:1-5; 9:1-5; Joshua 21:43-45). The Spiritual Living God reminds the Israelites they cannot mingle with other countries because

AMERICA WAS ESTABLISHED FOR THE SPIRITUAL LIVING GOD

they will turn their hearts away from Him (Deuteronomy 7:1-5; 8:11-20; 1 Kings 11:9-13). Joshua takes a stand (Joshua 24:14-15), reminding the people to be sincere and fear the Spiritual Living God out of honor and respect for His holiness. As for him and his house, they would serve the Spiritual Living God, without a doubt. The United States of America must take a stand regarding her nation, which was established with Christian principles.

We cannot allow other nations to influence the United States of America with their gods. We have already been warned of their ability to change the hearts of those living in the nation originally established by Christian principles. We had the religion of Judaism before Jesus Christ (Hebrews 1-2); only those the Spiritual Living God decided to communicate with heard from Him in order to reach His people. Someone greater than all who were before Him (Psalm 22; Isaiah 53; 56:3-8; Matthew 12:38-42; John 1:1-34; 3:16-21; 5:17-47; 6:44-65; 10; 14-16; 1 John 1-5) is now available to all nations (Isaiah 56:3-8; 66:18-20, 23; Matthew 24:13-15; Mark 13:10). The only begotten Son, Jesus Christ, provides the guidance of the Holy Spirit, which enlightens the Spirit within us as children (Romans 1:16-20; 8) of the Spiritual Living God; now we are allowed to communicate with Him in the Spirit. We have been provided with standards according to Jesus Christ; He is superior to all before His existence as the Spiritual Living God's only begotten Son (Hebrews 1; 3:1-4, 13; 4:14-7:28; 8:1-3; 9:1-10:18; 11:1-40). Stop whatever you are doing now, and pray for the Spiritual Living God to reveal unto you the inspired words of Truth (John 1:1-18; 3:16-21; 4:23-24; 5:17-47; 6:44-65; 10; 14-16; Acts 2; 1 Corinthians 2; Hebrews 8; 1 John 1-5). We are not dealing with things we can observe,

BECAUSE THE LORD IS YOUR SHEPHERD

but spiritual darkness (Ephesians 6:1-20). Children of the Spiritual Living God must desire to live a life of faith and obedience according to the purpose and plans of the Spiritual Living God. We must walk by faith (2 Corinthians 4; Galatians 5:16-26; Hebrews 1; 8; 11; James 2:14-26) and put on the whole armor of the Spiritual Living God (Ephesians 6:10-20). We should never invite someone into our home to disrupt our standards and rules. Otherwise, they should be put out and told never to return this way again. If we do not take a stand for the original plans and purpose the Spiritual Living God used to establish His country, the United States of America, we can look forward to the turbulence the past generations had to experience for being disobedient as a nation who represents the Spiritual Living God (2 Peter 2).

Our children and future generations will not have a country where they can sing "God Bless America," "My Country, 'Tis of Thee," or "The Battle Hymn of the Republic." They will not be able to understand others lost their lives so we could live in the land of the free and home of the brave. We need to teach the future generations about the Spiritual Living God's "Amazing Grace" and acknowledge "There is a fountain, filled with blood drawn from Emanuel's veins" (1 John 1-2). "Just as I am the blood, was shed for me, and there is no failure in the Spiritual Living God, because Jesus paid it all. All to him we owe; sin has left a crimson stain, but He washed it white as snow." These words have spiritual substance and will always stand forever; many generations before our birth understood it was necessary to teach future generation these songs. Just like Moses (Deuteronomy 32) provided a song for future generations, this was a reminder of the Spiritual Living God's blessings for obedience and consequences for choosing to live in disobedience. David provided a song also for future generations about being delivered from all his enemies (2 Samuel 22); this is very nice to know in this generation. There were others before our birth, spiritually guided to pen the words of truth for future generations, here in the United States of America. The Holy Spirit enlightened others to sing words of spiritual truth, helping the future generations remember past generations' experiences with the Spiritual Living God, reminding them to never forget where they came from and exactly who holds the future (1 John 5).

The songs written and sung were not confusing during past generations; they received spiritual insight about the world and spiritual lyrics. We did not dance in the world and worship the Spiritual Living God with the same music, like this current generation is experiencing. There was a difference in past generations' obedience, even if they failed sometimes. Maybe they were gifted without hardened hearts (Hebrews 3:7-11) to receive spiritual guidance regarding the wisdom to come up with different music, and they did not have to borrow music from their past generation.

We must continue to teach future generations; otherwise, the Holy Spirit will not allow them to recall a spiritual song to minister to them in times of trouble. The Spiritual Living God really does provide an anointing through songs, which ministers to each and every one of His children (Romans 8; Ephesians 4:14-32). We need to remember to stay focused (Proverbs 3:5-6; Matthew 6:25-33); just when we need Him and nothing else is working, the spiritual substance within each child of the Spiritual Living God is used to carry and strengthen you. The songs of Zion carried those who needed

BECAUSE THE LORD IS YOUR SHEPHERD

to be strengthened in past generations and still work in the twenty-first century. Regardless of how many songs they write in this generation, the songs the Holy Spirit usually brings to remembrance are the songs about the Spiritual Living God before our generation during times of need, especially if it is a heavy burden you need to leave at the feet of Jesus. The Spiritual Living God looks at our heart and current circumstances in this generation, allowing those spiritually enlightened to minister to the needs of the people in this generation, anytime someone writes songs with an anointing.

The past generations did not have as many gods as we have available today. Whenever they felt the Spirit of the Spiritual Living God ministering to them through any situation, we can tell the words were written from their hearts because the Spirit of Truth ministers to each person differently.

The Reverend James Cleveland (deceased) is another writer whose songs have a lot of spiritual substance that can be easily recalled in times of trouble for spiritual strength. We should thank the Spiritual Living God for His mercy and grace in this generation. If a person has been called into obedience in this generation, it is a blessing to lead according to the plans and purposes established before their birth (Jeremiah 1:4-10). Anytime someone desires to become the leader of a nation established by Christian principles, the person must realize the Spiritual Living God does not change for man's benefits (Deuteronomy 6-8:20; Hebrews 13:8). It is America's fault; she allowed other nations to corrupt her country, bringing their little gods and different beliefs to her country (Isaiah 56:3-8). She was established to

AMERICA WAS ESTABLISHED FOR THE SPIRITUAL LIVING GOD

be a Light to the nations living in darkness. She was not told to accept their standards over things the Spiritual Living God established in His country. They had a country before they arrived in this Christian nation. Just like God had to remind Israel there is a difference between Egypt and Israel (Exodus 12:13, 19-28, 36; 13:21-22), Isaiah had to remind the people in his generation (Isaiah chapters 1-4; 12-14; 25-33; 40-43) to stay focused on the Spiritual Living God, who is currently keeping the destroyer from our nation in this generation, surely not human beings with alarms. Let us hope it is the one and only Spiritual Living God, who never slumbers or sleeps (Psalm 121). He really can dispatch His angels to watch over His children (Romans 8; Ephesians 4:14-32) constantly (Isaiah 40:28-31).

We also need to understand, it was the blood (Colossians 1:14-22; 1 John 1:4-2:6) that was shed on Calvary's cross for this generation. The blood still has its power in this generation, covering the children of the Spiritual Living God (Romans 8; Ephesians 4:14-32). There is no reason for us to lie awake at night, so feel free to get some sleep without man-made medicinals. The Spiritual Living God will eventually remind the United Sates of America, He is the Spiritual Living God with one Son and one Spirit (John 3:16-21; Ephesians 4:4-7; 1 John 5). I hope those who know Him spiritually and personally are grounded in their faith and belief (2 Corinthians 4; Hebrews 11; James 2:14-26; 2 Peter 1:12-21).

Just like Daniel, who faced the lions in the lions' den (Daniel 6:14-27), knew his Spiritual Living God had closed the lions' mouths, therefore bringing him no hurt, harm, or danger, the Spiritual Living God always has an angel standing by, waiting to comfort and protect His children

BECAUSE THE LORD IS YOUR SHEPHERD

in times of need (1 Peter 5:6-10). We have been warned Satan is bored and needs to do something with his time (Job 1:6-2:8). Remember, Satan always needs the Spiritual Living God's permission before he can disrupt anyone's life here on Earth. We just make it easy for the Spiritual Living God to give the "go-ahead" in this generation. When we choose to be disobedient and still say we are being led by the guidance of the Holy Spirit (1 John 1-4), never forget, He is the one and only Spiritual Living God (Genesis 1:1-2; John 1:1-18; 3:16; 4:23-24; 5:17-47; Hebrews 1; 1 John 5). We are currently making excuses for other countries' little gods and their beliefs in this generation. We have been warned; He is a jealous Spiritual Living God (Exodus 20:5; Deuteronomy 4:4-40). The Spiritual Living God told Israel to go in and take the land; otherwise, "The Canaanites will turn your heart against Me," the Spiritual Living God (Numbers 33:50-56; Deuteronomy 7:1-11; 8 (Hello!)).

Do you think we are ready to handle the Spiritual Living God's anger in this generation? Deuteronomy 29-30 was written for future generations' benefit; the consequences for disobedience still exist today. He said we would rather entertain men and not follow His inspired words; surely, we are not doing this in this generation (Psalm 118:6-9; Acts 5:17-42). Many things took place before we were born. We really need to pay attention to the inspired words found in the Holy Bible, written for our benefit. Whenever we be still and observe past generations' experiences with the guidance of the Holy Spirit (Psalms 46-50; Isaiah 30), we can thank the Spiritual Living God for Jesus Christ and the guidance of the Holy Spirit. Psalm 112 reminds those who fear the Spiritual Living God out of honor and respect, His blessings

AMERICA WAS ESTABLISHED FOR THE SPIRITUAL LIVING GOD

are available to you as His child (Matthew 18:1-10; Romans 8; Ephesians 4:14-32). As children of the Spiritual Living God, you do not have to fear evil things because the Spiritual Living God has power over all things (Hebrews 2:14-18). The Holy Spirit is more powerful than the other spirits that exist in this world (Psalm 112:7; Acts 19:11-10; 1 John 4:1-6). Psalm 114 is a reminder of the power of the Spiritual Living God. He performed miracles for past generations to observe His power in their generation. They wrote about these situations for our generation, lest we forget and need a new reminder about the power of the Spiritual Living God.

If we are honest and realistic, we have experienced the Spiritual Living God in the twenty-first century many times already. America has experienced many disasters in this generation of the twenty-first century. The Spiritual Living God could have stopped any of those situations and spared the lives of those that were lost. Why would He do this when this is the only time we really acknowledge His power and strength (Romans 13:1-14)? Just about everyone that has breath (Genesis 2:7) will stop whatever they were doing and begin to focus on the power of the Spiritual Living God, in this generation (Proverbs 3:5-6; Matthew 6:25-33). He spoke to Solomon in his generation; He said, "If My people, which are called, by My name, shall humble themselves and pray, and seek My face, and turn from their wicked ways; then will I hear from Heaven, and I will forgive their sin, and will heal their land" (2 Chronicles 7:14). The message still holds true in this generation for those called into obedience as the children of the Spiritual Living God, in the name of Jesus.

There were others in the book of Isaiah (2:5-22) who forgot to walk in the Light of the Spiritual Living God. Isaiah

BECAUSE THE LORD IS YOUR SHEPHERD

reminded the future generations of the consequences for being disobedient, in his generation. Surely, we can learn from their mistakes in this generation (2 Timothy 3). Psalm 115 is a reminder for us to trust the Spiritual Living God and not idols. Anything you put before the Spiritual Living God is considered an idol (Matthew 22:37-40). Exactly who or what here on Earth can heal, deliver, or help you when your material possessions are no longer available to you? The book of Job provides insight regarding being blessed and forgetting who provided your blessing. Always remember, Satan has to obtain permission before he can interfere with the Spiritual Living God's children's lives here on Earth (Job 1-3). As a Christian nation, we can also forget and need reminders from the Spiritual Living God, just like Moses' generation (Deuteronomy 8:11-20). Just make sure you are grounded in your faith and belief of the Gospels (Matthew, Mark, Luke, and John), believing Hebrews 1-5; 8; and 11; 2 Corinthians 4; and 2 Peter 1:12-21. Otherwise, you are going to be tossed and driven like a ship without a sail. Try to remember, with the guidance of the Holy Spirit, how Jesus calmed the sea and made the waves behave (Matthew 8:23-27) in His generation; He really has wonder-working power.

When the United States of America experienced September 11, 2001 (9/11/2001), there were many who were in the right place at the right time (Romans 14:5-12). Testimonies were provided from families and friends about those who were in a position to lead others to the Christian faith before they left this world (John 3:16-36; Romans 1:16-20; 10:9; Hebrews 1). Remember, the Spiritual Living God provides for those who desire to know Him to be given an opportunity before we leave

AMERICA WAS ESTABLISHED FOR THE SPIRITUAL LIVING GOD

the land of the living (Romans 10:6-21; 1 Timothy 2:3-8; 2 Peter 3:8-10). The Spiritual Living God allowed us to observe His Spirit in those who redirected the last airplane to an open field, which minimized the loss of additional lives. Those Americans who stood and gave their lives would not have been successful with the spirit of fear (Romans 8:28-39; 2 Timothy 1:7-14). I personally think they knew where they were going after experiencing life here on Earth (1 John 5). I really believe they expect those whom they left behind as children (Romans 8; Ephesians 4:14-32) of the Spiritual Living God should look forward to seeing them when they arrive in heaven.

This was like Esther's experience (chapters 4-5) when she had to go before the king on behalf of the Jewish people (4:12). She asked the people to pray, and she came to the decision, "If I perish, I perish." It's like the Reverend James Cleveland (deceased) penned in a song, "He Always Comes Through with a Message for You." The children of the Spiritual Living God must be faithful in order to receive the promises provided in the Holy Bible (Romans 15:1-13; 2 Corinthians 7:1; Titus 1:2; 2:11-15; Hebrews 11; James 2:14-26). Psalm 111 reminds us to praise the Spiritual Living God because He really cares for you. Remember, the fear of the Spiritual Living God is the beginning of wisdom, knowledge, and understanding, provided by the guidance of the Holy Spirit, in this generation (1 Corinthians 2; Romans 9). As children of the Spiritual Living God, we must keep the commandments found in Matthew (22:36-40). These two provided by Jesus actually cover the Ten Commandments (Exodus 20:1-17) given to Moses in his generation. We really need to remember to always praise the Spiritual Living God for His mercy and grace (Psalm 113), thanking Him for His only begotten Son (John 1:1-18; 3:16-

BECAUSE THE LORD IS YOUR SHEPHERD

21; 5:17-47; Romans 1:16-20; Hebrews 1), Jesus Christ, our intercessor because the Spiritual Living God is a Spirit and must be worshiped in Spirit and Truth (John 4:23-24), which can only be accomplished by the guidance of the Holy Spirit (John 14-16; Acts 2; Ephesians 4; Hebrews 1; 1 John 1-5).

Whenever we choose to ignore the need to have spiritual guidance regarding spiritual things (1 Corinthians 2), we will experience the following Scriptures: Psalm 14; 53; Isaiah 6:8-10; Acts 28:26-28; Romans 1:21-32; 3:10-18; 10:1-5; 1 Corinthians 1:18-31.

When the Scripture speaks of the kingdom of God being within you (Jeremiah 31:31-35; Joel 2:28-32; John 1:1-18; 14-16; 1 Corinthians 2; Ephesians 1:13; Hebrews 1), remember, He is the Spirit (John 4:23-24) of the Spiritual Living God you choose to ignore. Nevertheless, the people did the exact same thing before you were born (Luke 17:21-32), just like Noah's generation and Lot's generation in Sodom and Gomorrah. The people were eating and drinking, marrying whomever their hearts desired, and worshiping idols before we were born, also (Genesis 18:16-33; 19:1-29). The Spiritual Living God reminded them He was still in control of the world; He designed us for His benefit (2 Kings 19:4-7). Hopefully, we can learn from their mistakes, in this generation, before the Spiritual Living God becomes too angry with the United States of America, which He established for other nations to observe (Deuteronomy 4), just like Israel was blessed in Moses' generation.

Remember, we are the richest nation in the world. Other nations look for America to lend a helping hand in times of need, and she usually comes through. Remember, charity does cover a multitude of sins (1 Peter 4:8). Thank the

AMERICA WAS ESTABLISHED FOR THE SPIRITUAL LIVING GOD

Spiritual Living God for His only begotten Son, Jesus Christ (Hebrews 1). He really does intercede on our behalf, asking the Heavenly Father to have mercy on the United States of America (Job 34:29; Romans 8:34; 1 Timothy 2:5; Hebrews 1:3; 2:14-18; 7:22-25). The Spiritual Living God would find fifty that really desire a life of obedience, according to His holy inspired words found in the Holy Bible (Genesis 18:16-33; 2 Peter 1:12-21), in this generation.

We ask in the name of Jesus, the Spiritual Living God hold off on the need to destroy the United States of America, in this generation. Nevertheless, Spiritual Living God, we accept Your need to constantly remind us about Your holiness, in this generation. Anytime a disaster occurs, people everywhere stop and pay attention in America. Those without spiritual insight (1 Corinthians 1:18-31) usually give man credit, but the Spiritual Living God is more powerful than any human (Hebrews 1-2). He can start any disaster and stop it when He decides to (Jeremiah 49-51). David experienced a disaster in his generation when the Spiritual Living God became angry (2 Samuel 11:27; 12:1-25; 24). Surely, we can learn from his mistake of provoking the Spiritual Living God to become angry, in this generation. If Isaiah had to remind the people in his generation apart from the Spiritual Living God, the people have no hope (Isaiah 41:21-29), there was no one among man or their idols who could answer their words of confusion. The Spiritual Living God's servant would come and provide the answers needed about all things past and present (Isaiah 42:1-16).

This servant means His Son, Jesus Christ, would glorify the Heavenly Father. Jesus would bring the covenant and Light for Gentiles. Nevertheless, Israel needs to remember the

BECAUSE THE LORD IS YOUR SHEPHERD

suffering she is experiencing is a result of her sin (Isaiah 42:17-25). Do you think America can sin against the Spiritual Living God without receiving consequences for her evil practices in this day and time? Heaven forbid, the Spiritual Living God decides not to remind us of His glory, in small doses. Otherwise, Sodom's and Gomorrah's experiences would be felt in this generation (Genesis 18:16-33; 19:24-29; Romans 1:21-32). Who would have ever thought the twenty-first century would be the generations to copy the homosexual lifestyles of Sodom and Gomorrah? It really does not take a lot to get our attention in America, in this generation. We will have fear or faith when it comes to experiencing consequences for being disobedient in the United States of America (Amos 5:13-15; Luke 12). Those other nations living in darkness will need to ask permission just like Satan. All evil spirits must ask permission from the Spiritual Living God (Job 1:5-2:8) before they can interfere with the children or nation, which belongs to Him. The Spiritual Living God always has at least fifty that would call on the name of Jesus, in this generation, asking Him to intercede on our behalf for the Spiritual Living God to have mercy on the United States of America (Job 34:29; Romans 8:34; 1 Timothy 2:5).

We must pray and teach future generations the Spiritual Living God is a Spirit (John 1:1-18; 3:16-21; 4:23-24; 5:17-47; 8:12-30; 12:28-50; Hebrews 1) and will be worshiped according to the inspired words provided for past generations (2 Peter 1:12-21). This is the Truth according to His purpose and plans for His people who reside here on Earth. **It is not about you!** It is all about Jesus, the only One capable of freeing humans from sin so they can have an abundant life (John 10; 1 John 1-5). We need to STOP taking man-made medicinals, which allow you to escape reality,

AMERICA WAS ESTABLISHED FOR THE SPIRITUAL LIVING GOD

only to return without changes, except more problems depending on your action during your escape. Your body belongs to the Spiritual Living God (Romans 8; 1 Corinthians 3:16-21). We are personally doing a disservice to our heirs, in our family, if we leave this life without planting the seed of hope for their generation (Genesis 18:19-21; Deuteronomy 4:10; 11:19-20; Joshua 24:14-15; Hebrews 1; 8; 10; 11). We should take the time and think about our generation and look at the current generation. Surely, you are thanking the Spiritual Living God right now! It will only get worse without spiritual guidance provided by Jesus Christ (John 14-16; Acts 2; 1 Corinthians 2; Hebrews 1).

Whenever the people chose not to listen to Jeremiah (chapter 8) and caused him to be in mourning of things to come, Jeremiah (chapter 9) helped our current generation reference how disobedience brings the Spiritual Living God's judgment. We are the generations provided with the guidance of the Holy Spirit (John 14-16). This Helper allows us to make the right decision, when we accept the Gospel by faith (Psalm 22; Isaiah 53; Romans 1:16-20; 2 Corinthians 4; Hebrews 1-2; 11-12; James 2:14-26), the birth, life, death, resurrection, and ascension of the only begotten Son. Nevertheless, the Galatians had a problem with the Gospel until Paul provided inspired words to strengthen their faith (Galatians 3:1-4:31). The Scriptures found in Galatians (chapter 5) were provided with details of how to live by faith. The following Scriptures provide insight regarding Jesus being connected with the Gospel: Genesis 1:1-2; Psalm 22; Isaiah 53; John 1:1-18; 3:16-21; 4:23-24; 5:17-47; Romans 1:16-20; Galatians 1:6-24; Ephesians 1:13-23; 2-3; Colossians 1:14-29; 3; 1 Thessalonians 2:14; and Hebrews 1.

BECAUSE THE LORD IS YOUR SHEPHERD

The Spiritual Living God's only begotten Son (John 1:1-18; 3:16-21; Hebrews 1-2; 8), Jesus Christ, canceled the need for anyone else to mediate between the Spiritual Living God and His people. Jeremiah tried to get the people to repent in his generation and turn back to the Spiritual Living God (chapter 7). Nevertheless, America can identify with that generation, in this generation (chapters 8-9); he speaks about being disobedient.

If we do not teach the future generation who the Spiritual Living God really is--"I am that I am"; He is Jehovah, sufficient all by Himself, as a Spirit (Exodus 3:13-15; 6; John 4:23-24)--they will eventually live as Barbarians (Acts 28:2-10; Romans 1:13-15; 3:10-20; 1 Corinthians 14:10-12) without Him. We can have a spiritual personal relationship with Him through His Son (John 5:17-47; 14-16; Romans 8; Hebrews 1; 8; 11;), Jesus Christ. This knowledge of the Spiritual Living God is the beginning of wisdom (1 Corinthians 2). Jeremiah reminds the people to trust the Spiritual Living God and not idols in (chapter 10) his generation. He reminded them of the broken covenant the Spiritual Living God made with Abraham and Moses in their generations (Exodus 3:9-22). He told Jeremiah (chapter 11) the relationship the people had with idols caused Him displeasure. The Spiritual Living God warned him not to pray or cry for them (11:14).

Surely, we are not this disobedient in the twenty-first century (Philippians 4:6-9, 13, 19; 1 John 1-5). This generation has access to the guidance of the Holy Spirit. Surely, we do not want the Spiritual Living God to become angry in this generation. As children of the Spiritual Living God, we must recall the 23rd Psalm, at all times, and remember John 10. Psalm 100 reminds us to always praise the Lord GOD in all generations for His Truth.

Notes for the next Generation

Notes for the next Generation

Notes for the next Generation

Notes for the next Generation

Notes for the next Generation

Notes for the next Generation

About the Author

My personal Christian experiences with guidance from the Holy Spirit are from the following places of worship: First New Mount Calvary Baptist, where, at the age of eight, I accepted Christ and was baptized (I was there from eight to twenty-five years of age); South Post Oak Baptist under the teachings of Rev. C. Southern and Rev. R. Wright (I accepted my call to teach while attending South Post Oak Baptist); and I was inspired to attended Second Baptist under the teachings of Dr. Ed. Young for about seven or eight years. I taught the divorce single parents Bible study class and held the position of layman prayer coordinator for this group also.

I am currently attending Wheeler Ave. Baptist under the teachings of Rev. Dr. M. Cosby. I am serving as one of the Bible study teachers for the senior choir class; the age group is probably between forty and eighty-plus. Recently, I obtained a degree in leadership from the College of Biblical Studies (April 2005). This degree provided insight regarding personalities and characteristics of people regardless of race or culture.

Please feel free to contact me. It would be nice to speak with you as we try to make a difference in the future generations (lwalker32008@yahoo.com).